T0128863

GOD
AND THE
HUMAN
ENVIRONMENT

GOD
AND THE
HUMAN
ENVIRONMENT

Catholic Principles of Environmental Stewardship as a Template for Action in Nigeria

Osunkwo Jude Thaddeus Ikenna, PhD

GOD AND THE HUMAN ENVIRONMENT
Catholic Principles of Environmental Stewardship as a Template for Action in Nigeria

iUniverse books may be ordered through booksellers or by contacting:

iUniverse
1663 Liberty Drive
Bloomington, IN 47403
www.iuniverse.com
1-800-Authors (1-800-288-4677)

ISBN: 978-1-4917-6912-6 (sc)
ISBN: 978-1-4917-6913-3 (e)

Library of Congress Control Number: 2015910059

Print information available on the last page.

iUniverse rev. date: 6/29/2015

DEDICATION

This Book is thankfully dedicated:

To St. Pope John Paul II of venerable memory and His Holiness Pope Benedict XVI (*Emeritus*), whose teachings on and commitment to the environment, inspired me to write this Book;

AND, to my Parents: Mr. Sylvester Mputam Osunkwo and late Mrs. Christiana Okwuchukwu Osunkwo, who influenced me from infancy on the necessity to respect nature and maintain a dignified and healthy environment.

ACKNOWLEDGEMENT

This book developed from my original doctoral dissertation *The Theology of Environment: Issues in Nigeria and the Response of the Church.*

The writing of this book was undertaken at a period of profound challenges in my life. My inexpressible gratitude, therefore, goes to God Almighty for the life and the inspiration that enabled me to complete this book.

My appreciation goes as well to my family and friends for all the support, affection, criticisms, useful contributions and encouragement I received in the course of my research and in realizing this project.

I am indebted to the paternal love of my Bishop *incumbent,* Most Reverend Dr. Augustine Ukwuoma, and my Bishop *emeritus,* Most Reverend Dr. Gregory Ochiagha, for the privilege, opportunity and support given to me.

My unalloyed thanks are equally extended to the authority, staff and students of Pontifical Urban University, Rome, and the GTF/Oxford for the formation, sharing, inspiration and exchanges that helped to ground me in my areas of specialization and scholarship.

I also extend a note of gratitude to all my priest-colleagues in Nigeria, Rome and the United States of America with whom I shared ideas in the course of writing this book, and who provided me the concern, conducive environment, encouragement and the intellectual engagement I needed.

I am no less appreciative to the Library Personnel of the following Libraries – the *Pontificia Università Urbaniana* Library Rome, the *Angelicum* Library Rome, the Urban Archives Rome, the Fordham University Library New York, the JFK Presidential Library and Museum Massachusetts, and The 21st Century On-Line and Site Library of GTF,

Indiana – who made their facilities available and accessible to me for the actualization of this Book.

Very Special thanks go to my hard-working and diligent supervisors, friends and colleagues: Prof. Carmelo Dotolo, Prof. Benedict Kanakappally, Prof. Anthony O. Nwachukwu, and Dr. Luke Emehiela Ijezie for the wisdom, time and patience that went into supervising, editing, and fore-wording this book respectively, and for their sharpening and constructive ideas and criticisms.

I invoke God's special blessings upon all of them in their entire lives and endeavors, including those others I have in mind but failed to mention their names in this little space.

CONTENTS

FOREWORD I

In recent years religious thinkers of diverse shades have been confronted with the problem of the role of religion in the face of environmental challenges of the contemporary world. One of the Christian responses to these challenges is the development of the type of theologizing called "eco-theology". In the face of monumental ecological disasters and their concomitant effects, many scholars are convinced that it can no longer be business as usual with theology. Jude Thaddeus Osunkwo, in the present book, takes up the challenge by suggesting the principles. With particular focus on Africa and his own country, Nigeria, Osunkwo laments the immense ignorance regarding environmental issues among the people but also sees this as an opportunity for the Church to fill the gap since the protection of creation has been recognized as an essential aspect of the Church's missionary apostolate.

The book sees the main role of the Church in this regard as that of influencing the civil society to adopt more responsible and ethical approaches to the environment. In a nation like Nigeria this becomes very relevant as most environmental disasters and pollutions are caused by the reckless attitudes of the civil society and the environmentally unfriendly or insensitive policies and activities of the civil authorities. The abuse of the environment in Nigeria has its peculiar features. It has to do with the general societal attitude to hygiene which goes far beyond industrial pollution. The issue has provoked a number of researches and public discussions in recent times. Osunkwo's book joins the ranks of such researches. He helps the discussion with very inspiring recommendations as he proposes a systematic, holistic and organic approach by the Church which will influence the people to develop renewed ways of thinking that would in turn orient them to take greater positive commitments towards the common good in their overall relationship with the environment.

In this book, Osunkwo recognizes the fact that many ideologies of both political and economic orientations compound the problems of the environment today. It is a fact that some groups due to selfish political considerations either deny or underestimate the ecological problems confronting the modern world. Many others, for fear of not continuously maximizing their profits on the economic level, continue to pollute the environment and sometimes with false theories that try to persuade whoever wants to believe that the situation is not as bad as being trumpeted. The book encourages the local Church to address such political and economic ideologies as they often constitute the structural roots of the problem. On the other hand, the Church is also challenged to address the often exaggerated attention to the environment which tends to divinize nature and reduce human persons to insignificant elements in creation. In fact, Pope Benedict XVI appears to respond to this malaise when, in his Post-Synodal Apostolic Exhortation on the Second General Assembly of the Synod of Bishops for Africa, popularly called the Second African Synod, he includes under his treatment of environmental issues the fact of poverty and misery ravaging large parts of the African society. The Pope first addresses the issue of poverty by calling on all members of the Church "to work and speak out in favor of an economy that cares for the poor and is resolutely opposed to an unjust order which, under the pretext of reducing poverty, has often helped to aggravate it" (*Africae Munus*, 79). After this injunction, the Holy Father goes on to say on the environment: "Some business men and women, governments and financial groups are involved in programmes of exploitation which pollute the environment and cause unprecedented desertification. Serious damage is done to nature, to the forests, to flora and fauna, and countless species risk extinction. All of this threatens the entire ecosystem and consequently the survival of humanity" (*Africae Munus*, 80). In this way, the Pope beautifully links the campaign for the elimination of poverty to the campaign for the respect for creation and the eco-system. Contemporary Africa is faced with a myriad of problems emanating from the way people treat the environment. The ever increasing menace of diseases, the scourge of hunger and allied malnourishment, the incessant, violent conflicts ravaging many groups often trace their origins to the abuse or lack of proper care of the inhabited environment. As a matter of fact, some international groups consider the mineral resources of Africa and her rich trove of tourist attractions as more important than the African persons inhabiting those ecological areas. The local Church is thus challenged in this book to balance cosmocentrism with anthropocentrism and to avoid the unethical absolutization of one to the detriment of the other.

All these challenges call for an inculturated environmental theology in the African context. This is the type of theology that Osunkwo has done in this book and which he has encouraged the Church in Africa and Nigeria to keep doing so as to salvage the environment for better living and peaceful coexistence. The book is very well written and addresses issues in a way that recommends it to all readers in both academic and non-academic circles.

Dr. Luke Emehiele Ijezie
Lecturer in Biblical Studies
Catholic Institute of West Africa, Port Harcourt, Nigeria

FOREWORD II

The need to have an environmentally based Church or Theology is important today. It is possible to enhance the teaching and practice of Theology in the manners we handle our environments. In this book, *GOD AND THE HUMAN ENVIRONMENT*, OSUNKWO Jude Thaddeus Ikenna has presented Theology in the light of everyday activity. He ex-rayed the subject matter, outlined and examined the synopsis and contextual analysis of the matter at hand and the various constraints that impact negatively on achieving positive results or utilizing the benefits of the environment to the fullest. Our cooperation is the key. The author's methodology was scientifically organized with detailed strategies that could create immediate consciousness for the preservation of the environments.

The book carefully examined the enormity and nature of problems facing society today due mainly to the neglect of our environments, and the possibility of actualizing and realizing his hypothesis by suggesting certain measures that could be taken or implemented to curb possible constraints and degradation of our most cherished gift of God - the environment. In the author's opinion, we are our environments and our environments essentially shape us. He has not only informed us of the necessity of our environment but also the need to preserve it because without a healthy environment, life will obviously come to extinction and the worship of God, inconsequential. Osunkwo wrote with great passion emphasizing the danger society would face if nothing is done to respect and preserve our environment. He equally went ahead to proffer some solutions to the problem.

While I must say that the book did not claim to have exhausted the questions and problems with our environment today, it has attempted to handle this topic in a special way that has made him unique in this field. The book has not only alerted society of the greatest treasure she has, but it has also furnished each of us with the basic guidelines we need to live peacefully with our environments. We need to pray that our environments may protect our efforts on daily basis.

This book has classically ventured into an urgent area that seemed to have challenged theologians and scholars for so many years. The summary of his work was systematic, logical, and consistent to his area of specialty – "Environmental Theology" – a functional theology that addresses the human problem in the moment.

Therefore, based on the enormity of work Osunkwo has done on the above subject, and the relevance of this topic and its contributions to scholarship in general, without any equivocation, I say that succinctly, Jude Osunkwo's book is ad rem and has made him a Scholar in the true sense of the word.

Anthony O. Nwachukwu, PhD, PsyD

PREFACE

The thought of how to make theology go beyond the models of "sitting" and "kneeling" theology, to a model of theologising that can address the concrete possibilities and challenges of today's world, and turn these possibilities and challenges into opportunities for humanity's well-being, has been a preoccupying thought and driving force for me. This has led me to think of developing a work that can apply theology to our concrete natural environment.

Since theology has three definitive modes - theology as proclamation or dogmatics, theology as correlation, and theology as advocacy - it must, without neglecting Proclamation and dogmatics (Revelation and Church), Correlation (Culture and Dialogue) as key contexts for theologising, also listen to the concrete voices of the vulnerable and suffering and respond by affirming and expressing God's liberating Will for humanity and for creation. Theology that matters today is theology rooted in Tradition, but responsive to the concrete sufferings and possibilities of today's World, and is inspired by the vision of God's *basileia*, of life abundant for all.

Today, the Church's theology of the environment expresses greater concern about environmental matters. This is because the environmental challenges that we face today are not only technological and economic but also theological and ethical.

In the face of the so many conflicting voices and ideologies today on environmental issues, which revolve between the economic and the power blocks, I re-present the articulated and unmitigated Catholic principles of environmental Stewardship to Christians and to the world. And in the face of the persistent calls by the *Magisterium* of the Church in recent times that Particular and Local Churches engage in environmental matters in line with her project of holistic evangelisation,

I have, in a contextualised survey, challenged the Catholic Church in Nigeria to help rescue the Nigerian environment by translating the environmental principles for a theology of the environment into concrete contextual social engagements in the spirit of "think globally and act locally". This is 'operational and functional' theology that addresses human issues from their roots.

This means that in view of the proposition on the environment of the Second Special Assembly for Africa of the Synod of Bishops, this book has tried to use the principles of the Church's theology of environment, espoused in the first part of the research, to give impetus to a practical engagement by the Catholic Church in Nigeria and indeed any other particular or local Church. This is to assist in salvaging our environment from human induced degradation and reducing its human impacts. This is because commitment to reconciliation, justice and peace (which is the main trust of the Second Special Assembly for Africa of the Synod of Bishops), and the task of transforming social realities, must also consider seriously environmental issues.

The contextual inquest is: Since responsibility for the environment is an integral aspect of the Christian faith, how can the Church, applying her principles of environmental stewardship, play a specific and concrete role in educating the people in environmental responsibility? How can the Church inject ethical values into environmental considerations? The above questions are very relevant as this is another important area of life where local and particular churches can immensely augment the efforts of Nation States.

In sum, this book represents an attempt to promote/foster the theological principles of Environmental stewardship, its biblical, magisterial and doctrinal principles, and to sell it to my context with the objective of facilitating the realisation of a healthy environment for all.

This book represents one of the first attempts to link the Church's environmental principles to concrete environmental practice, and an effort to enlarge the discussion base to the socio-religious, socio-political, socio-economic and health realms in order to discover the individual, corporate, government and church dimensions to the subject. This makes the subject-matter an engaging one for all. Therefore, the laid out principles and the proposals made represent an original contribution to an unfolding environmental debate and engagement from the Church perspective, and present a systematic, integral and organic approach to environmental issues.

However, though situated in the Nigerian environment, this book addresses the global challenges facing peoples and the Church in different continents of the world in the area of the environment even if the dimensions of the problem may vary from place to place. This is more so in the developing and industrialising regions. Therefore, a broader perspective of analysis and judgement would certainly admit that the concerns addressed in this Book are of global and regional relevance and application. And the proposals made are of equal relevance everywhere. Borrowing from Tom Sheridan, God's *basileia* has no single face: It is not the mostly well-off Western society. It is not the torn and bleeding developing nations with their poverty, illness and deprivation. Nor is it the struggling former Soviet Union sinking into pollution and civil strife. But in each, the connection between the environment and the people who live and work in that environment is a rich opportunity to appreciate the link with the God of Creation ("*Environment: A Compact between the Creator and the Created*", in The Pilot, 2014: Vol. 185, n.11).

OUR SHARED HOME FACES CRISES

The Opening Premise

According to the Environmental Literacy Council, "The environment has become one of the most important issues of our time and will continue to be well into the future. The challenge is to find approaches to environmental management that give people the quality of life they seek while protecting the environmental systems that are also the foundations of our well being"[1].

Hence, in page one of his book, *Ecology at the heart of faith*, Denis Edwards says: "One of the gifts we have received from the twentieth century is a picture of Earth as our shared home....At the same time we are confronted by the damage human beings are doing to the atmosphere, the soil, the rivers.... We are in the midst of a process that, if allowed to continue, will end in the destruction of much of what we have come to treasure...it is obviously far more than a human problem...is a theological issue."[2]

The Catholic Church also recognizes today, more than at any time in history, that the environmental question is theological too. Environmental concerns in the Church has, however, gone through a "...historical progression, from the time of the second Vatican Council through the beginning of the new millennium, and includes flashbacks to earlier eras of the Christian story."[3] The last one hundred years

---

[1] ENVIRONMENTAL LITERACY COUNCIL http://www.enviroliteracy.org/category.php/5.html (accessed 08/27/11).
[2] D. EDWARDS, *Ecology at the heart of faith*, Orbis Books, MaryKnoll (NY) 2006, 1.
[3] J. HART, *Environmental theology?*, Paulist Press, Mahwah (N.Y) 2004, 5.

1

in particular attest to this progression: from Pope Leo XII encyclical *Rerum Novarum* in 1891, to Pope Pius XI encyclical *Quadragesimo Anno* in 1931, to Pope John XXIII encyclical *Mater et Magistra* in 1961, to Second Vatican Council Conciliar document *Gaudium et Spes* in 1965, to Pope Paul VI encyclical *Populorum Progressio* in 1967, to St. Pope John Paul II encyclicals and messages – *Laborem Exercens* in 1978, *Sollicitudo Rei Socialis* in 1987, *Message for World Day of Peace* in1990, and *Centesimus Annus* in 1991. All these in particular have prepared the way for the emergence of the *Compendium of the Social Doctrine of the Church* in 2004 and the *Ten Commandments of the Environment* in 2005. The compendium devotes an entire chapter to the environment.[4] The appearance of Pope Benedict XVI encyclical *Caritas in Veritate* in 2009 and his Message for World Day of Peace 2010, *If you want to cultivate Peace, Protect Creation*, are yet other feathers added to the wings of the Church's theology of environmental stewardship. Today, theology of environmental stewardship of the Universal Church expresses greater concern about environmental matters, and so ought all local and particular churches.

Authentic environmental concerns rest on a three-fold consideration: that nature cannot be used with impunity; that natural resources are limited and some non renewable; that environmental degradation has serious consequences for humanity.[5] This book focuses attention on this consideration. The principal components of the natural environment are: Soil, Water and Air. And the right to a safe and healthy environment is based on two fundamental principles: the respect for human life and the integrity of creation. This right is basic to a healthy and peaceful world.

The Problem

According to St. Pope John Paul II, a great problem facing humanity today and affecting society is the environmental question, the problem of ecology.

---

[4] Cf. A. FOSHEE, *"Environmental issues"* in M. COULTER et al (eds.), *Encyclopedia of catholic social thought, social science and social policy*, 1, The Scarecrow Press Inc., Lanham (Maryland) 2007. 360-361.
[5] Cf. JOHN PAUL II, Encyclical letter *Sollicitudo Rei Socialis* (30 December 1987), n. 34.

He identifies the environmental crisis as a direct consequence of an ethical crisis which calls for a mobilisation of the will of citizens to this issue which is vital for human survival.[6] This means that the environmental challenges that we face today are not only technological or economic but also theological and ethical, and they are not only global, but also regional and national. In the words of Paul Haffner, "What actually constitutes the environment for human beings… cannot be reduced to purely physical elements, but should take into account…theological considerations."[7] For Kathleen Ray, "Without the material bases for existence – the elemental forces of earth, air, water, and fire – there would be no economics, no religion, no anything at all…. Our God-talk cannot afford to ignore the elemental forces upon which we all depend for our very life…. If Earth is to continue to support life as we know it, then it needs theology. Earth needs theology's imaginative capacities, its conceptual and rhetorical power, and its insights into and access to the hearts and minds of humanity…. Theology that matters is theology that makes ecology a primary partner…theology's three definitive modes: theology as proclamation or dogmatics, theology as correlation, and theology as advocacy".[8] What Kathleen is saying here is that theology, without neglecting Proclamation and dogmatics (Revelation and Church), Correlation (Culture and Dialogue) as key contexts for theologising, must also listen to the concrete voices of the vulnerable and suffering and respond by affirming and expressing God's liberating Will for humanity and for creation. Theology that matters is theology rooted in Tradition and dialectics, responsive to the concrete sufferings and possibilities of today's World, and is inspired by the vision of God's *basileia*, of life abundant for all.

Haffner, Kathleen, like so many other scholars who call for an existential and pragmatic theology, are only re-echoing the voice of *Gaudium et Spes* which asserts that "…although we must be careful to distinguish terrestrial progress clearly from the development of the kingdom of Christ, such progress is of vital concern to the kingdom of

[6] Cf. JOHN PAUL II, Encyclical letter *Sollicitudo Rei Socialis* (30 December 1987), n. 26; cf. also JOHN PAUL II, Message for world day of peace *Peace with God the creator, Peace with all of Creation* (1 January 1990), nn. 5&13.
[7] P. HAFFNER, *Mystery of creation*, Cromwell Press, Broughton Gifford 1995, 186.
[8] K. RAY, "*Prologue*" in RAY Kathleen (ed.), *Ecology, economy, and God: theology that matters*, Fortress Press, Minneapolis (MN) 2006 (1-7), 3.

God, insofar as it can contribute to the better ordering of human society".[9] Emphasising this theological and ethical dimension to existential issues, Pope Benedict XVI has this to say: "If the moral principles underpinning the democratic process are themselves determined by nothing more solid than social consensus, then the fragility of the process becomes all too evident; herein lies the real challenge for democracy. The inadequacy of pragmatic, short-term solutions to complex social and ethical problems has been illustrated all too clearly by the recent global financial crisis. There is widespread agreement that the lack of a solid ethical foundation for economic activity has contributed to the grave difficulties now being experienced by millions of people throughout the world. Just as every economic decision has a moral consequence, so too in the political field the ethical dimension of policy has far-reaching consequences that no government can ignore."[10]

In recent times, studies and researches on the environmental question from the Church perspective and beyond are being undertaken. Some awareness is being created. But beyond mere awareness, the human conscience must be sufficiently stimulated to respond. This is because the environmental question today is three dimensional: context (where human interventions and exploitations occur), consciousness (awareness of the effects of our way of life on the broader environment; what is happening to our environment) and conscience (accepting human responsibility to remedy the harm and reject negative and exploitative practices and to pursue more positive and environmental friendly alternatives).[11] Pope Benedict XVI sends out this message of urgency: "We must awaken consciences….We have to face up to this great challenge and find the ethical capacity to change the situation of the environment for good".[12]

Nigeria is also experiencing the crises. But Nigeria is one of the countries of the world where not much has been achieved by way of education

---

[9] VATICAN II DOCUMENT, Pastoral Constitution on the Church in the Modern World, *Gaudium et Spes* (7 December 1965), n. 39.
[10] POPE BENEDICT XVI, Address to Parliament, Westminster Hall, England 2010.
[11] Cf. J. HART, *op. cit.*, 1.
[12] KOENIG-BRICKER Woodeene, *Ten commandments for the environment: pope Benedict XVI speaks out for creation and justice*, Ave Maria Press, Notre Dame (IN) 2009, 8.

and concrete initiatives to safeguard the natural environment. There is a pervading ignorance about environmental issues in Nigeria. This is another important area of life where the Church can immensely augment the effort of the State. The urgency to tackle the issue of environment in Nigeria today comes, particularly, from its link to injustice and conflicts in the country. There is a fundamental link between peaceful co-existence in today's world and the covenant between human beings and the environment as designed by God.[13] Because of the prevalence of hatred, injustice and war in the continent of Africa, the whole issues of reconciliation, justice and peace become central to evangelisation in Africa today and create opportunities to the Church for new frontiers in mission to its peoples.[14] Environmental degradation has become one of the predominant problems causing a greater part of these conflicts and wars in Africa, a continent endowed with tremendous natural resources. This is especially so in those African countries (like Nigeria) that have the numerous natural resources, and which provide the much needed raw material needs of today's world. In the final message of the Second Assembly for Africa of the Synod of Bishops in Rome, the Church in Africa observes: "We live in a world full of contradictions and deep crisis…. In all this, Africa is the most hit. Rich in human and natural resources, many of our people are still left to wallow in poverty and misery, wars and conflicts, crisis and chaos. These are very rarely caused by natural disasters. They are largely due to human decisions and activities by people who have no regard for the common good and this often through a tragic complicity of local leaders and foreign interests".[15]

The Scope of the Book

The question then is: Since responsibility for creation is an integral aspect of the Christian faith,[16] and since beyond mere awareness, the human conscience must be sufficiently stimulated to respond, how can

---

[13] Cf. POPE BENEDICT XVI, Message for world day of peace, *If you want to cultivate peace, protect creation* (1 january 2010), n. 1

[14] Cf. LINEAMENTA, II Special Assembly for Africa of the Synod of Bishops: *The Church in the Service of Reconciliation, Justice and Peace*, Vatican City 2006, n. 10.

[15] L'OSSERVATORE Romano, *Final message of the second special assembly for Africa of the synod of bishops* nn. 4&5, 43 (2117), Vatican City 28 October 2009, 3.

[16] Cf. JOHN PAUL II, Message for world day of peace, op. cit, n. 15.

the local churches play specific and concrete role in educating the people on environmental responsibility? How can the local and particular churches inject ethical values into environmental considerations? How can the local and particular churches champion an environmental education, which can propel the civil society to concrete and positive environmental habits?

Contextualising the above inquests, one asks: How can the Church in Nigeria play a specific and concrete role in educating the people in environmental responsibility? How can this Church inject ethical values into environmental considerations? Since responsibility for the environment is an integral aspect of the Christian faith, this book has sought to clarify the ethical-pastoral obligation of the Church to champion an environmental education, which can propel the civil society to concrete, and positive environmental habits through healthy lifestyles. The Church has to do this by pursuing a systematic, holistic and organic approach to environmental issues, which will inspire people to that profound commitment to the mutual responsibility of delivering a healthy environment for the common good.

The above questions are very relevant as this is another important area of life where the local churches can immensely augment the efforts of Nation States. In this duty, the Church would be playing the role of the liberator. She would also be conscientising the people to be vehicles of their own liberation and that of their environment. The challenge is to develop every potential aspect of the Gospel message so as to liberate the peoples from "structures of sin".[17] The Church plays this liberating role through her social engagements which favor movements of social change.

Moreover, environmental stewardship is rooted in the concept of sacred space. As in the case of the biblical merchants in the temple whose tables were downturned by Jesus for intruding into the sacred space of God[18], the Church sees the true temple of God as including the Earth in which life takes root. Justifying the Church's concern for and involvement in the socio-political and economic problems of the world, one could say that the Temple of God is the entire humanity and every

---

[17] LINEAMENTA, II Special Assembly for Africa of the Synod of Bishops, n. 32.
[18] Cf. Matt. 21:12.

single person, in which God is seeking to build a definitive image of him. In this sacred space, the merchants are proposing cruel commerce and negotiating unjust bargaining. This is the reason for which the Church raises its protest and invites all men to proper responsibility.

Therefore, in the face of the so many conflicting voices and ideologies today on environmental issues, which revolve between the economic and the power blocks, this book has re-presented in an articulated manner the unmitigated Catholic theological principles of environmental stewardship to her members and to the world. And in the face of the persistent calls by the *Magisterium* of the Church in recent times, that particular and local churches engage in environmental issues in line with her project of holistic evangelisation, this book has challenged the Catholic Church, especially in Nigeria, to help save the environment. This she does by translating the principles of environmental stewardship into concrete contextual social engagements in the spirit of "think globally and act locally". This is operational and functional theology that addresses human issues from their roots.

In view of the proposition on environment by the Second Special Assembly for Africa of the Synod of Bishops, the author of this book has used the theological principles of environmental stewardship, as espoused in the first part of this book, to give impetus to a practical engagement by the Catholic Church. Especially in Nigeria, this will assist in salvaging our environment from human induced degradation and reducing its human impacts. The author believes that commitment to reconciliation, justice and peace (which is the main trust of the Second Special Assembly for Africa of the Synod of Bishops), and the task of transforming social realities, especially in Africa, has to consider seriously environmental issues.

In this regard, firstly, this book has tried to explore in brief the teaching of the Catholic Church on the environment (in the face of a secular ideological environmentalism that divinises nature, diminishes the centrality of the human person and sacrifices him on the altar of nature). Secondly, the book has attempted to present the environmental situation in Nigeria, having in mind the Church's teaching on the environment. And finally, in the spirit of concrete responsibility, the book has endeavoured to proffer concrete proposals for the Church's involvement, especially in Nigeria, towards the realisation of a relatively safe and secure environment for all.

In sum, this book represents an attempt to promote and foster the theology of environment, its biblical, magisterial and doctrinal principles, and to sell it to the world and to my context (Nigeria) with the objective of facilitating the realisation of a healthy environment. It is the uncompromising position of this book that in order to help achieve the objectives and strategies, the Church has to give clear ethical guidance on environment by evolving an engaging pastoral catechesis of environment, by embarking on public education and sensitization, by designing a rescue package for victims of the human induced environmental degradations, by dialoguing with the Government and the operators of major degradation outfits, by co-operating with pro-environment N.G.O's, and by ownership and use of radio and television stations as indispensable tools of effective ministry in today's world.

Motivation and Investigation Questions

The motivation of the author of this book hinges on two convictions: (i) Environmental harmony is a key to peaceful co-existence. (ii) Countries still developing and industrialising can be guided to avoid the mistakes of the past and reduce drastically the incidents of environmental damage and its consequent hazards.

In alignment with this motivation, the author has proposed two Investigation questions:

1) Is there a relationship between environmental harmony and peaceful co-existence?
2) Can the Church play a concrete pastoral role in shaping positive environmental behaviour that will promote peaceful co-existence and harmony in Countries?

By the time the reader of this book has finished dissecting through the pages, the answer to both questions will surely be in the affirmative.

The Division of Work

Any deep reflection on the natural environment within our context of investigation must address these issues: The ethical dimension of the environmental crisis, the link between environment and development, the poor and the disadvantaged persons whose lives are often affected by misplaced priorities, environmental abuse and compromises, a deep reflection on the spiritual/religious bond between humans and their environment, and on the potential contribution of the Church to environmental questions and issues. This book has attempted to do justice to these issues by following a work plan with three strategies: the strategy of ethical standing (describes the ethically significant environmental features in the Church's teaching on the environment); the strategy of nature's standing (accesses multivalent human practices within the environment itself); and the strategy of human subjectivity (integrates that environment and the practices into some model of a renewed human response).[19]

Therefore, the first chapter of the book looks at the Catholic principles of environmental stewardship, systematically and logically sets out themes, and evaluates also some contemporary challenges to it. The second chapter explores the principle of Creation-Redemption in order to explain the concepts of Dominion and Stewardship. The third chapter examines the Fundamental Principles of Respect for Human Life and Integrity of Creation. The forth chapter deals with the Notion of Development and its Underlying Ethical Questions. The fifth chapter discusses Environmental Conversion and Developmental Solidarity. The sixth chapter captures the Current State of Degradation of the Nigerian Environment. The seventh chapter exposes the kinds and sources of environmental degradation in Nigeria. The eighth chapter exposes the ethical-spiritual, economic, political, socio-cultural and health consequences of environmental degradation in Nigeria. The ninth chapter of the book discusses the environmental challenge in Nigeria that environmental degradation poses and offers proposals for pastoral action to the Church. The tenth chapter reviews Nigeria and Africa in relation to the rest of the world on the issue of environment.

---

[19] Cf. W. JENKINS, *Ecologies of grace: environmental ethics and christian theology*, Oxford University Press, New York (NY) 2008, 59.

The eleventh chapter takes a cursory look at the Church of the future in Nigeria and Africa. A general evaluation and conclusion caps up the book.

Originality and Contribution of Work

The author truly submits, *ab initio,* that the domain of exploration of *God and the Human Environment* is indeed a "virgin area" in Church circles. *God and the Human Environment* represents one of the first attempts to broadly link the Catholic principles of environmental stewardship to environmental practice. This book equally represents an effort to enlarge the discussion base to the socio-political, socio-economic, socio-cultural, socio-religious and health realms in order to discover the individual, corporate, government and Church dimensions to the subject. This makes the subject matter one engaging for all. Therefore, the proposals made represent an original contribution to an unfolding environmental debate and environmental engagement from the Church perspective. This book also in clarifying the ethical-pastoral obligation of the Church to champion an environmental education which can propel the civil society to concrete positive environmental habits, has proposed and articulated a systematic, integral and organic approach to environmental issues in the Church. In line, therefore, with the Proposition of the Second Special Assembly for Africa of the Synod of Bishop[20], the author intends this book to be a ready "handbook" and "blueprint" for the Church, especially in Africa, in the area of environment. It is a unique contribution and roadmap offered to Church leadership.

The Definition of Environment in Context

In speaking of the word environment, many aspects come to mind: spiritual environment, biological environment, human environment, animal environment, plant environment, natural environment, *et cetera.* These have their various definitions and descriptions. A coherent and

---

[20] SECOND SPECIAL ASSEMBLY FOR AFRICA OF THE SYNOD OF BISHOPS, The 57 propositions op. cit. 22.

comprehensive understanding, therefore, would include the material, biological, intellectual, cultural and spiritual elements. But for the purpose of this work, we are concentrating on the natural environment.

We now look at a few definitions of the natural environment, and make some deductions from them. The WordReference.com English Dictionary defines the natural environment as "the area in which something exists or lives"; "The totality of surrounding conditions".[21] YourDictionary.com sees the natural environment as "a surrounding or being surrounded", "something that surrounds, surroundings".[22] The Merrian-Webster Online Dictionary defines the natural environment as "The circumstances, objects, or conditions by which one is surrounded"; "The complex of physical, chemical and biotic factors that act upon an organism or an ecological community and ultimately determine its form and survival".[23] The New Age Encyclopedia defines the natural environment as "The complex of factors to which living organisms are subjected comprises their environment or surrounding."[24]

From the definitions, we can deduce the following: that the natural environment includes a place (static) and conditions of a place (dynamic); that the natural environment includes all the conditions, circumstances and influences surrounding and affecting the development of an organism or group of organisms, or that influence life on earth.

Section 38 of the Federal Environmental Protection Agency Act of the Federal Republic of Nigeria defines environment as "(including) water, air, land and all plants, beings or animals living therein and the inter-relationships which exist among these or any of them".[25] This definition, in essence, indicates that life depends on the environment.

---

[21] WORDREFERENCE.COMENGLISHDICTIONARY, http://www.wordreference.com/definition/environment (accessed 26/11/09).

[22] YOURDICTIONARY.COM, http://www.yourdictionary.com/environment (accessed 26/11/09).

[23] THE MERRIAN-WEBSTER ONLINE DICTIONARY, http://www.merrian-webster.com/dictionary/environment (accessed 26/11/09).

[24] E. HUMPHREY Edward et al (eds.), *New age encyclopedia* vol. 6, Lexicon Publications 1963, 487.

[25] FEPA (Federal Environmental Protection Agency), *National guidelines and standards for environmental pollution control in Nigeria*, Federal Government Press, Lagos 1991.

Archbishop Renato Martino adds another dimension to the earlier definitions. According to him:

> The word environment itself means 'that which surrounds'. This very definition postulates the existence of a centre around which the environment exists. The centre is the human being, the only creature in this world who is not only capable of being conscious of itself and of its surroundings, but is gifted with the intelligence to explore, the sagacity to utilize, and is ultimately responsible for the choices and the consequences of those choices. The praiseworthy heightened awareness of the present generation for all components of the environment, and the consequent efforts at preserving and protecting them, rather than weakening the central position of the human being, accentuates its role and responsibilities.[26]

This definition differentiates more clearly between what is surrounded and what surrounds, and singles out the human person as the centre of that which is surrounded. From the above, we can conclude that the natural environment involves a place that is exposed to certain conditions that affect life, and at the centre of this life is the human person.

Linking the above phenomenological definition to the degradation or pollution of environment, the American Heritage Dictionary of English Language talks of "the act or process of polluting or the state of being polluted, especially the contamination of soil, water, or the atmosphere by the discharge of harmful substances".[27] The American Heritage Science Dictionary describes the degradation or pollution of the environment as "The contamination of air, water and soil by substances

---

[26] ARCHBISHOP RENATO MARTINO, Addresses at the *Earth Summit* in Rio De Janiero, Brazil, June 1992, n.1.
[27] THE AMERICAN HERITAGE DICTIONARY OF ENGLISH LANGUAGE, Houghton Mifflin Company 2009, http://www.thefreedictionary.com/pollution (accessed 26/11/09).

that are harmful to living organisms. This can occur naturally…or as a result of human activities".[28]

In this description, we can clearly identify the three broad categories in environmental anatomy: air, water and soil as representing that which surrounds; living organisms as representing that which is surrounded; and substances as representing the dynamic conditions affecting that which surrounds and is surrounded.

This book is concerned with environmental degradation precipitated through human activities. The World Health Organisation (WHO) in 1974 observed: "The environment is considered polluted when it is altered in composition or condition directly or indirectly as a result of activities of man so that it becomes less suitable for some or all of the uses for which it would be suitable in its natural state.[29] The FEPA Act also decries environmental degradation, i.e., any "man-made or man-aided alteration of chemical, physical or biological quality of the environment to the extent that is detrimental to that environment or beyond acceptable limits and 'pollutants' shall be construed accordingly".[30]

Degradation or Pollution of the environment is, therefore, the introduction of substances into the environment that alter its physical, chemical and biological properties in such a way that is harmful to living organisms. In this circumstance, the substances are termed as pollutants. It is also important to note that this introduction produces an undesirable and objectionable change. This undesirability and objectionable change is the concern of this book in the final analysis, as it investigates God and the Human Environment and tries to discover the Christian theological principles for sound environmental practice and its contextual relevance.

---

[28] THE AMERICAN HERITAGE SCIENCE DICTIONARY, Houghton Mifflin Company 2005, http://www.thefreedictionary.com/pollution (accessed 26/11/09).
[29] World Health Organisation (WHO) 1974,
[30] FEPA (Federal Environmental Protection Agency), *National guidelines and standards for environmental pollution control in Nigeria*, Op. cit.

Review of Related Literature

As stated earlier, environmental concerns in the Church has gone through decades of progressive development[31]. This unfolding growth in Catholic environmental thought has prepared the way for the emergence of the *Compendium of the Social Doctrine of the Church* in 2004 and the *Ten Commandments of the Environment* in 2005. The compendium devotes an entire chapter to the environment.[32] The appearance of Pope Benedict XVI encyclical *Caritas in Veritate* in 2009 and his Message for World Day of Peace 2010, *If you want to cultivate Peace, Protect Creation*, are yet other feathers added to the wings of the Church's Social Teaching. The most eloquent Church magisterial documents on environment among them, and which have inspired the author most to undertake the writing of this book include: *Sollicitudo Rei Socialis* (1987), *Centisimus Annus* (1991), and *Caritas in Veritate* (2009). In this condensed review, the author summarily captures their historical antecedents, highlights briefly on their significant feature contributions and notes some reactions to them.

- **Encyclical *Sollicitudo Rei Socialis* (On the Social Concerns of the Church)**

On December 30, 1987, Pope John Paul II (now St. Pope John Paul II) issued the second of his social encyclicals, *Sollicitudo Rei Socialis*. *Sollicitudo Rei Socialis*, was issued to commemorate the twentieth anniversary of Paul VI's *Populorum Progressio*. *Sollicitudo Rei Socialis* would build on *Populorum Progressio* (The Development of Peoples) to discuss global development and its ethical/moral dimensions; survey the synergic relationship between the developed and poor countries. It would underscore the ethical nature of development that must lead humanity to the "fullness of being".

The Significant contributions of *Sollicitudo Rei Socialis* to the environmental debate include:

---

[31] J. HART, *Environmental theology?* Op. Cit, 5.
[32] Cf. A. FOSHEE, *"Environmental issues"* in M. COULTER et al (eds.), *Encyclopedia of catholic social thought, social science and social policy*, 1, Op. Cit. 360-361.

- It discusses the ethical question and identifies what it calls "structures of sin" as obstacles to development and enemies of environment. The road chosen for development must be the one which provides that human dignity is properly respected, and integrity of creation is promoted.
- It calls for Environmental Conversion and Developmental Solidarity: urges the developed world to take responsibility for present environmental crisis and to work for a truly just and humane world; but far from exempting the developing nations themselves from a share in the blame for the present state of things. It sees the way forward in Environmental conversion and Developmental solidarity.
- It clearly differentiates the Church's theology of environment from ecologism as an ideology: the Church's theology of environment is not an ecological ideology (ecologism); rather, it is the result of careful reflection in the light of Gospel principles at concrete situations that confront humanity in order to suggest/ proffer viable solutions to real human problems.[33]

This encyclical brought profound theological perspective into environmental discussions. The Christian creation/redemption-centred perspective leads it to a pronounced holistic view of humanity and humanity's place within the earth's ecosystems. Competing political and economic power blocs, with all their social and economic reverberations, violate this ecological web[34].

According to Thomas Storck, this encyclical presents development as having not only political and economic implications; Development is also theological and moral[35]. Thus, this Magisterial Document has taken debates on Environment and Development beyond the political and the economic to the theological and the ethical realms.

In his critical review, Matthew Habiger observes: "The obstacles

---

[33] Cf. JOHN PAUL II, Encyclical letter *Sollicitudo Rei Socialis* (30 December 1987), n 41.
[34] Cf. *National Catholic Reporter* (4 March 1988) 12, http://www.shc.edu/theolibrary/resources/comments_srs.htm (accessed 05/09/2011)
[35] Cf. T. STORCK, *The Catholic Faith*, vol. 4, no. 3 (May/June 1998)

to development also have a moral character. This is Pope John Paul's contribution to the advancement of Catholic social teaching. He singles out the moral causes, which retard development and hinder its full achievement. By dealing with the behaviour of individuals considered as responsible persons, obstacles to development will be overcome only by means of essentially moral decisions."[36]

Commenting on the contribution of *Sollicitudo Rei Socialis*, Peter Henriot has this to say: "Solidarity, the political response to the political analysis of John Paul II, is in my view the new encyclical's major contribution to development of the church's social teaching. His discussion of solidarity poses serious challenges...the emphasis on solidarity also has profound implications for the community we call church and its structures of relationships.... A church of solidarity is more liable to be both sign and instrument for a world of solidarity."[37]

I completely agree with Philip Land and Peter Henriot that the major contribution of *Sollicitudo Rei Socialis* to the development of Catholic theology of environment is, precisely, its methodology: experientially in touch with today's reality through a reading of the signs of the times, analytically focused on the global structures of development, theologically sensitive to both tradition and scripture, and pastorally open to whatever system respects authentic human development[38]. This encyclical demonstrates an approach to theology of environment that will have long-term consequences as the author espouses in the course of this book.

- **Encyclical *Centesimus Annus***

Centesimus Annus was issued in May 1, 1991 by Pope John Paul II (now St. Pope John Paul II) and written to commemorate the hundredth anniversary of *Rerum Novarum*. Drawing strength from *Sollicitudo Rei Socialis*, this magisterial document stretches the environmental and

---

[36] M. Habiger, *Social Justice Review* (September-October 1988)139, http://www.shc.edu/theolibrary/resources/comments_srs.htm (accessed 05/09/2011)

[37] P. Henriot, *National Catholic Reporter* (27 May 1988)8,http://www.shc.edu/theolibrary/resources/comments_srs.htm
(accessed 05/09/2011).

[38] P. Land & P. Henriot, (eds), The Logic of Solidarity (1989)74,
http://www.shc.edu/theolibrary/resources/comments_srs.htm (accessed 05/09/2011).

developmental argument to the factoring triad: the Human Person, Society and God. According to this document, from the proper notion of the human person, there necessarily follows a correct picture of society. Moreover, if we correctly perceive the truth about God and the human person, we will correctly perceive the truth about society and development.[39] *Centessimus Annus* argues that although developmental activity must have a legitimate sphere of autonomy, at the same time it must respect certain necessities of the human person, and there must be some means to guarantee that this is done. There must be a strong juridical framework to orient development toward the total good of humankind.[40] This encyclical removes environmental discussions from the clutches of environmental ideologies that tend to "thingnify" the human person and "deify" nature.

• Encyclical *Caritas in Veritate* (Charity in Truth)

In 2009, the encyclical *Caritas in Veritate* (Charity in Truth) of Pope Benedict XVI appeared on the horizon of Catholic theology of environment. This magisterial document puts particularly strong emphasis on issue of development and social justice, which the learned Pope extends to the discussion on environmental questions. The encyclical brings insightful thinking and contributions to human ecology and the natural environment. And the issues treated are logical and consistent with the preceding encyclicals and Catholic social engagements, applying them to today's arena. The encyclical notes: "The risk for our time is that the *de facto* interdependence of people and nations is not matched by ethical interactions of consciences and minds that would give rise to truly human development. Only in charity, *illumined by the light of reason and faith*, is it possible to pursue development goals that possess a more humane and humanizing value. The sharing of goods and resources, from which authentic development proceeds, is not guaranteed by merely technical progress and relationships of utility, but by the potential of love that overcomes

---

[39] Cf. JOHN PAUL II, Encyclical letter *Centesimus Annus* (May 1, 1991) no 13.
[40] Cf. JOHN PAUL II, Encyclical letter *Centesimus Annus* (May 1, 1991) no 15.

evil with good (cf. Rom 12:21), opening up the path towards reciprocity of conscience and liberties."[41]

Consequently, one sees the encyclical breaking new grounds and addressing issues as micro-financing, intellectual property rights, globalisation, *unions*, the principle of *subsidiarity*, energy sufficiency and the moral duty to reduce energy consumption, redistribution of wealth, intergenerational justice and environmental resources, international markets and agriculture. *Caritas in Veritate* subsequently harps on the following points:

- Solutions to the world's numerous crises must include strategies to meet people's human and spiritual needs. An overemphasis on technology or giving in to a sort of "supremacy of technology", which finds its highest expression in some practices opposed to life, could in fact spell out disturbing scenarios for the future of humanity.
- The solutions to the current problems of humanity cannot be merely technical, but must take into account all the needs of the person who is endowed with a soul and body," (this point was also stressed by Pope Benedict XVI to the Group of Eight (G8) summit in L'Aquila, Italy, which wrapped up July 10).
- There is an urgent duty to share the earth's resources equitably and safeguard the environment for future generations.
- Not only does the stockpiling of natural resources hinder the development of poorer nations, but also it gives rise to exploitation and frequent conflicts between and within nations.
- The international community has an urgent duty to find institutional means of regulating the exploitation of non-renewable resources, involving poor countries in the process, in order to plan together for the future.
- Ethical values are needed to overcome the current global economic crisis as well as to eradicate hunger and promote the real development of all the world's peoples.
- The truth that God is the creator of human life, that every life is sacred, that the earth was given to humanity to use and protect

[41] POPE BENEDICT XVI, Encyclical letter *Caritas in Veritate* (29 June 2009), no. 9.

and that God has a plan for each person must be respected in development programs and in economic recovery efforts if they are to have real and lasting benefits.

Reviewing this magisterial document, Cardinal Francis George of Chicago affirms: *"Caritas in Veritate*, Pope Benedict XVI's new encyclical, provides helpful guidance for finding answers to the social, economic and moral questions of the contemporary world in a search for truth…. It analyzes the current global economic crisis in light of traditional moral principles. The letter affirms the progress that has been made in world development yet notes that other challenges exist given newly emerging problems in the global society…. The encyclical offers sound reflections on the vocation of human development as well as on the moral principles on which a global economy must be based. It challenges business enterprises, governments, unions and individuals to re-examine their economic responsibilities in the light of charity governed by truth."[42]

These three Church documents demonstrate an approach to theology of environment that has long term consequences as espoused in some details by the author in the course of this book. In fact, it is particularly from these literatures that the author has systematically gleaned out, logically articulated and sequentially expatiated on the fundamental Catholic principles of Environmental Stewardship such as Creation/Redemption-Dominion/Stewardship, Fundamental Principles of Respect for Human Life and Integrity of Creation, Development and its Ethical Questions, Environmental Conversion and Developmental Solidarity.

The Methodology

The author followed a phenomenological methodology plan with three logical strategies: the strategy of ethical standing, the strategy of nature's standing, and the strategy of human subjectivity.[43]

---

[42] CARDINAL FRANCIS GEORGE, in http://www.usccb.org/caritasinveritate/ (accessed 05/09/2011).
[43] Cf. W. JENKINS, *Ecologies of grace: environmental ethics and christian theology*, Op. Cit. 59.

- **The Strategy of Ethical Standing**

In this scientific research methodology strategy, the author has articulated and described in some detail the ethically significant environmental features in the Church's theology of environment. Therefore, this section of the book has explored the Church's theology of environment, evaluating also some contemporary challenges to it. Under this strategy, the author has articulated in some systematic and logical detail the fundamental core principles or themes. They include: Creation–Redemption and Environment, Dominion and Stewardship, Fundamental Principles of Respect for Life and Integrity of Creation, Authentic Development and its ethical questions, and Environmental Conversion and Solidarity. These core themes of environmental stewardship are to guide and inspire environmental practices of peoples and the concrete environmental initiatives of local Churches.

- **The Strategy of Nature's Standing**

In this scientific research methodology strategy, the author has accessed the multivalent human practices within the Nigerian environment. In view of the fact that the above principal themes as presented under the strategy of ethical standing are to guide and inspire environmental practices of peoples and the concrete environmental initiatives of local Churches, the author has gone further in this section, in the spirit of contextual relevance, to examine the prevailing environmental practices in Nigeria in the light of the Church's environmental principles. The author examined environmental practices in Nigeria (which mostly contravene the above principles), the major areas of environmental degradation in Nigeria (soil, water, air and noise) and their sources, and the consequences of such degradation to human life and the overall environment. The author noted that Nigeria has neither measured up to the principles of environmental stewardship in so many areas of environmental management and development, nor complied fully with international standards concerning environmental management, whether at the level of hygiene consciousness of its citizens, or at the level of her developmental strides, or at the level of the exploitation of her natural resources. To a greater extent, the author observed that ignorance about environmental issues is largely responsible. Therefore, the author strongly recommends that an education in environmental responsibility is urgent since education is a dynamic instrument of change and authentic development.

- **The Strategy of Human Subjectivity**

In this scientific research methodology strategy, the author has attempted to integrate the environmental principles developed in the strategy of ethical standing and the multivalent practices investigated in the strategy of nature's standing into some model of renewed human response. Logically, therefore, in view of the incessant calls today by the Church's *Magisterium* that Local or Particular Churches get really involved in environmental issues within their own contexts, this book turned attention in this section to the Catholic Church in Nigeria and how she can, through her environmental initiatives augment the efforts of State in this direction, by using the Church's principles to assist in environmental education that will reverse the grim picture of the Nigerian environment. Concretely, the strategy of human subjectivity which addresses renewed human response, therefore, proposes the conservation, prevention and remedial programs and projects that would be put in place to realise the vision of a healthy environment for all. It is the uncompromising position of the author that the Church has to give clear ethical guidance on the environment by evolving an engaging pastoral catechesis of the environment, by embarking on public education and sensitisation, by designing a rescue package for victims of the man-made environmental pollutions, by dialoguing with the Government and the operators of major pollution outfits, by co-operating with pro-environment N.G.O's, and by ownership of radio and television stations to help achieve the above. It is indeed my conviction and remains the optimism of this work that the Church's involvement in environmental issues, through championing education and dialogue, is one principal road to guarantee peace and harmonious co-existence among peoples. This work believes strongly that a healthy environmental practice is a sure route to lasting peace and genuine progress.

In pursuing the above methodology and strategy, this piece of scholarship therefore is historical, descriptive, analytico-deductive, synthetic, evaluative and prescriptive. It is also necessary to indicate that the numbering in the *footnotes* is continuous according to the headings and chapters, while the *Bibliography and Resources* follow at the end of the entire work.

The Limitation of Thesis

This book is an attempt to promote/foster the theological-pastoral orientations of the Church on the environment, its biblical, magisterial and doctrinal principles, and to sell it to my context (Nigeria) with the objective of facilitating the realisation of a healthy environment, above all in Nigeria. So, the book has tried to respond to the questions deriving from the environment in Nigeria and has evaluated what ought to be the pastoral response of the local Church. This work is, therefore, limited in scope to the Natural Environment. It is not intended to be a research on the interrelationship between human ecology, natural ecology, social ecology and even ecology of the spirit. Such a vast area of intimate interrelationship will be left for further research and educational inquiry. Furthermore, this book does not claim to exhaust the entirety of Catholic documents, literatures, ideas and authors in this chosen area of research. Nor does it claim that the suppositions and proposals made in this project are absolute for the resolution of all the problems of environment in Nigeria. Moreover, there are yet, some open questions that are unanswered by this project, e.g.: How can we develop a catechesis of the environment that can enter into dialogue with the peoples' cultures? And how may we propose a catechesis of the environment that can overcome the problem of religious and cultural pluralism in Nigeria? These are big questions. Certainly, therefore, those questions and those others agitating your minds that are not addressed in this work indicate that there is still room for further exploration and research scholarship in the area under investigation.

CHAPTER ONE

CATHOLIC PRINCIPLES OF ENVIRONMENTAL STEWARDSHIP: THEOLOGICAL-PASTORAL ORIENTATIONS

The real obstacle or stumbling block today in arriving at an objective cause-effect assessment of environmental issues is the interplay of forces and fisting of muscles between economic interests, environmental fanaticism and genuine concerns for environment. Who is sincerely and truly concerned with environmental problems? Certainly the Catholic Church is.[44]

Environmental destruction and degradation involves a lot of human disaster oriented attitudes. The position has been asserted by some environmentalists that Christianity is axiomatically guilty for environmental ruin based on the scriptural command that humans hold dominion over the entire earth[45]. These environmentalists claim that this axiom gave Christians the theological impetus for destroying both earth and the environment.[46] This very recent position's argument, which has generated a lot of debate for and against, has its root in Lynn White who in 1967 charged that the roots of the ecological crisis

---

[44] Cf. P. HAFFNER, *Towards a theology of the environment*, Lightning Source UK Ltd, Leominster (UK) 2008, 71.
[45] Cf. Genesis 1:28; Psalm 8:5-6.
[46] Cf. S. MOREAU et al (eds.), *Evangelical dictionary of world missions*, Baker Books, Grand Rapids (MI) 2000, 296.

could be attributed in large part to Christianity.[47] On the above debate, the positions of Mark Wallace and D. Edwards are informative. Mark Wallace argues rather that Christianity is primarily a biblical faith that is nature-cantered. He affirms that exploitative environmental habits belong to the greed of the human race and not Christianity: "Christianity's primary sacred document, the Bible, is suffused with rich ecological imagery that stretches from the Cosmic Potter in Genesis who fashions Adam from the dust of the ground and puts him in a garden, to the river of life in Revelation that flows from the throne of God, bright as crystal, vivifying the tree of life that yields its fruit to all of earth's inhabitants."[48] It has to be stated that "While Christianity has to accept some responsibility for the ecological crisis, a list of major contributors would need to include the Enlightenment view of the natural world in instrumental terms, the rise of capitalism, the industrial revolution, technological society, an economy based uncritically on endless growth, uncontrolled corporations, and unrestrained greed."[49]

While the debate is raging on, the Catholic Church, in its global, regional and national communities, has begun to evaluate her responsibility to care for creation relative to the exigencies of its historical and ecological contexts, so that creation might both meet human needs and retain its integrity as God's good work. She assesses human role in creation as 'images of God'. This renewed effort has provided for Church theologians and Church leaders the window to 'scrutinize the signs of the times'. The result has been an evolutionary theology of environment, which offers ideas about the intrinsic value of all creatures, responsible use of the earth's resources, a sense of inter-generational responsibility, and a heightened consciousness of the immanence of the creator in creation.[50]

It has to be said, *ab initio*, that the Church's theologizing on environment is neither a mid-way between liberal capitalism and Marxist collectivism, as some scholars tend to argue, nor is it an ecological ideology

---

[47] Cf. D. EDWARDS, *Ecology at the heart of faith*, Op.Cit. 20.
[48] M. WALLACE, "Crum creek spirituality, earth as a living sacrament" in RAY Kathleen (ed.), Ecology, economy, and God: theology that matters, Fortress Press, Minneapolis (MN) 2006, 121.
[49] . D. EDWARDS, *Ecology at the heart of faith*, Op.Cit. 20.
[50] Cf. J. HART, *What are they saying about environmental theology?*, Op. Cit. 10.

(ecologism) with all the "isms" under its umbrella - egalitarianism, conservatism, libertarianism, conservationism, ecopopulism, ecomarxism, ecofeminism, ecosocialism, ecofascism, etc. Rather, the Church's theologizing on environment is the result of careful reflection in the light of Gospel principles at concrete situations that confront humanity in order to suggest/proffer viable solutions to real human problems.[51] It is functional and operational. The Church, therefore, carries out the mandate to evangelise when she applies her social teaching to make her contributions to the solution of the urgent problems facing humankind.

The Catholic Church views as unacceptable two primary ideological pollutants: a renewed philosophical and theological pantheism and a materialistic scientism; these two tendencies lead to a reductionism which does not accept openness to the transcendent dimension of existence.[52] Between the ecological pessimism of a philosophical and theological pantheism and the ecological optimism of a materialistic scientism, therefore, comes the Church's prognosis which this book tends to expose.

The question then is: How has the Church's theologizing on environment faired especially in the face of secular ecological ideologies that mischievously misrepresent the Sacred Scriptures and the Christian position, try to divinise nature, diminish the centrality of the Human Person and sacrifice same at the altar of Nature? Because of the need to give clear theological-pastoral orientations to the environmental debate, the last three decades in the Church has produced landmark documents in Catholic environmental efforts. These documents have attempted to articulate her concerns on environment. Among these documents are:

- Encyclical letter *Sollicitudo Rei Socialis*.[53]
- Message for World Day of Peace 1990.[54]
- Encyclical letter *Centisimus Annus*.[55]

---

[51] Cf. JOHN PAUL II, Encyclical letter *Sollicitudo Rei Socialis* (30 December 1987), n 41.

[52] Cf. P. HAFFNER, op. cit., 93.

[53] JOHN PAUL II, Encyclical letter *Sollicitudo Rei Socialis* (30 December 1987), AAS 80 (1987), 513-586.

[54] JOHN PAUL II, Message for world day of peace *Peace with God the Creator, Peace with all of Creation (1 January 1990)*.

[55] JOHN PAUL II, Encyclical letter *Centisimus Annus* (1 May 1991), AAS 83 (1991), 793-867.

- *Earth Summit* address 1992 and *World Summit on Sustainable Development* address 2002.[56]
- A Christian reflection on the "New Age" *Jesus Christ the Bearer of the Water of Life.*[57]
- Compendium of the Social Doctrine of the Church.[58]
- Ten Commandments for the Environment.[59]
- Encyclical letter *Caritas in Veritate*[60]
- Message for the World Day of Peace 2010[61]

These official documents of the Church have, among others, set out far reaching environmental principles leading to a progressive development of a Catholic Theologizing on environment or Environmental Theology. They have set out clearly the theological-pastoral orientations towards the development of a solid Christian theology of environment. These theological-pastoral orientations "... reveal that shifts in understanding – some gradual, some more abrupt – have occurred in some aspects of Catholic thought on environmental issues, on human's relation to creation, and on awareness of the immanence of God in creation and the concrete implications of that awareness".[62]

---

[56] ARCHBISHOP RENATO MARTINO, Address at the *Earth Summit* in Rio De Janiero, Brazil, June 1992, and at the *World Summit on Sustainable Development* in Johannesburg, South Africa, 2002. Archbishop Martino represented the Vatican as Apostolic Nuncio and head of the delegation of the Holy See (the Vatican's designation as a Nation State in the United Nations) to the Rio De Janiero and Johannesburg conferences hosted by the United Nations.

[57] PONTIFICAL COUNCIL FOR CULTURE – PONTIFICAL COUNCIL FOR RELIGIOUS DIALOGUE, *Jesus Christ the Bearer of the Water of Life, a christian reflection on the "new age"*, Libreria Editrice Vaticana, Vatican City 2003.

[58] PONTIFICAL COUNCIL FOR JUSTICE AND PEACE, *Compendium of the Social Doctrine of the Church*, Libreria Editrice Vaticana Vatican city 2004.

[59] WOODEENE KOENIG-BRICKER, *Ten commandment for the environment, Pope Benedict XVI speaks out for creation and justice*, Ama Maria Press, Notre Dame (IN) 2009.

[60] POPE BENEDICT XVI, Encyclical letter *Caritas in Veritate* (29 June 2009), AAS

[61] POPE BENEDICT XVI, Message for world day of peace, *If you want to cultivate peace, protect creation* (1 january 2010), Libreria Editrice Vaticana 2009.

[62] J. HART, op. cit., 60.

These Universal Church documents have elaborated fundamental themes of environmental stewardship such as:

- Creation-Redemption: Dominion and Stewardship.
- Fundamental Principles of Respect for human life and Integrity of Creation.
- Notion of Development and its underlying ethical question.
- Environmental Conversion and Developmental Solidarity.

These themes and core principles of Catholic environmental theologizing have addressed specific environmental issues and inspired practical political and pastoral efforts to transform perspectives on practices towards the environment among communities of faith all over the world. The significant social implications of this integrated vision are that peoples of the world are invited to care for both humanity's common good and God's creation as a whole drawing from the Sacred Scriptures and the Church's Social Teaching in a mode which engages the Church *ad intra* and *ad extra* into constructive and concrete historical and contextual environmental projects. The aim is "...to confront and remedy current problems and injustices, conserve the earth and protect the community of life, and construct communities that will think about and work both to prevent future human-caused problems and to inspire and strengthen people to care for all creation."[63]

This book will logically navigate, examine and elaborate on these fundamental environmental themes subsequently.

---

[63] J. HART, op. cit., 3.

CHAPTER TWO

CREATION-REDEMPTION: DOMINION AND STEWARDSHIP

The theological and ethical starting point for a responsible engagement with the environment and an adequate response to the environmental crisis is the Catholic theology of Creation. This is of particular importance for our subject. From it, we learn not only why we should care for the environment but also with what attitude we should do so.

The critique given to modern industrial and technological culture that it puts in danger humans and the environment does not spare Christianity. The critique includes the Judeo-Christian religion in its list of prosecutable offenders, and passes a judgment on her as a religion that has provoked an aggression against the environment by the doctrine of creation in Genesis chapters One and Two. This is joined to another, the supposed Western Christian mentality and the degradation of the third world countries they colonized. Whatever is the truth or non-truth here, a common consensus today is that there is need to save humanity from a self-imposed suicide, and therefore a need for a proportionate ethical response by all, indeed an ethic of responsibility for creation.

There are, therefore, two points which this book has to investigate: whether a true interpretation of Creation in the Bible (which must go beyond the book of Genesis to embrace the whole Sacred Scripture and the wider biblical tradition) ought to be read always in simultaneously analytic, comparative and synthetic manner? And whether a distinction can be made between Western technological mentality (that could have the propensity to plunder the environment) and the Christian religion?

It cannot be sustained from biblical data that Christianity has a plundering anthropology when the whole phenomenon of human-nature-God (religion) is read within the ambit of the whole history of salvation ending at the new creation in Christ. In the letter to the Romans[64], Paul talks of Creation in need of liberation. This spasmodic expectation of the whole created order invokes the Genesis account of the subjugation of Nature to Humans within the context of humans, not only as the image of God (*imago Dei*) through the divine breath, but also humans as molded from the dust of the earth. Thus, humanity cannot operate outside the plan of God. To do that would be to fracture humanity's covenant with God and harmony with nature. This would alienate humanity from both the "divine breath" and "the dust of the earth".

The plan of God, in putting humanity at the centre of the garden (at the headship of Nature or Environment) cannot be to destroy it. Paul Haffner asserts: "The theology behind the *imago Dei* affirms man's crucial role in the realization of God's eternal abiding in the perfect universe. Human beings, by God's design, are the administrators of this transformation for which all of creation yearns."[65]

A deviation, therefore, will be humanity's choice as a free being. While Genesis 1:26 talks of 'dominate', 2:15 talks of 'take custody' and 'take care'. Therefore, human dominion is not presented as absolute, a nature sorely for human use. Rather, the image of God is to preserve the integrity of creation with which humanity is in harmony from the "dust". As Jürgen Moltmann puts it, before the earth is humanity's, the earth is first God's. This means that a theology of creation that is biblical, Christological and ecological has also to be ecclesiological.[66] Jürgen Moltmann seems to affirm here the Church's teaching that humanity's supreme position is based on God's prior and original gift of things that are.[67] And so, it was the creator's will that humans should communicate with nature as an intelligent and noble 'master' and 'guardian' and

[64] Cf. Romans 8:19-22.
[65] P. HAFFNER, *Towards a theology of the environment*, Op. cit. 201.
[66] Cf. J. MOLTMANN, *La giusticia crea futuro*, Queriniana 1990.
[67] Cf. PONTIFICAL COUNCIL FOR JUSTICE AND PEACE, *Compendiun of the social doctrine of the church*, Libreria EditriceVaticana, Vatican City 2004, 281.

not as a heedless 'exploiter' and 'destroyer' ".[68] As a matter of fact, the contemporary society can develop better to the extent human beings recognize their responsibility in creation and respond with fidelity to the divine ordinance.[69]

Genesis 2:8-9 read together with Gen. 2:15-17 would bring out much more clearly the harmony-tension between 'God-nature-humanity' in the tree placed at the center of the garden. The harmony-tension lies between humanity's limited dominion and the choices humans must make in freedom that define humanity's future, and the harmony that must exist between God, nature and humanity. This means that the earth cannot be cultivated in truth when it is separated from humans and from God as auto-sufficient. The earth, on the contrary, is not auto-sufficient. The environment is indeed the context of human culture and divine glory.

Therefore, the principle of dominion, guardianship and custody must in responsibility strike equilibrium between the parties – divine intension, human need and nature's integrity. Thus the Catholic Church teaches: "At the summit of this creation which "was very good" (Gen. 1:31), God placed man. Only man and woman, among all creatures, were made by God "in his own image" (Gen. 1:27). The lord entrusted all of creation to their responsibility, charging them to care for its harmony and development (cf. Gen 1:26-30)." [70]

In the texts of Genesis, therefore, natural environment is the context of cultural and historical realization. Since of all creatures only humanity is capable of taking a distance from nature, humans must guard the earth not only as an entity of material utility but also as home. This responsibility for the earth understood as 'care' and as 'consciousness of the good of life' is the true sense of the Genesis dialogue between the Divine will/command, and the human freedom/choice. Whenever dominion is separated from stewardship which entails our responsibility to God, exploitation and destructive

[68] JOHN PAUL II, Encyclical letter *Redemptor Hominis* (4 March 1979), AAS 71 (1979), n. 15
[69] Cf. M.N. NWACHUKWU, *et al* (Eds), African Journal of Contextual Theology, Vol 2. Change Publications Ltd, Lagos 2010, 42.
[70] PONTIFICAL COUNCIL FOR JUSTICE AND PEACE, *Compendium of the Social Doctrine of the Church*, Op. cit., n. 451, p. 276.

power take over. But this is only a part of the analysis. Creation must be understood within the whole context of salvation history. This is because the design of creation has as summit not the Adam of Eden, but Jesus, the second Adam properly called, who has come to reconcile the entire intra-mundane reality (i.e. Jesus as new Adam of new creation). The work of the first Creation culminates, therefore, in the greater work of Redemption. St. Pope John Paul II in the encyclical *Dominum et Vivificantem* teaches:

> The incarnation of God the son signifies the taking up into unity with God not only of human nature, but in this human nature, in a sense, of everything that is 'flesh': the whole of humanity, the entire visible and material world. The incarnation, then, also has a cosmic significance, a cosmic dimension. The 'first born of all creation', becoming incarnate in the individual humanity of Christ, unites himself in some way with the entire reality of man, which is also 'flesh' – and in this reality with all 'flesh', with the whole creation.[71]

This cosmic dimension of the Christ event is well articulated in the Compendium of the Social Doctrine of the Church: "The definitive salvation that God offers to all humanity through his son does not come about outside of this world....The whole of creation participates in the renewal flowing from the Lord's Paschal Mystery...nothing stands outside this salvation."[72] Capturing this divine kenosis, Paul Haffner said: "The happy message of God's creation is maintained, recapitulated and surpassed through the happy message of Jesus Christ. There is no more profound reason, more radical measure or greater assurance for man's task concerning creation than Jesus Christ himself."[73]

Paul Haffner stretches this further by asserting that the environment is considered in the context of *oikumene*: the object of the new divine economy is the *oikumene* – all the inhabited earth. All of creation is

---

[71] JOHN PAUL II, Encyclical letter *Dominum et Vivificantem*, (18 May 1986), n. 50.
[72] PONTIFICAL COUNCIL FOR JUSTICE AND PEACE, *Compendium of the Social Doctrine of the Church*, Op. cit., nn. 443&445, pg. 277-278.
[73] P. HAFFNER, op. cit., 148.

recapitulated in Christ.[74] In Jesus Christ humanity re-reads its original call to subdue the earth, as a continuation of God's work of creation rather than the unbridled exploitation of it.

Karl Rahner in his *Self Transcendence of the Cosmos*[75] sees in the human nature of the Son of God, Jesus, the place of meeting of creation with the Eternal Word. For him, the Son calls to profound communion again the whole of creation after the rupture by the first Adam. So, the whole of nature participates in the redemptive work of the *First Born Son*, new Adam of the new creation.

Humanity's participation in this created nature that is redeemed must, therefore, bring up new dimensions to whole issues of dominion and stewardship, respect for human life and integrity of creation, authentic development and its ethical questions, and the issue of environmental conversion and developmental solidarity. The question is: Within the ambience of Christian responsibility to the environment, what does it mean for the ministry of the Church in the world that God's earth is in danger of being destroyed by human induced activities? Can the Church do something in this regard or must she remain a simple spectator? Is the Church to remain the stainless heavenly city, or must she become stained by the predicaments of the present? The point is that salvation in Jesus Christ is an incarnated salvation. It is a divine deed in time, within the vicissitudes of this world. It is the truth that the relationship of the person of Jesus with the suffering nature and the suffering humanity is not only ontological but also soteriological.

In the view of Emmanuel Levinas, in his classical metaphysics, time is not abstract but concrete. Our responsibility is not also abstract but inserted into the concrete daily existence of humans (cf. Rom 8:21-22). For Levinas, the coming of the kingdom preached by Jesus and his resurrection are all inserted into concrete daily life, and his passion lives on in men and women who suffer the consequences of the wickedness of the powers of this world. Hence in his Paschal Mystery, the reality of God enters into contact with the reality of this world. Both are not opposed. There does not exists a world reality outside the reality of

[74] Cf. P. HAFFNER, op. cit., 167.
[75] Cf. K. RAHNER, "The theological problem entailed in the idea of 'the new earth'" in *Theological investigation*, 10, Darton, Longmann & Todd, London (1973), 270.

Christ and of God, and therefore not outside of the Church. This means that the Church has to be visible in the world, not only in the sense of 'spacio' but also in service to the kingdom of God in Christ through the Spirit. This is the real sense of Church as Sacrament of God in the world. To separate these two aspects of God-world-in-Christ is to betray the gospel.

If the love of God is implicated (made concrete) in creation this way, this creation then becomes the environment of our salvation, and therefore to degrade it is to go contrary to the natural context in which we realize our salvation. Of consequence, nature/earth comes into the context of responsibility and decision. The responsibility of the Church becomes responsibility in Christ in the totality of the life of Christ for us. Therefore, a theology of creation (cosmology) and a theology of incarnation or redemption (Christology) are not opposed.

If the Church must continue to speak of the totality of the life of Jesus Christ – the incarnate Jesus crucified and risen – she must speak out against the destruction of our vital environment. In this, we have a responsibility towards God and in favor of God, and towards humanity and in favor of humanity. For Christians, therefore, the emphasis on otherworldly concerns present in some readings of the New Testament needs to be balanced with its complementary consideration of being in the world and transforming it.[76]

For D. Bonheoffer, responsibility to the environment is always connected to Jesus Christ. And this responsibility means entering into the totality of this reality that Christ gives life for the whole humanity including nature. This responsibility involves representation and accommodation: the one about the liberty of God that we know in Christ, the other about the liberty of man that we manifest in historical witness.[77]

In his existential perspective, Karl Rahner holds that responsibility to the 'absolute future' (God) does not diminish or suppress responsibility for the 'intra-mundane future'. The future in which God comes does

---

[76] Cf. E. LEVINAS, *Of the God who comes to mind*, Stanford University Press, Palo Alto 1998,
[77] Cf. W. ELNELL (ed.), "D. bonhoeffer" in *Evangelical dictionary of theology*, Baker Academic, Grand Rapids (MI) 2009, 181-182.

not frustrate the present in which man lives. Man realizes openness to the absolute future through a relation to the present, i.e. the future is realized in responsible availability to the present.[78]

In this connection, G. Kaufman also holds that the Divine future in which God comes does not negate the human future towards which humanity goes – devotion to bringing about a more humane and ecologically rightly-ordered world to which we all aspire. He holds that our human past, present and future are drawn together in this overall vision – a vision that helps us identify and address the problems in today's world most urgently demanding our attention.[79]

Paul Haffner also assents to these views when he observes: "The announcement of redemption, which offers a hope of salvation beyond a merely earthly future, cannot avoid having consequences for ecological ethics, which, among other things, invites everyone to take responsibility for the future of this world. Faith in Jesus Christ does not excuse man from concern for the world…but does form him to an attitude of service to the world"[80]

Redemption theology is bringing a totally new vision into humanity's attitude to the world around us. Today, humanity's consciousness of responsibility, a responsibility 'to our world', is that of supremacy and creativity. In this mode, humanity's relationship with the environment conditions the relationship with God and not vice-versa. But in Christ, as we have tried to analyze in creation-redemption investigation, humanity's rapport with the environment is conditioned by the rapport with God. This is, indeed, the supremacy of biblical anthropology over pragmatism.[81]

---

[78] Cf. K. RAHNER, "The eternal significance of the humanity of Jesus for our salvation" in K. RAHNER, Theological investigations 3, Seabury (NY) 1974, 43-44; cf. also K. RAHNER, "The theological problems entailed in the idea of 'the new earth'" in K. RAHNER, Theological investigations 10, Darton, Longmann and Todd, London 1973, 270; cf. also K. RAHNER, "Resurrection" in RAHNER Karl (ed.), Encyclopedia of theology: a concise sacramentum mundi, Burns & Oats, London 1975, 1438-1442.
[79] Cf. G. KAUFMAN, "The human niche in earth's ecological order" in RAY Kathleen (ed.), Ecology, economy, and God, theology that matters, op. cit. 119.
[80] P. HAFFNER, op. cit., 221
[81] Cf. JOHN PAUL II, Address to participants in the congress on environment and health, 24 march 1997 4, 1.

In the gospel periscope of Luke[82], we remember the question the rich man asks about eternal life, the answer Jesus supplies to him, and what his reaction is. The response from Jesus indicates that the rich man of this narration has two things to offer to this world: religion and material well-being. Is he forthcoming? He is willing to offer the former and to shy away from the later.

Of logical consequence to this text, therefore, the mission of the Church as *Sacramentum Mundi* touches on both. It extends to the suffering humanity and the suffering nature. The Church assists to better the situations and conditions through which men and women come meeting with the God of Jesus Christ who makes all things new. She, therefore, participates in the historical processes that promote respect for human life and integrity of creation.

For John Hart, "Creation-affirming teachings that emerge from a careful consideration of the implications of God's incarnation in Jesus Christ affirm the goodness of the corporeal reality of human existence. In this connection, the perception of theology in conversation with environmental issues is that God is both transcendent (distinct from the created world) and immanent (present to the world)....This divine presence is seen in a unique way in Jesus Christ."[83] This sense of God-immanent is not limited sorely to human-divine personal engagement. It extends across and deep within creation. All creation, in some way, has the potential to be revelatory of divine presence.[84] This is what is meant by *sacramental universe*.

To the environmentalists, who claim that Christianity is axiomatically guilty for environmental ruin based on the scriptural command that man holds dominion over the entire earth (cf., Gen 1:28; Psalm 8:5-6) and go ahead to affirm that this gave Christians theological impetus for destroying both earth and the environment, we say, from the foregoing investigation, that it is an interpretative error. As a matter of fact, the notion of senseless and limitless progress hasn't its origin in Christianity; they are characteristic of Hegel and Marx and of neo-Darwinism.[85]

---

[82] Cf. Luke 18:18-23.

[83] J. HART, op. cit., 102.

[84] Cf. J. HART, op. cit., 102.

[85] Cf. P. HAFFNER, op. cit., 188.

Their theories tried to remove God from the equation as man becomes "God" to himself.

In the Catechism of the Catholic Church (CCC) §299 we read that God created an ordered and good world, and because creation emerges from God's goodness, it is also good. It goes further to affirm that God willed creation as a gift to humanity, entrusted to humans[86]

The issue under interrogation here is whether this biblical goodness means an "intrinsic goodness" or an "instrumental goodness"? "Good", "Gift", "Entrust" must be understood within the contexts of stewardship and responsibility. The CCC §373 in clearing the ambiguity and harmonizing both views asserts that man and woman have the vocation of "subduing the earth" as stewards of God not with an arbitrary and destructive domination, but since they are made in the image of the Creator who loves everything that exists, with responsibility for the world God has entrusted to them.[87] Adding voice to this, Paul Haffner said: "Creation is 'very good' only after God places a central reference point on it: man, through whom it all becomes a meaningful whole, with a unitary and comprehensive order....The idea of equality, equivalence and autonomy of all creatures does not accord with the faith of the Church. There is a hierarchy of participation and solidarity in the cosmos."[88]

Having tried to analyse creation-redemption in relation to God-nature-humanity, the question becomes: what then does dominion and stewardship mean for the human person in his relationship to the environment?

Dominion (Gen 1:26-28), which comes from the Hebrew word *răda*, means "to herd", "to conduct", "to guide", and "to govern".[89] Dominion, therefore, means to have sovereignty over and responsibility for the well-being of God's Creation.

Stewardship ensues from the biblical concept of *care* (Gen. 2:15), a concept that comes from the Hebrew word šamar, which expresses

---

[86] Cf. THE CATECHISM OF THE CATHOLIC CHURCH, Paulines-Africa/Libreria Editrice Vaticana, Cittá del Vaticano 1994, 100.
[87] Cf. THE CATECHISM OF THE CATHOLIC CHURCH, Op. cit., 114.
[88] P. HAFFNER, op. cit. 202.
[89] Cf. P. HAFFNER, op. cit. 203.

loyalty.[90] Stewardship, therefore, is the careful and responsible management of something entrusted to one's care by another.

Commenting further on these two etymological roots, Paul Haffner says that the etymological significance is captured in the symbolic naming by the man (Gen. 2:19) of all the animals created by God: "In the Hebrew mentality…giving a name is a sign of a right of sovereignty, a role of dominion….Man welcomes the animals just as God made them, but, giving them a name, they become part of his own world. A demythologizing occurs in this process: the animals lose any divine quality, and are ordered to man as part of his living space to be organized freely and responsibly."[91]

This analysis disagrees with the stance taken by Denis Edwards on the same text of Genesis 2:19. For Edwards, the text is fundamentally God-centered (theocentric) and not human-centered (anthropocentric).[92] But it is both, in *trust* and in *responsibility* respectively.

Dominion, as it applies in Genesis 1:26, does not imply unrestricted exploitation; rather it is a term describing a 'representative' and how that person is to behave on behalf of the one who sends the representative. We are God's representatives. Therefore we are to treat nature as the Creator would, not for our own selfish consumption but for the good of all creation.[93] Thus, dominion understood in this proper context, far from being a license to exploit, becomes an invitation extended to humans to accept a sacred trust as responsible agents in God's creative dynamism. This divine dynamism in which humanity participates always restores and renews. It does not destroy and annihilate. Thus the environmental fundamentalists' view that the dominion perspective gives other creatures merely an instrumental value is again erroneous. They tend to confuse responsible dominion with absolute domination. Human beings are not to be masters of the environment only in the sense of the things that it contains, but as persons, humans ought to act responsibly. Consequently, dominion

---

[90] Cf. P. HAFFNER, op. cit. 204; cf. also W. JENKINS, *Ecologies of grace: environmental ethics and christian theology*, op. cit. 80

[91] P. HAFFNER, op. cit. 205.

[92] Cf. D. EDWARDS, *Ecology at the heart of faith*, op. cit. 19.

[93] J. HART, op. cit. 46.

matched with the theocentric term stewardship puts the concepts hierarchy and human hegemony and control in a context of ultimate responsibility to God.[94]

That is why the fundamental elements of the Church's environmental ethics include: the earth and the natural environment as a trust (which is more fundamental, engaging and demanding than a gift) since it is ultimately held on behalf of another; human responsibility to care for the natural environment (to edify it and employ it for humanity's progress); intergenerational responsibility (on the part of those who own or manage the natural environment where the good of future generations are also included in present-day decisions); Conservation of the natural environment and its goods; and an implied cooperation with God (a participation in God's creative action so that the earth might become ever more fruitful and ever more renewed).[95]

Stewardship, therefore, is the exercise of responsibility for a trust. And it includes the capacity and responsibility to affect, modify, and control many aspects of the ecosphere.[96] But this is to be exercised, as defined in the book of Wisdom[97], with holiness and justice.[98] It means that humans must respect the laws and structures, the framework of meaning and values of the created world. The pre-established structures of the world make it possible for humanity to develop a meaningful and fruitful existence. But this interaction excludes the possibility of absolute autonomy for humans.

Unfortunately, if one takes a look at the various regions of the world, it becomes immediately evident that humanity has fallen short of this expectation. Especially in our time, humans have uncontrollably devastated the environment through forms of dehumanizing industrialization.[99]

Today more than ever, humanity has to be redirected from an

---

[94] J. HART, op. cit. 54.
[95] Cf. J. HART, op. cit., 42; also JOHN PAUL II, "Address at Living History Farms, Iowa" in Origins vol. 9,18 (1979) 293- 294).
[96] Cf. S. MOREAU et al (eds.), Evangelical dictionary of world missions Op. cit. 296.
[97] Cf. Wisdom 9:3.
[98] Cf. PONTIFICAL COUNCIL FOR JUSTICE AND PEACE, Compendium of the Social Doctrine of the Church, Op. cit., n. 473. pg. 288.
[99] Cf. P. HAFFNER, op. cit., 132.

anthropological error. This error hunts not only the environment but also humans themselves. Humanity which discovers the capacity to transform and in a certain sense create the world through human work, forgets that this is always based on God's prior and original gift of the things that are. Humans think that they can make arbitrary use of the earth and subject it without restraint to their whims. But the earth has its own requisites and a prior God-given purpose which humanity can indeed develop but must not betray. Instead of carrying out this role as co-operator with God in the work of creation, humanity sets himself up in the place of God.[100]

Hence, the Church brings the good news of God's love for the cosmos (John 3:16) and Jesus' cosmic redemption and reconciliation (John 1, Col 1, Heb 1) to bear on the environment. The Church cannot be a complicit bystander and participant in the degradation and defilements of the world that God loves and recreates. Meeting human needs without caring for the environment is not only impossible but also unbiblical. This responsibility entails that we must use the earth, the atmosphere, the land, and the water so as to maintain their purity and to conserve and renew their systems. This is because the earth is not a commodity to be bought and sold at the altar of greed and exploitation. That is why the Church as salt of the earth would continue to call all humanity to righteousness and justice in a deteriorating society, and caretaking of an ailing environment.[101] For W. Jenkins, since the earth is the environment of God's action, stewards must be led to know what God's action means for the earth, so that they can know how the earth should shape their own actions in response.[102] According to the U.S Conference of Catholic Bishops: "On a planet conflicted over environmental issues, the Catholic tradition insists that we show our respect for the Creator by our stewardship of creation. Care for the earth is not just an Earth Day slogan; it is a requirement of our faith. We are called

---

[100] JOHN PAUL II, Encyclical letter *Centisimus Annus* (1 May 1991), AAS 83 (1991), n. 37.
[101] Cf. S. MOREAU et al (eds.), Op. Cit. 296-297.
[102] Cf. W. JENKINS, *Ecologies of grace: environmental ethics and christian theology*, op. cit. 90.

to protect people and the planet, living our faith in relation with all of God's creation."[103]

Conclusively, we have tried to establish that human stewardship of and responsibility over the environment is rooted in the biblical creation-redemption anthropology. Pope Benedict XVI summarizes this position thus: "The Redeemer is the Creator – and if we do not proclaim God in his total grandeur, as creator, then we also debase Redemption….That is why a renewal of the doctrine of Creation and a new understanding of the inseparability of Creation and Redemption is of great importance."[104] Based on this Creation-Redemption theology, there can be no confession of Christ without care for creation, and environmental stewardship is Christian discipleship.[105]

Having established this basis, we now turn to the fundamental principles of application that must guide responsible stewardship of the environment: respect for human life and integrity of creation.

---

[103] U.S. CATHOLIC BISHOPS, "*Sharing catholic social teachings: challenges and directions*" in *Origins* 28, 7, 102-106, pg. 104.

[104] BENEDICT XVI, *Message to Priests, deacons and seminarians of the diocese of Bolzano-Bressanone*, 6 August2008,http://www.vatican.va/holy_father/bebedict_xvi/speeches/2008/august/documents/hf_benxvi_spe_20080806_clero-bressanone.en.html (accessed 21/ 09/09).

[105] Cf. W. JENKINS, *Ecologies of grace: environmental ethics and christian theology*, Op. Cit. 82.

CHAPTER THREE

FUNDAMENTAL PRINCIPLES OF RESPECT FOR HUMAN LIFE AND INTEGRITY OF CREATION

Let us examine respect for human life.

The moral factor underlying the environmental problem is the lack of respect for human life evident in many patterns of environmental degradation and callousness. Often, the interests of production prevail over concern for the dignity of persons, while economic interests take priority over the good of individuals and even of entire peoples. In these cases, environmental degradation and destruction are the results of an unnatural and reductionist vision, which at times lead to real contempt for man.[106] For St. Pope John Paul II , "No peaceful society can afford to neglect either respect for life or the fact that there is integrity to creation".[107]

The Church has always maintained that the care and protection of the environment must be approached from the point of view of the human person. It is affirmed that respect for human life and integrity of creation are inextricably linked. And the reverse is also true: Our lack of respect for life extends also to the rest of Creation. This is, in fact, the underlying cause of social injustice and environmental destruction.

Within the exegetic interpretation of the divine breath of the "old

---

[106] Cf. JOHN PAUL II, Message for world Day of Peace: *Peace with God the Creator, Peace with all of Creation* (January 1990), n. 7.
[107] Ibidem.

creation" in Genesis 2:7 and the breath of the Holy Spirit of the "new creation" in Jesus Christ recorded in the gospel of John 20:21-23, human life receives a unique identity. In its analysis, therefore, the idea of human life assumes a specific form of reality different from that of the other creatures. The uniqueness of human life, image of God, is most manifest not only because the human person possesses intelligence, but even in the zone of sensation which he shares with other creatures, he operates at a higher level: while other creatures can feel the content of sensation, only the human person can perceive the origin of the perceived content. Thus the human person feels and sees not only things but also their totality. Because of the above qualities, the human person cannot be 'thingnified' (reduced to a "thing") without great damage to his true nature. St. Pope John Paul II alludes to this when he affirms: "Among all other earthly beings, *only a man or a woman is a "person", a conscious and free being* and, precisely for this reason, the "centre and summit" of all that exists on the earth."[108]

The great paradox of the technologico-industrial modernity is, despite its obvious advantages, to have reduced the human person to an object, a 'thing'. In contrast to the hedonist, individualistic and materialistic mentality of today, the primacy of the human person in the web of life as a unique creation as emphasized by the Social teachings of the Catholic Church, is at the heart of the solutions to today's environmental problems. Environmental issues have to place in top priority the promotion of human life in its personal, familial, social and cultural dimensions.

Therefore, in the different world situations that are contrary to life, we are called to opt for a culture of life and resist developments that are incompatible with life. Protection and promotion of human life and respect for the dignity and fundamental rights of the person are responsibilities of everyone, both individually and collectively. If we close our eyes to them, we are also the promoters of the culture of death. Paul Haffner articulates the fundamental principle of respect for human life, or absence of it, this way:

---

[108] JOHN PAUL II, Apostolic exhortation *Christifideles Laici* (30 December 1988), n. 37.

Instead, many environmentalists give the impression that they believe human beings are a 'scar' or 'cancer' of the planet, a violation of the otherwise perfect natural order. This idea finds no support in revelation.... Considering the existence of other people a misfortune or even a violation of nature is an idea that radically distances itself from Judeo-Christian ethics...The idea that people are simply a drain on... resources not only contradicts our faith, but negates the true contribution of human beings to the common good of human society and to the entire environmental realm.[109]

The Christian view continues to hold that the human person is ontologically and axiologically different from other creatures in a biotic unity of differentiated value. This view is superior to the view which demeans the human person as a scar and an enemy. The truth is that within the dignity of all living beings, the human person is a superior being with superior responsibility.[110]

We must, therefore, reject any ideological approach to environmental issues, which ignores the centrality of the human person, or tries to subordinate the human person to the environment.

Both the entire Social Teaching of the Church and Catholic Theology today do not conceive a Christian vision without the dynamism of integral salvation, of humanization, of reconciliation and of social insertion. Here we are confronted with one of the fundamental principles of Christian ministry: gospel becomes life in total donation. In sum therefore, respect for life, and above all for the dignity of the human person, is the ultimate guiding norm for any sound and authentic economic, industrial or scientific progress.

The history of our time has shown in a tragic way the danger which results from forgetting this truth about the human person. Before our eyes we have the results of ideologies such as Marxism, Nazism and Fascism, and also of myths like racial superiority, exclusivist nationalism and ethnicism. No less pernicious, though not always as obvious, are

---

[109] P. HAFFNER, op. cit., 62.
[110] Cf. PONTIFICAL COUNCIL FOR JUSTICE AND PEACE, *Compendium of the Social Doctrine of the Church*, Op. cit., n. 463, pg. 282.

the effects of materialistic consumerism, in which the exaltation of individual interests and the selfish satisfaction of personal aspirations become the ultimate goal of life. In this outlook, the negative effects on others are considered completely irrelevant. On the contrary, it must be said that no affront to human dignity can be ignored, whatever its source, whatever actual form it takes and wherever it occurs.

Moreover, to choose life involves rejecting every form of violence: the violence of poverty and hunger often from unjustifiable deprivation which afflicts so many human beings; the violence of armed conflict in place of constructive dialogue; the violence of criminal trafficking in humans, human organs, drugs and arms which destroy the psyche and fabric of society; and the violence of mindless damage to our natural environment which ultimately demeans human dignity in preference for senseless development. In every circumstance, the right to life must be promoted and safeguarded with appropriate ethical, legal and political instruments, for no offence against the right to life, against the dignity of any single person, is ever unimportant. The promotion of human dignity is particularly linked to the right to a healthy and life-sustaining environment, since this right highlights the dynamics of the symbiotic relationship between the individual and society. The question comes: What are the implications this respect for human life has for the rest of creation?

Respect for human life and for the dignity of the human person extends also to respect for the rest of creation, which is called to join humanity in praising God (cf. Ps 148:96).[111] Conserving the integrity of God's 'good' creation is a specific responsibility of the human person. The Book of Genesis describes the creation of man and woman as "very good". But the creation of non-human creatures is also described as "good." In other words, the material world has its own value. Consequently, though not equal to humans, nature may not be abused by man.

In the encyclical *Evangeliun Vitae*, we read: "As one called to till and look after the garden of the world (cf. Gn. 2:15), man has a specific responsibility towards the environment in which he lives, towards the

---

[111] Cf. JOHN PAUL II, Message for world Day of Peace: *Peace with God the Creator, Peace with all of Creation*, Op. Cit. n.16.

creation which God has put at the service of his personal dignity, of his life...."[112] This means that human beings are responsible *for* the environment but not responsible *to* it, as if it shared in the dignity and fundamental rights which human beings themselves enjoy as persons made in God's image.

In CCC 2415 and 2416-2418, the Catholic Church affirms the integrity of Creation and the importance of respect for animals. However, this is not to be confused with the so called "animal rights" - the Catholic social teaching does not reduce human beings to the level of animals and elevate animals to the dignity of human beings. Before the human person, the integrity of the rest of creation advances more within the realm of duty than right. In a critical evaluation between rights and duties, Pope Benedict XVI strongly observes: "Individual rights, when detached from a framework of duties which grants them their full meaning, can run wild....Duties set a limit on rights because they point to the anthropological and ethical framework of which rights are a part, in this way ensuring that they do not become license. Duties thereby reinforce rights and call for their defense and promotion as a task to be undertaken in the service of the common good."[113]

Duties here place the human person at the center of consideration within the hierarchy of values and of truth.

The world's present and future depend on the safeguarding of creation, because of the endless interconnection and interdependence between human beings and their environment. The two fundamental principles that ought to guide humanity in its relationship to the natural environment, viewed together in their interconnectedness, extends the concept of the "common good" beyond the human family to include the common good of all people, the common good of the entire environment, and the common good of the entire web of life, in fact, a relational consciousness and commitment to the well-being of humans and of all creation.[114] The Compendium of the Social Teaching of

---

[112] JOHN PAUL II, Encyclical letter, *Evangelium Vitae*, (1995), AAS 87 (1995), 401-552, n. 27.
[113] POPE BENEDICT XVI, Encyclical letter *Caritas in Veritate* (29 June 2009), AAS, n. 43.
[114] Cf. J. HART, op. cit., 45.

the Church synthesizes it thus: "A central point of reference for every scientific and technological application is respect for men and women, which must also be accompanied by a necessary attitude of respect for other creatures."[115]

This implies that the goods of the earth and all the resources of the environment might not be used for the good of humanity independently of considerations about how human activities impact on the environment or effect the human and biotic communities. But this does not suggest in any way putting at par the human person with other creatures, worse subordinating him to the environment. Paul Haffner underscores this strongly when he said:

> It is grossly inconsistent to oppose the destruction of the environment while allowing, in the name of comfort and convenience, the slaughter of the unborn and the procured death of the elderly and the infirm, and the carrying out, in the name of progress, of unacceptable interventions and forms of experimentation at the very beginning of human life. When the good of science or economic interests prevail over the good of the person and ultimately of the whole society, environmental destruction is a sign of a real contempt for man.[116]

Within the necessary connection that must, therefore, exist between the two fundamental principles in consideration here – respect for human life and integrity of creation – St. Pope John Paul II affirms: "The essential meaning of this "kingship" and "dominion" of man over the visible world, which the Creator himself gave man for his task, consists in the priority of ethics over technology, in the primacy of the person over things, and in the superiority of spirit over matter."[117] This priority, this primacy, this superiority, ought always to guide and determine the direction which authentic development takes. This must have informed Luke Emehiele Ijezie, a biblical scholar, to hold that "The whole

---

[115] PONTIFICAL COUNCIL FOR JUSTICE AND PEACE, *Compendium of the Social Doctrine of the Church*, Op. cit., n. 459, pg. 280
[116] P. HAFFNER, op. cit., 130.
[117] JOHN PAUL II, Encyclical letter *Redemptor Hominis*, Op. cit. n. 16.

creation account attests to how the Creator progressively empowers different cadres of creation to function as agents of cosmic control and governance. This reaches its climax in the creation of humans. The creation of human beings has the express aim of establishing competent and efficient leadership personnel for the continued governance of the universe."[118] Any appeal to creation's integrity has to take off from the creation- redemption theology.

We now look at the direction which development should take in order to be truly sustainable and authentic, especially as it relates to the dignity of the human person and to the integrity of the environment.

---

[118] L. E. IJEZIE, *"Creation account in genesis 1:1-24 as a model of political governance"* in African Journal of Contextual Theology, Op. Cit. 41.

CHAPTER FOUR

NOTION OF DEVELOPMENT AND ITS UNDERLYING ETHICAL QUESTION

At the root of any meaningful development lie these fundamental principles: respect for human life and integrity of the environment. These two bring inescapably ethics into the realm of development and humanity's management of the environment. In her presentation at the United Nations Conference on Environment and Development in *Rio De Janiero*, the Catholic Church, through her spokesperson Archbishop Renato Martino, affirms that the problems of environment and development are at their root, issues of a moral, ethical nature, from which derive two obligations: the urgent imperative to find solutions and the inescapable demand that every proposed solution meet the criteria of truth and justice.[119] St. Pope John Paul II in the encyclical *Sollicitudo Rei Socialis* states: "The limitation imposed from the beginning by the Creator himself and expressed symbolically by the prohibition not to 'eat of the fruit of the tree' (cf. Gen 2:16-17) shows clearly enough that, when it comes to the natural world, we are subject not only to biological laws but also to moral ones, which cannot be violated with impunity."[120] The United States Conference of Catholic Bishops (USCCB) also underlines the ethical aspect of development when it says: "At its core the environmental crisis is a moral challenge. It calls us to examine

---

[119] Cf. ARCHBISHOP R. MARTINO, Addresses at the *Earth Summit* in Rio De Janiero, Op. cit. n. 2.
[120] JOHN PAUL II, Encyclical letter *Sollicitudo Rei Socialis*, Op. cit. n. 34; Cf. also JOHN PAUL II, Encyclical letter, *Evangelium Vitae*, Op. cit. n. 42.

how we use and share the goods of the earth, what we pass on to future generations and how we live in harmony with God's creation."[121]

But this ethical imperative, which ought to be at the core of development, has often, not been on the table, as the encyclical *Redemptor Hominis* observes: "The development of technology and the development of contemporary civilization, which is marked by the ascendancy of technology, demand a proportional development of morals and ethics. For the present, this last development seems unfortunately to be always left behind."[122]

Within this ethical-moral concept of development, the Church goes beyond the concept of sustainable development of the United Nations to develop the notion of authentic development. In the encyclical *Populorum Progressio*, Pope Paul VI defines authentic development as the complete, integral promotion of the good of every person and of the whole person.[123] Bearing the above in mind and developing the definition further in its holistic sense, Cardinal Jean-Louis Tauran underscores the position of the Church on development when he said: "Authentic development must be integral, i.e. advance towards the true good of every individual, community and society, in every single dimension of human life: social, economic, political, intellectual, spiritual and religious."[124]

What we are saying is that development and environment cannot be exclusive concerns but must be considered jointly: Christian love forbids choosing between people and the environment. We need development policies that are socially just, environmentally benign and economically efficient. A just and sustainable society and world are not an optional ideal, but an ethical and practical necessity. Without justice, a sustainable

---

[121] U.S. Catholic Bishops, *Renewing the earth: an invitation to reflection and action in the light of catholic social teaching*, Washington DC, November 14 1991, pg. 1.
[122] John Paul II, Encyclical letter *Redemptor Hominis*, Op. cit. n. 15.
[123] Cf. Paul VI, Encyclical letter *Populorum Progressio*, (26 march 1967), AAS 59 (1967), 257-299, n. 14.
[124] Card. J. Tauran, President of the Pontifical Council for Interreligious Dialogue, L'Osservatore Romano 43 (2117), Vatican City 28 October 2009, 22.

economy will be beyond reach. Without an environmentally responsible world economy, justice will be unachievable.[125]

A group of Scientists are arguing that in the face of increased energy and natural resource consumption due to accelerated development, we have a limited window of opportunity to change our environmentally destructive ways. But the proponents of this argument ought to understand that the problem confronting the human environment today is more ethical than statistical, and any balanced solution does not ignore this ethical perspective. A concept of development that thinks and acts only in terms of economics and profit inflicts damage on the environment and limits humanity's deserved authentic growth. The Catholic Church has a concept of authentic development, which offers a direction for progress that respects human dignity, the limits of material growth, the serenity of the environment and openness to transcendence. Pope Benedict XVI in the encyclical *Caritas in Veritate* argues:

> But it should also be stressed that it is contrary to authentic development to view nature as something more important than the human person. This position leads to attitudes of neo-paganism or a new pantheism…it is also necessary to reject the opposite position, which aims at total technical dominion over nature, because the natural environment is more than raw material to be manipulated at our pleasure; it is a wondrous work of the creator containing a "grammer" which sets forth ends and criteria for its wise use, not its reckless exploitation. Today, much harm is done to development precisely as a result of these distorted notions. Reducing nature merely to a collection of contingent data ends up doing violence to the environment and even encouraging activity that fails to respect human nature itself.[126]

In line with this argument, the post-synodal exhortation, *Ecclesia in Asia*, affirms: "The protection of the Environment is not only a

---

[125] Cf. U.S. CATHOLIC BISHOPS, Renewing the earth: an invitation to reflection and action in the light of catholic social teaching, op. cit. 14.
[126] POPE BENEDICT XVI, Encyclical letter *Caritas in Veritate* Op. cit, n. 48.

technical question; it is also and above all an ethical issue. All have a moral duty to care for the environment, not only for their own good but also for the good of future generations."[127]

In the encyclical *Solicitudo Rei Socialis*, the Catholic Church recognises four objectives for an environment-friendly development: Proper use of the things of nature, continuous renewability of renewable resources, proper management of industrial and domestic hazardous wastes, and prevention of haphazard industrialization.[128] Authentic Development also takes into consideration the issue of the common good. The CCC §1906 defines 'Common Good' as "the sum total of social conditions which allow people, either as groups or as individuals, to reach their fulfilment more fully and more easily." These social conditions available to individuals, families and communities must include a healthy natural environment.

There has to be development; And Science and Technology has to be applied to enhance the world and make it ever more useful for the perfection of human beings and society. The Catholic Church has always supported this view. But she objects with passion to the use of same science and technology to destroy or threaten the environment (or not even to use them when difficulties or new and varied challenges arise, in the bid to keep nature sacrosanct) as a contradiction and an abuse of the divine plan, and an affront to the will of the Creator who is absolute Lord of the earth and humankind. The compendium of the social teaching of the Church warns, therefore, against both extreme errors: a mechanistic view of the environment as something sorely to be exploited, and an ecocentric and biocentric view of the environment which ignores the qualitative difference of the human person from other creatures founded on the dignity of the human person.[129] In fact, the key to avoiding these two errors is maintaining the Christian environmental perspective that is theological, Trinitarian, christological, eschatological and anthropological.

Another ethical issue on development and the environment

---

[127] JOHN PAUL II, Post-Synodal Apostolic Exhortation *Ecclesia in Asia* (1999), n. 41.
[128] Cf. JOHN PAUL II, Encyclical letter *Sollicitudo Rei Socialis*, Op. cit. n. 34.
[129] Cf. PONTIFICAL COUNCIL FOR JUSTICE AND PEACE, *Compendium of the Social Doctrine of the Church*, op. cit., n. 462, pg. 282.

is their connection to the poor, as *"... hunger and poverty make it virtually impossible to avoid an intense and excessive exploitation of the environment."*[130] Authentic Development, therefore, is to be guided above all by these ethical values: the dignity of the human person, the universal common good, respect for the natural environment, an option for the poor, and a sense of inter-generational and intra-generational obligation.[131] In the encyclical *Sollicitudo Rei Socialis*, The Church outlines some factors she calls *"structures of sin"* which she describes as obstacles to authentic integral development of peoples: selfishness, short-sightedness, mistaken political calculations, imprudent economic decisions, the all-consuming desire for profit, the thirst for power, the absolutizing of human attitudes with all its possible consequences, and modern imperialism.[132] Pope Benedict XVI, in his message for the celebration of the World Day of Peace in 2007, also said:

> The destruction of the environment, its improper or selfish use, and the violent hoarding of the earth's resources cause grievances, conflicts, and wars, precisely because they are the consequences of an inhuman concept of development. Indeed, if development were limited to the technical-economic aspect, obscuring the moral-religious dimension, it would not be an integral human development, but a one-sided distortion which would end up by unleashing man's destructive capacities.[133]

This means that we are capable of facing a human failure in development when human power over the environment does not include the protection of the environment in the technological-economic

---

[130] PONTIFICAL COUNCIL FOR JUSTICE AND PEACE, *Compendium of the Social Doctrine of the Church*, Op. cit., n. 482, pg. 292

[131] Cf. http://www.wcr.ab.ca/bin/eco-lett.htm.1998, (accessed 01/11/09); Cf also POPE BENEDICT XVI, Message for world day of peace, *If you want to cultivate peace, protect creation*, op. cit. n. 8; cf. also R. GAGLIANONE, PUU Dispensa Corso MLE 1005 "Evangelizzazione e promozione umana: pastorale della promozione umana e dello sviluppo" op. cit. 10-11.

[132] Cf. JOHN PAUL II, Encyclical letter *Sollicitudo Rei Socialis*, op. cit. nn. 36, 37, 38.

[133] POPE BENEDICT XVI, Message for the Celebration of the World Day of Peace, 1 January 2007, n. 9.

calculations and equations, due to a philosophy of life according to which "being is having" and having is a sign of fulfilled existence.[134] The above concerns must have informed the joint declaration on the environment signed by St. Pope John Paul II and Patriarch Bartholomew I of Constantinople in 2002 which states: "The problem is not simply economic and technological; it is moral and spiritual. A solution at the economic and technological level can be found only if we undergo, in the most radical way, an inner change of heart. A new approach and a new culture are needed, based on the centrality of the human person within creation and inspired by environmentally ethical behaviour."[135]

For them and for the Church's Theology on Environment, the way out of or solution to the current environmental degradation and developmental crisis is the way of environmental conversion and developmental solidarity.

We now turn our attention to environmental conversion and developmental solidarity. What do these mean in the context of the Church's theology on environment?

---

[134] Cf. JOHN PAUL II, Encyclical letter *Sollicitudo Rei Socialis*, op. cit. n. 28; Cf. also JOHN PAUL II, Encyclical letter *Centisimus Annus*, op. cit. n. 37.
[135] JOHN PAUL II and BARTHOLOMEW I of Constantinople, *Declaration on the environment*, 10 June 2002.

CHAPTER FIVE

ENVIRONMENTAL CONVERSION AND DEVELOPMENTAL SOLIDARITY

The entire human community - individuals, States and international bodies - has to take responsibility for current environmental hazards.[136] This responsibility calls for environmental conversion and developmental solidarity.

Environmental conversion and developmental solidarity rests on what the Church calls the "ecology of the Spirit" which recognizes the fundamental ethical character of the environmental crisis. Ecology of the Spirit sees the relationship between environment and development as serving the common patrimony of humanity and responds to the challenges with a creativity that guarantees holistic care of the environment and re-establishment of environmental balance in the process of development.[137]

Within the ecology of the spirit, therefore, both environmental conversion and developmental solidarity entail serious ethical obligation, which has direct practical consequences as regards the promotion of a sound environment.

Environmental conversion (environmental *metanoia*) is not to be understood as simply (though does not exclude) turning away from sin. It rather signifies the ability of the mind and heart to adapt to new

---

[136] Cf. JOHN PAUL II, Message for world Day of Peace: *Peace with God the Creator, Peace with all of Creation*, Op. cit. 6.

[137] Cf. S. UZOUKWU, *Peace through dialogue and solidarity*: the basis of true humanism, Snaap Press, Enugu 2004, 218-219.

realities and situations in the light of Gospel principles and motivated by the common good. It is an ecological change of heart and resolve of will from each and from all, personally and collectively, to work together to preserve and protect our environment for the common good. Environmental conversion engages the individual, the Church and the Government: the individual reclaiming his or her vocation as God's steward of the environment through change of lifestyle, the Church committing herself to teaching and promoting environmental ethics especially in her parishes and institutions and in her interactions with the larger society, and Government seeking the common good by observing healthy development strategies, eradicating actions and policies which perpetrate various forms of environmental racism, and working for an economy which focuses more on equitable sustainability rather than on the unbridled consumption of natural resources and the scramble and acquisition of the goods of the earth with such a lion-like ferocity.[138]

Paul Haffner captures this co-responsibility to the environment as it applies to the needed environmental conversion this way: "Public authorities and all people of good will... to examine their daily attitudes and decisions, which cannot be directed towards an endless and unbridled search for material goods that does not take into account the environment in which we live.... Such an approach to the environment basically demands the grace of conversion".[139] Pope Paul VI who also discussed concrete environmental questions struck the cord when he said that the problem of the environment cannot be tackled with technical measures alone, but a mentality change is necessary.[140] This mentality change is one of personal conversion and of social change. It is about a true concept of development, which cannot ignore the proper use of the things of nature, the continuous renewability of resources and the consequences of industrial hazards and haphazard industrialization - three considerations which alert our consciences to the ethical dimension of development.[141]

---

[138] Cf. POPE BENEDICT XVI, Encyclical letter *Caritas in Veritate* Op. cit. n. 51.

[139] P. HAFFNER, op. cit., 130.

[140] Cf. PAUL VI, *Message to the Stockholm conference on human environment*, 1 June 1972).

[141] Cf. JOHN PAUL II, Apostolic exhortation *Christifideles Laici* (30 December 1988), n. 43.

Developmental Solidarity, on the other hand, and as a follow-up to environmental conversion does not mean failing to accept responsibilities and postponing decisions; it means being committed to making joint decisions after pondering responsibly the road to be taken. Talking of this commitment, Walter Grasier says that individuals, communities, cultures can no longer survive on the paradigm of individualism without commitments. He hinges this commitment, from the Christian point of view, to the central mystery of the Trinity – the communion between the Father, son and Holy Spirit.[142]

This commitment is individual, national and international. It, therefore, includes a global human accountability for the fate of the environment and a call for global interdependence in tackling the global environmental crisis (since what happens in one part can quickly affect the rest). This is the point in Walter Grazier's book where he states: "When it comes to environmental problems, everyone is affected and everyone is responsible".[143]

Thus, the Church speaks of an international coordination regarding environmental questions which does not, however, lessen the responsibility of individual nations and states to monitor their own environment and pay greater attention to the most vulnerable sectors of society:

> Not only should each State join with others in implementing internationally accepted standards, but it should also make or facilitate necessary socio-economic adjustments within its own borders, giving special attention to the most vulnerable sectors (victims) of society. The State should also actively endeavour within its own territory to prevent destruction of the atmosphere and biosphere, by carefully monitoring, among other things, the impact of new technological or scientific advances. The State also has the responsibility of ensuring that its citizens

---

[142] Cf. GRAZER Walter, *Catholics going green: a small guide for learning and living environmental justice*, Ave Maria Press, Notre Dame (IN) 2009, 74; Cf. also THE CATECHISM OF THE CATHOLIC CHURCH, Op. Cit. n.259.
[143] GRAZER Walter, Catholics going green: a small guide for learning and living environmental justice, Op. Cit, 36.

are not exposed to dangerous pollutants or toxic wastes.
THE RIGHT TO A SAFE ENVIRONMENT is ever more
insistently presented today as a right that must be included
in an updated Charter of Human Rights.[144]

There is a call, therefore, for the "…renewal of the model of global
development in such a way that it be capable of 'including within its
range all peoples and not just the better off'".[145] The Second Special
Assembly for Africa of the Synod of Bishops describes this type of
solidarity as "globalization of solidarity."[146]

The obligation for authentic Developmental Solidarity within
Nation-States and in International Relations based on our common
humanity, therefore, implies that humanity ought to be united in
both the enjoyment of the benefits of valid choices and in bearing the
responsibility for consequences of actions planned on wrong choices.
Developmental Solidarity is simply, therefore, a call to collective
responsibility for our common humanity based on the sound logic that
the world is one world despite geographical boundaries. This translates
into interdependence. In principle, therefore, Developmental Solidarity
must include four principal implications: a de-emphasis on equality
(as this can foster an individualism in which one claims one's rights
without concern for others); equal treatment (which assumes that all are
involved); unequal treatment (which arises from the recognition that the
circumstances of all peoples' life are not identical, and sometimes some
desperate circumstances dictate disparate treatment); a demarcation
between those policies that unjustly discriminate (which should be
fought and gotten rid of) and those that require recognition of differences
among people (which should be developed to ensure justice).[147] This
places humanity before the throne of "conscience", a fundamental

---

[144] JOHN PAUL II, Message for world Day of Peace: *Peace with God the Creator,
Peace with all of Creation*, Op. cit. 10.
[145] L'OSSERVATORE ROMANO 43 (2117), Vatican City 28 October 2009, 12.
[146] SECOND SPECIAL ASSEMBLY FOR AFRICA OF THE SYNOD OF BISHOPS, The
57 propositions published on October 24 at the conclusion of the Second Africa
Synod and presented to Pope Benedict XVI, 31.
[147] Cf. ALASKA CATHOLIC BISHOPS, "*A catholic perspective on subsistence*" in
Origins vol. 31, 45, pp. 745-752.

aspect of the "God-image" which should take humanity today away from the unethical choice of Cain (cf. Gen. 4:9).

In line with this reasoning, the Compendium of the Social Teaching of the Church outlines some fruits of authentic Developmental Solidarity: equitable commercial exchange, promotion of the development of most disadvantaged peoples, exchange and transfer of scientific and technological knowledge, and political leaders of developing nations taking responsibility for the good of their peoples. It assumes that authentic integral development is achievable only by assuming a shared responsibility and seriously engaging in collaborative actions based on mutual respect.[148]

Today the environmental question is the responsibility of everyone and it demonstrates the need for concerted efforts aimed at establishing duties and obligations that belong to individuals, peoples, Nation-states, and the International community. It reveals the urgent ethical need for a new solidarity which must take into consideration not only the needs of all peoples but also the protection of the environment in view of the good of all. Thus humanity learns again to live in harmony, not only with God and with one another, but with Creation itself.

Environmental Conversion and Developmental Solidarity in sum represent a moving away from consumerist mentality, an adoption of a universal horizon of perspective, and an option for the poor. This holds for humankind a lot of advantages: it will produce the fruits of progress, humanisation and civilization of love; humanity will rediscover the meaning and value of the environment as a hospitable dwelling; it will usher in a harmonious form of societal development which respects and values the natural environment; it will stair Christians to rediscover the profound meaning of the creative plan revealed in the scriptures.

It must be said that in the last three decades of environmental reawakening, connections between theology and the environment have been made not only in official Catholic Church documents but also by independent theologians and thinkers. While the insights of some have influenced the Church's evolving self-understanding of human relationship to the environment, some have broken link with

---

[148] Cf. PONTIFICAL COUNCIL FOR JUSTICE AND PEACE, *Compendium of the Social Doctrine of the Church*, op. cit., nn. 475 & 476, pp 289 & 290.

the Church's theology on environment. I want to look briefly at the environmental thoughts of two contemporary theologians, Matthew Fox[149] and Leonardo Boff[150]. One reason I want to do this is because of their attractiveness at first sight, and another, because of their inherent danger.

Matthew Fox feels that at this critical time in human and planetary history, when the earth is being ravaged by the violence of war, poverty, sexism, homophobia, and eco-destruction, religion ought to be part of the solution, not the problem. For Fox, Christian tradition "...does not teach believers about the new creation or...about justice-making and social transformation... fails to teach love of the earth and care for the cosmos."[151] He elaborates what he calls 'a theology of new creation and original blessings' in which he dismisses original sin as a farce. He holds that God is in every thing and every thing is in God. Fox writes:

---

[149] Matthew Fox was born in Madison, Wisconsin. He entered the Order of Preachers (the Dominicans) and was ordained to the priesthood in the Roman Catholic Church in 1967. He received masters degrees in both philosophy and theology from the Aquinas Institute of Theology and later earned a Ph.D. from the Institut Catholique de Paris. Due to controversy surrounding his denial of original sin, he was forbidden to teach theology by Cardinal Joseph Ratzinger (now Pope Benedict XVI) of the Holy See in 1988. In 1992 he was dismissed from the Dominican order after refusing to appear when being summoned to discuss his writings with his superiors. He was received in 1994 into the Episcopal Church (Anglican Communion) by Bishop William Swing of the Episcopal Diocese of California. He articulates his environmental concerns in his book, Original Blessings, a Primer in Creation Spirituality (1996).

[150] Leonardo Boff was born on December 14 1938 in Concórdia, Santa Catarina State, Brazil. He is a liberation theologian, philosopher and writer, known for his active support for the rights of the poor and the excluded. Boff entered the Franciscan Order in 1959 and was ordained a Roman Catholic priest in 1964. He later abandoned the Franciscan religious order and the priestly ministry. He believes that open confrontation instead of dialogue, besides being a strategic error, is also a theological error. And if we must dialogue with philosophies and ideological currents, in the first place, the elements of light and positiveness that are in them must be identified, because, whether they come through Marx, Freud, Luther or Lyotard, if they are true, in the final analysis they come from God. His environmental theology is articulated in his two books: Ecology and liberation: a new paradigm, Orbis Books, MaryKnoll (NY) 1996; and Cry of the earth, cry of the poor, Orbis Books, MaryKnoll (NY) 1997.

[151] M. Fox, Original blessings, a primer in creation spirituality, Bear and Co, Santa Fe (NM) 1996, 11.

"There is one flow, one divine energy, one divine word in the sense of one creative energy flowing through all things, all time, and all space. We are part of that flow and we need to listen to it rather than to assume arrogantly that our puny words are the only words of God.... A creation-centred spirituality is cosmic.... We are in the cosmos and the cosmos is in us."[152]

John Hart captures his position this way: "Fox believes that the Christian tradition has focused too strongly on fall/redemption theology and spirituality. He rejects the fall/redemption approach to human relations with God and the cosmos.... What follows from Fox's focus...is a reconsideration of the meaning of the incarnation and understanding of who Jesus is and what his role among us in creation is."[153] Fox's theology of *new creation* and *cosmic Christ* influences his approach to environmental concerns which has three principal demerits: Firstly, in shying away from the fall-redemption theology, he runs into the temptation of elaborating a creation theology that has no real basis in salvation history. Secondly, the logical consequence is a panentheism that places humanity at par with other creatures denying the human person of his uniqueness. Thirdly, he thus posits an approach to social transformation and environmental engagement that is rigidly individualistic.[154]

Leonardo Boff's environmental thought, on the other hand, developed within the perspective of his theology of liberation. For him, human power over nature is really the power exercised by some people over others using nature as a tool. From this argument, he affirms an intrinsic connection between social justice and ecological justice: "Social injustice leads to ecological injustice and vice versa"[155] For him, just as the present dominant social model of relating leads to the rupture of social relations, the existing ecological model also leads to rupture of relations between humankind and the environment.[156] Logically for him then, "Rights do not belong only to humankind and to nations, but

---

[152] M. Fox, *Original blessings, a primer in creation spirituality*, op. cit. 38-39, 69.
[153] J. HART, op. cit., 67.
[154] Cf. J. HART, op. cit., 68.
[155] L. BOFF, *Ecology and liberation: a new paradigm*, Orbis Books, MaryKnoll (NY) 1996, 21.
[156] Cf. L. BOFF, *Ecology and liberation: a new paradigm*, Op. cit. 27.

also to other beings in creation. There is a human and social right, but there is also an ecological and cosmic right. We do not have the right to what we have not created."[157] From the above conclusions, he connects the cry of the oppressed with the cry of the environment, and laments that humans can commit not only homicide and ethnocide, but also biocide and genocide.[158] Because of this link between environmental degradation and human oppression, ecological justice has to go hand in hand with social justice. The two are thoroughly intertwined, as social (in) justice cannot be separated from ecological (in) justice.[159]

Though attractive at first sight as Boff's theory might look, we must be careful of its inherent tendency towards natural deism, which is both unbiblical, and against common sense. From the foregoing we must treat with suspicion and consider as "bad teachers" of our time any environmental ideology that subordinates the human person to a presumed centrality of nature, and tries to see the later as sacrosanct. This opinion sounds risky and blocks development, above all the right to development of poor countries. Archbishop Renato Martino underscores this point this way:

> Responsible **stewardship** and genuine **solidarity** are not only directed to the protection of the environment, but, equally so, to the inalienable right and duty of all peoples to development. The earth's resources and the means to their access and use must be wisely monitored and justly shared. The demands for the care and protection of the environment cannot be used to obstruct the right to development, nor can development be invoked in thwarting the environment. The task of achieving a just balance is today's challenge.[160]

Any solutions to the environmental question must be based on firm evidence and not on dubious and spurious ideologies. The world needed to care for the environment, but not to the point where the

---

[157] L. BOFF, *Ecology and liberation: a new paradigm*, op. cit. 30.
[158] Cf. L. BOFF, *Cry of the earth, cry of the poor*, Orbis Books, MaryKnoll (NY) 1997, xi.
[159] Cf. L. BOFF, *Cry of the earth, cry of the poor*, op. cit. 132.
[160] ARCHBISHOP RENATO MARTINO, Addresses at the *Earth Summit* in Rio De Janiero, op. cit. 2.

welfare of animals and plants was given a greater priority than that of humankind. A balanced approach to the environment should begin with the recognition that creation is entrusted to humanity's responsibility and care. Not to admit this is to risk having a vision of humanity and of nature that in the end is against both humanity and nature.

In planning solutions to environmental problems, therefore, faulty approaches ought to be avoided. The romantic dread of a 'virgin world' and a nature that must be worshipped as Mother Earth, *Gaia*, and cannot be touched ignores history and underestimates the demands that the right to human life and dignity places on all.[161] In his critique of all forms of natural deism, while he accepts that there is a great deal Christian theology can learn from people who hold this position and other contrary positions, Denis Edwards said: "In abandoning the uniqueness of human beings made in the image of God, it undermines a fundamental basis for the struggle for social justice. This view also undermines a powerful source of ecological commitment. Human beings have a unique moral responsibility for other creatures."[162] Reasoning along this line, the African Journal of Contextual Theology says, "In their governance of created nature, human beings need wisdom to understand the interconnections that make up the integrity of the ecosystem and which enhance its generative potentials."[163] Thus the Church avoids a parallelogram-like cosmological dualism (heaven and earth, God and world, super-nature and nature) and an anthropological dualism (body and soul, mind and matter). The Church continues to teach that our human existence in its purposiveness, its social, ethical, cultural, spiritual and religious values and meanings, its glorious creativity and historicity, even its horrible failures and gross evils, attests to the significantly distinctive and unique position of the human person in the whole cosmic arrangement.

In this chapter, in line with the Church's theology of environment, I have tried to articulate her concerns:

[161] Cf. PONTIFICAL COUNCIL FOR CULTURE – PONTIFICAL COUNCIL FOR RELIGIOUS DIALOGUE, *Jesus Christ the bearer of the water of life, a christian reflection on the "new age"*, Libreria Editrice Vaticana, Vatican City 2003, Appendix 7.1.
[162] D. EDWARDS, *Ecology at the heart of faith*, Op.Cit. 22.
[163] M.N. NWACHUKWU, *et al* (Eds), African Journal of Contextual Theology, Vol 2. Op. Cit. 14

- Environmental consciousness: remaining aware of what is happening in one's area.
- Stewardship and duty: The stewardship granted by the creator is not a licence to misuse God's creation.
- Authentic development: Going beyond mere economic and demographic considerations when dealing with issues concerning the human person and his environment.
- Pursuance of authentic human development: The development of the whole person and of every human being which refers also to the correct relationship of individual persons with God, with nature and with society.
- The Ethical Question: Ethical issues are, therefore, involved for adequate safeguards and ecological integrity.
- Inculturated ecology: sensitivity to living worlds, diverse cultures and religious heritage.
- Ecological conversion: remaining pro-life in all environmental considerations.
- Christians' vocation: They are called by faith to practice stewardship of God's creation.

I have also gone further to highlight the ethical nature of environmental issues and to propose the following solutions:

- Good education.
- Integration of science and faith: Scientific solutions to environmental issues must recognise faith dimensions.
- Harmonising mastership of creation with responsible stewardship.
- Integration of culture, science and technology: the efforts of science and technology in environmental matters must be permeated by authentic human and cultural values, in order to put them at the service of humanity and in the protection and stewardship of our fragile environment.
- Positive ecological life-style is a healing to the consumerist and materialistic attitude of today's world of economic globalisation.

We have also seen a development in Catholic environmental thought: the use of the term *sacramental universe* to emphasise the immanence of God in creation; the emerging shift of emphasis from an anthropocentric-dominion ideas to a stewardship-care taking perspective in an interdependence with other creatures, and with creation as a whole; a recognition of the relationship between environmental degradation and human poverty; a prophetic and evangelical invitation to all humanity, particularly the Church, in their respective zones and regions to asses environmental issues and devise concrete and engaging tools and means to handle them. These ideals should serve to stimulate concrete projects in and for the environment. Faith based environmental efforts will have a profound impact on eliminating environmental degradation and enhancing environmental health.

What is the expected overall result of this endeavour: a renewed effort on the part of all, especially Christians, to seek to understand God's will for creation; facing the challenge of conversion, i.e. the courage to change not only our own attitude and way of life but also to commit ourselves to social change; an education in environmental responsibility - this education can be formal or informal. It should also be part of our catechetical programs and educational approach at all levels. We have also tried to argue that the real enemies of man and his environment are the views that promote human domination and see the earth as mere instrument on the one hand, and the views that divinize nature, and sunder the human person from transcendence on the other hand.

The concrete issue now for next consideration would be: Since the Catholic principles of environmental stewardship are to guide and inspire environmental practices of peoples and the concrete environmental initiatives of local Churches, what are the prevailing environmental situations and practices in Nigeria? The Church in Nigeria, to help realise the vision of a healthy environment for all Nigerians would put in place conservation, prevention and remedial programs and projects. The next section and chapter will address these questions and issues.

CHAPTER SIX

CURRENT STATE OF THE ENVIRONMENT IN NIGERIA

Environmental Degradation in Nigeria.

In this section, I have x-rayed the environmental situation in Nigeria. What are the prevailing environmental practices in Nigeria? I have examined the four principal types of environmental degradation that are prevalent in the country – soil, water, air and noise.

In "proposition" 22 of the Second Special Assembly for Africa of the Synod of Bishops presented to Pope Benedict XVI on October 24 2009 in Rome, Bishops and Church leaders from all over the continent of Africa affirmed unequivocally: "Our Christian faith teaches that God the Creator made all things good (cf. Gn 1); and gave the earth to us humans to cultivate and take care of as stewards (cf. Gn 2:15). We observe that many human beings, at all levels, have continued to abuse nature and destroy God's beautiful world by exploitation of natural resources beyond what is sustainable and useful. There is an irresponsible degradation and senseless destruction of the earth, which is "our mother".[164]

We must immediately classify two major kinds of environmental degradation harmful to humans and the biotic community - natural and human induced. In agreement with this categorization, John Hart

---

[164] SECOND ASSEMBLY FOR AFRICA OF THE SYNOD OF BISHOPS, *The 57 propositions published on October 24 at the conclusion of the Second Africa Synod and presented to Pope Benedict XVI*, 22, in http://www.ecs.org.et/Doc/Propositions_Synod.htm (accessed 12/12/09).

states: "Wars, terrorism, torture, political and economic oppression afflict human communities across the world, where people harm people; earthquakes, tornadoes, hurricanes, floods, and volcanic eruptions alter the landscapes and kill, hurt, and dislocate people and other living beings with natural disasters. In the first instance, human evil is expressed; in the second, natural catastrophes take their toll."[165]

God has blessed Nigeria with the least natural disasters in the world. Here, we are considering the human evil of environmental degradation generated by human activities in Nigeria. The primary areas are soil, water, air and noise. It is proper to mention that because of their interconnectedness, the effects of the degradation of one can affect the other. According to the New Age encyclopedia: "The multiplication of environmental crisis – air, water, soil…pollution…reflects uncritical progress and disregard on man's part for the role natural systems play in his own survival."[166]

In Nigeria, the general situation of the natural environment is moving towards a disaster. The picture is gloomy. It is part of the overall post-independence decay of our society. I.M Osuagwu paints the picture this way:

> Our environment has been left to decay, and both the government and the people in general do not seem to react sufficiently. Alarmingly, our king trees, birds, animals, insects, reptiles, fruits, crops, waters, seasons, landscapes, atmosphere, are diminishing or have disappeared completely. Deforestation, erosion, landslides, pollution, are setting in ecological destabilisation from a possible economic, socio-political, cultural and even human disaster. Shall we talk of our health system corroded by innumerable fatal viral infections?[167]

Here it is often a matter of chemical and other toxic wastes, of industrial by-products, of the poor management of energy sources, of

---

[165] J. Hart, op. cit. 107.

[166] E. Humphrey et al (eds.), *New age encyclopedia* vol. 14, Lexicon Publications 1963, 496.

[167] I. Osuagwu, *"Overcoming Nigerian obstacles to justice and peace"* in *The Leader*, 18 January 1988; quoted in S.Uzoukwu, Op. Cit. 292.

lack of effective safety standards, of mentality and of ideology. It is about degradation in all its ramifications. Some apparently innocuous activities of humans also contribute to the problem – domestic and commercial refuse carelessly disposed about residential and business areas, including aerosol cans of cosmetics and insecticides; discharge of emissions of vehicles, industrial fumes and other effluents into the environment; construction of structures without appropriate authorisation and/or compliance with health regulations, etc. It is indeed a state of chaos.

In the area of domestic wastes, all individuals in the society are culpable; in industrial wastes, companies and government are largely culpable; in air and noise pollution, individuals, businesses and companies are culpable; in water pollution, all are culpable. Let us now go into some details in presenting and analysing the issues involved here.

Soil Degradation

Soil degradation is the presence of man-made chemicals or other alterations in the natural soil environment. According to UNEP, "Harmful and persistent pollutants, such as heavy metals and organic chemicals, are still being released to the land...from mining, manufacturing, sewage...from the use of agro-chemicals, and from leaking stockpiles of absolute chemicals".[168]

In Nigeria, soil degradation typically arises from the presence of poisons, sedimentation of waste, excessive use of fertilisers, rupture of underground pipes and storage tanks, application of pesticides, leaching of wastes from landfills, and direct discharge of industrial wastes into the soil like petroleum hydrocarbons, solvents, lead and other heavy metals. The concern over soil degradation in Nigeria also stems primarily from health risks, both of direct contact and from secondary pollution of water supply. The land as one of the gifts God entrusted to humanity is not only God's gift but also man's responsibility as underscored in Chapter four(a) of this work, and ought to be conserved with care. This is an urgent task in today's Nigeria.

---

[168] UNITED NATIONS ENVIRONMENT PROGRAMME (UNEP), *Global environment outlook (GEO), environment for development 4*, Progress Press Ltd, Valletta 2007, 82.

Water Degradation

Water plays a central and critical role in all aspects of life. It is a social good, an economic good and an environmental good. Access to safe water and sanitation is one of the pressing needs and concerns in Nigeria and of crucial importance to every Nigerian family. Access to safe water is not only a natural endowment; it is also a fundamental human right the provision of which is not a humanitarian gesture but a legal responsibility to citizens. In line with this view, the Pontifical Council for Justice and Peace in a contribution at the Fourth World Water Forum held in Mexico affirms:

> Water is a natural resource vital for the survival of humanity and all species on earth. As a good of creation, water is destined for all human beings and their communities.... Human beings, and the communities in which they live, cannot do without water since it corresponds to their primary needs and constitutes a basic condition of their existence. All depend upon the fate of water. Access to safe water and sanitation is indispensable for the life and full development of all human beings and communities in the world....Water is much more than just a basic human need. It is an essential, irreplaceable element to ensuring the continuance of life. Water is intrinsically linked to fundamental human rights such as the right to life, to food and to health. Access to safe water is a basic human right.... Access to safe water is made a legal entitlement rather than a service or commodity provided on a humanitarian basis.[169]

Water degradation is the introduction of a wide spectrum of chemicals, pathogens and physical elements into the water ways from industrial discharges and spillages, thermal power stations, construction sites, refinery operations, agricultural processes, domestic chores and underground sewages directly done or indirectly induced. These pollutants can be divided into organic, inorganic and thermal.

---

[169] PONTIFICAL COUNCIL FOR JUSTICE AND PEACE, *Water, an essential element for life*, The Fourth World Water Forum, Mexico City, 16-22 March 2006, nn. 2&3.

Organic water pollutants include insecticides and herbicides, bacteria from sewages and livestock, food processing and domestic wastes, fuels (gasoline, diesel, lubricating oils), lubricants (from oil fields, refineries, and pipelines), underground storage tanks and detergents. Inorganic water pollutants include heavy metals from various industrial processes and acidity caused by industrial discharges. Thermal pollution is heat from hot water that is discharged from a factory into a river, lake or flowing stream. It can also occur when a water source is used as coolant and returned to the natural environment at a higher temperature, which endangers aquatic life.[170] According to a UN Environmental Programme statistics, cited by Paul Haffner, water degradation: "...cause the deaths of more than a million seabirds every year, as well as more than 100,000 marine mammals. Syringes, cigarette lighters and toothbrushes have been found inside the stomachs of dead seabirds, which mistake them for food. The slowly rotating mass of rubbish-laden water poses a risk to human health too...the raw materials for the industry...are...spilled every year working their way into the sea. These pollutants...enter the food chain."[171]

According to the United Nations Environment Programme (UNEP), "Water quality degradation from human activities continues to harm human and ecosystem health. Three million people die from water-borne diseases each year in developing countries".[172] The situation of the Nigerian Waters is glimmer. The Nigerian waters and waterways have become refuse dumps. A greater percentage of the wastes, some immensely dangerous, are thrown off ships and oil platforms, canoes and boats. The rest come from land. Oil spillages and purposeful dumping into our waters by companies operating in Nigeria often remain either unchecked, or unnoticed or ignored. Unfortunately many refineries, industries, factories, companies, take to this type of water dumping as an easiest and cheapest alternative in waste disposal. Quite a number of individual households also dump domestic wastes and faeces into

---

[170] Cf. THE AMERICAN HERITAGE SCIENCE DICTIONARY, Houghton Miffin Company 2005, http://www.thefreedictionary.com/pollution (accessed 26/11/09).
[171] P. HAFFNER, op. cit. 28.
[172] UNITED NATIONS ENVIRONMENT PROGRAMME (UNEP), *Global environment outlook (GEO), environment for development 4*, op. cit. 116.

our waters from which same water they draw for all kinds of domestic uses including their drinking water. Olanike K. Adeyemo captures the situation in this way:

> Major cities in Nigeria face serious water pollution crises, in which lack of environmental control of water-dependent activities (including domestic, agricultural, and industrial) play an important part. Fish and marine resources in the country face total collapse or extinction, due to destruction of marine life and natural habitats by pollution of water bodies. Unregulated and excessive use of pesticides for fishing and the deliberate disposal and dumping of toxic and hazardous wastes into water bodies are significant causes of massive fish kills and loss of aquatic life and habitats in the country. The protection of water quality and aquatic ecosystem as a vulnerable resource, essential to sustain life, development and environment is of utmost importance to prevent further pollution and degradation of Nigeria's freshwater resources.[173]

These actions lead to algal collapse. They choke the waters of the oxygen, which the organisms need. They in turn emit toxic decomposing gases responsible for most of our waters in Nigeria having water hyacinths (shades of green, yellow and brown and red colourings). There is no doubt that this situation is hazardous for the 'chain of life'. These illegal and inhuman activities inject very dangerous substances into the Nigerian waters, which choke aquatic vegetation, decrease the resource value of the Nigerian waters and create health related problems. The contamination contributes greatly to the spread of infectious diseases such as typhoid, cholera, amoebic infections, bacillary dysentery, diarrhoea and guinea worm, et cetera.

Because of the inability of Government at all levels – Federal, State and Local – to provide portable water to a greater number of the citizenry, these contaminated waters and natural streams still remain the main sources of water for drinking, cooking and other domestic uses.

---

[173] A. OLANIKE, "Consequences of pollution and degradation of Nigerian aquatic environment on fisheries resources," in *The Environment* 23 (2003), 297.

Today as never, the protection of water quality and aquatic ecosystem as a vulnerable resource, essential to sustain life, development and environment ought to be declared a state of emergency in Nigeria. It is of utmost importance that we join forces to prevent further pollution and degradation of Nigeria's freshwater resources.

Air Pollution
According to Paul Haffner:

> Air pollution is the human introduction into the atmosphere of chemicals, particulates, or biological materials that cause harm or discomfort to humans or other living organisms, or damage the environment. Air pollution is often identified with major stationary sources, but the greatest source of emissions is actually mobile sources mainly automobiles.[174]

These pollutants or substances in the air (which may harm the health of humans, animals and plants) are not naturally found in the air, but mainly introduced into it through human activities. We can classify these pollutants into primary and secondary pollutants.

Primary pollutants are substances directly emitted from a process into the air, such as the carbon monoxide gas from a motor vehicle exhaust. Secondary pollutants are pollutants not emitted directly, but they form in the air when primary pollutants react or interact such as formation of photochemical smog in the air. However, some pollutants may be both primary and secondary, i.e. they are both emitted directly and formed from other primary pollutants.[175]

Major primary pollutants produced by human activity and introduced into the atmosphere are identified as: Sulphur oxides emitted from coal burning and oil; Nitrogen oxides produced in high temperature combustion; Carbon monoxide which is a colourless, odourless, non-irritating but very poisonous gas generated by incomplete combustion of

[174] P. HAFFNER, op. cit. 15.
[175] Cf. P. HAFFNER, op. cit. 16.

fuel such as natural gas, coal and wood; Carbon dioxide, a gas emitted from combustion; Volatile organic compounds such as Hydrocarbon vapours and solvents emitted into the air; Particulate Matters (PM) generally known as smoke that are capable of entering the nasal cavity and the bronchial tubes and lungs; Toxic metals such as lead, cadmium and copper; Ammonia (NH3) emitted from agricultural processes; Unpleasant odours from sewage, refuse and industrial processes.[176]

According to UNEP, "more than 2 million people globally are estimated to die prematurely each year due to indoor and outdoor air pollution... many areas still suffer from excessive air pollution".[177]

Air degradation in Nigeria is going to be an environmental issue that we are dealing with for a long time and there are going to be more and more regulations that pollution outfits will have to follow. Anti-air-degradation equipments are going to have to keep up with the demand for new and better equipments to replace old equipments, meet new regulations, deal with preventative maintenance issues, deal with the issue of emergency repairs, and be serviced and maintained, and upgraded to keep them in good working order. The initial air degradation control equipments that came out years ago will not meet the new stricter environmental regulations that are being passed today so the equipments will have to be either rebuilt or replaced with new air degradation control equipments.

In Nigeria, air degradation come principally from gaseous discharges from oil prospecting companies, industries, indiscriminate and open burning of wastes, bush burning, gas flaring, indoor cooking, emissions from generators and vehicle exhausts, mining activities, etc. Nigerians suffer from very high levels of pollutants in the air they breathe, particularly from very fine particulate matter (PM), the main air pollutant affecting human health in Nigeria. According to the UNEP assessment on air pollution in 2007, Nigeria is in the red.[178]

---

[176] Cf. P. HAFFNER, op. cit. 16-17.
[177] UNITED NATIONS ENVIRONMENT PROGRAMME (UNEP), Global environment outlook (GEO), environment for development 4, op. cit. 40.
[178] Cf. UNITED NATIONS ENVIRONMENT PROGRAMME (UNEP), Global environment outlook (GEO), environment for development 4, op. cit. 53.

Noise pollution

The automobiles, industries, and the entertainment systems generate another kind of environmental degradation – Noise pollution. It is difficult to say whether it is the noisy nature of Nigerians that is transferred into these sources, or whether these sources have turned Nigerians into 'a noisy folk'. This analysis is left to Nigerian psychologists and sociologists. Suffice to say that Nigeria is a very noisy country. Noise pollution refers to the introduction of noise into the domestic or external environment such that it bothers or disturbs rest and other human activities, constitutes a danger to human health, and interferes with the legitimate enjoyment of the environment itself.

The sources are: Transportation, poor urban planning, factory machinery, and audio entertainment systems which include loud noise emanating from loudspeakers used by record and recording stores, generating plants, television sets, musical sets, intruder alarms, night parties, and with the proliferation of religious places of worship in Nigeria, noise emanating from religious activities. These religious activities are becoming one of the most potent sources of neighbourhood noise in the country. The effects are numerous. Some of them are; damage to physiological and psychological health, cause annoyance, irritation and aggression, hypertension, high stress levels and hearing loss.[179] We shall revisit this in the section on generators.

Solutions towards reducing noise pollution in Nigeria include: Real adjustment in human behaviour, use of noise barriers, supervised limitation of vehicle speeds, limitation of heavy duty vehicles from residential and thickly populated areas, use of effective traffic control that smoothen vehicle flow. But for these to be attainable, there must be, first, sensitisation, education, conscientization, and political will.

---

[179] Cf. P. HAFFNER, op. cit. 58.

CHAPTER SEVEN

SOURCES OF ENVIRONMENTAL DEGRADATION AND EFFECTS ON THE ENVIRONMENT IN NIGERIA (WASTE GENERATING CORRIDORS)

I have in this chapter exposed the sources of environmental degradation in Nigeria. Sources of human induced degradation in our context of study refer to the various locations, activities and factors, which are responsible for the releasing of pollutants into the soil, water and air. They are technically called "waste generating corridors". They include stationary sources such as power plants, manufacturing facilities and municipal waste incinerators, and mobile sources such as motor vehicles, aircraft, and marine vessels.[180] These are the main anthropogenic sources of environmental degradation in Nigeria:

- **Industries and Chemical Plants**

Nigeria is a developing country that is facing the challenges and opportunities of industrialisation. Industrial activities, which have grown over the years, especially with the discovery of oil in Nigeria, have been identified as a major contributor to environmental degradation in Nigeria. More than 80% of industries in Nigeria discharge liquid, solid and gaseous wastes directly into the environment without adequate treatment that meets the basic

---

[180] Cf. P. Haffner, op. cit. 17.

standards.[181] Industrial wastes are generated from industrial activities such as pesticides, paints, grease, inorganic materials, oil sludge, falloff or unused chemicals and raw materials, expired products and contaminated or substandard goods, heavy metals from metal smelting and refining industries, etc.

- **Hospital Waste**

Packaging materials and containers, used syringes and sharps, biological waste and pharmaceuticals are dumped recklessly in the open for long periods allowing scavengers to have contact with them. This constitutes high risk to public health and a disturbing source of environmental degradation.

- **Oil Exploration and Refineries**

The Nigerian environment has been degraded by oil spills. Oil spillage is a major and frequent hazard especially in the Niger Delta Regions of Nigeria. The main Trans-National oil exploration outfits in Nigeria are: Shell (Netherlands/UK), Exxon Mobil (US), Chevron-Texaco (US), Agip (Italy), and Elf-Aquitaine (France). The activities of these oil companies, in conjunction with their State counterparts like the Nigerian National Petroleum Corporation, do not observe in most cases international best practices in their exploration and oil prospecting activities which accounts for the devastation of the environment more especially in the States and communities of Nigeria where they operate.[182]

One conservative estimate, for example, put the number of spillage incidents in the oil producing areas between 1970 and 1999 at three thousand and eighty two (3,082).[183] More spillages have occurred between 1999 and today. There are not less than fifty seven oil and chemicals related waste dumps in the oil producing regions of Nigeria.[184]

---

[181] B. IBRAHIM, "Strategic approach to reducing vehicle emissions in Nigeria: role of fleet operators, Jos, 28 August 2009
[182] Cf. NIGERIAWATCH.ORG, http://www.nigeriawatch.org/media/htm/NGA-watch-Report07.pdf (accessed 22/01/2010).
[183] Cf. ADENUGA Ade et al (eds.), "Sustainability of the environment and water pollution in nigeria: problems, management and policy options," in *Bullion* 23 (October 1999), 4.
[184] NTA INTERNATIONAL, September 13, 2011.

This constitutes a major source of environmental degradation, and indeed an environmental terrorism.

The release of a UN report in 2011 into the state of oil-induced environmental pollution in Nigeria by the United Nations Environmental Programme (UNEP) has revealed a devastating indictment of the oil giants' reckless Nigerian adventure. In Ogoniland alone, the report's study involved 4,000 samples analyzed, 142 groundwater monitoring wells drilled, 264 formal community meetings conducted, and 780 boreholes monitored. Its headline conclusion projected that cleaning up the spillage mess in Ogoniland alone will take 25-30 years.[185]

The report discovered extensive contamination of soil and groundwater, extraordinarily high levels of dangerous chemicals in some areas and a devastating impact on aquatic life. The drinking water of one community contained 900 times the recommended level of benzene, a known carcinogen. The report lays part of the blame for this on Nigeria's muddled regulations and regulatory bodies which interpret the rules differently and often through backdoor smart practices connive with oil magnets to environmentally oppress the citizens. The oil industry has taken advantage of this to put the bare minimum of effort into clean-up operations and hazard preventive measures thus neglecting international best practices.

- **Automobiles**

Road transport in Nigeria is without doubt a major contributor to environmental degradation. More than 95% of the vehicles in Nigeria are old vehicles with internal combustion engines: the gasses emitted from the exhausts, noise from the prevalent old engines, car horns blown indiscriminately, car stereos, door slamming, all contribute to inestimable pollution. This is worsened by the near absence of good roads and number of discarded automobiles. Africa is becoming the dumping ground for used vehicles (popularly called *Tokumbo* in Nigeria) from the developed world because of pervading poverty in a blessed continent. According to B.G. Ibrahim:

---

[185] http://dailymaverick.co.za/article/2011-08-05-a-brief-look-un-says-nigerian-oil-pollution-worse-than-first-thought (accessed 08/15/11).

At a conference on clean air, clean fuels and vehicles in May 2006, the then Minister of Transport, Dr, Abiye Sekibo revealed that Nigeria's transport sector as a whole accounted for 83% of carbon monoxide, 41% of Carbon Dioxide, 59% of Nitrogen Oxide, 98% of Sulphur Oxides, 22% of volatile organic compounds and 98% of Particulate matter and Lead respectively in Nigeria's atmosphere. It was also revealed that in 1998, a single car in Nigeria emitted 29,600kg of hydrocarbons, 34,000kg of Nitrogen Oxides and 4,029kg of different carbonate gasses over its average lifespan.[186]

The provision of an effective, affordable, physically accessible, evenly distributed and environmentally friendly public transport system by the Government can minimise private ownership of vehicles and thus drastically reduce automobile pollution.

- **Generators**

Engine exhaust is a major source of carbon monoxide in Nigeria. Electricity supply in Nigeria is very erratic and grossly inadequate. This has forced many Nigerians to use fossil fuel electric generators. Unreliable power supply in the country has seen most households and businesses resort to the use of power generating sets as their primary means of electricity, while the Power Holding Company of Nigeria (PHCN), a Government parastatal obligated with the generation and distribution of electricity (which is essentially a Government monopoly for now) is viewed as a standby source. The use of the generators has resulted in having to cope with the hazards associated with it. These private fossil fuel generating sets (now a dominant part of the Nigerian landscape) have become major sources of anthropogenic greenhouse gas emissions constantly being released into densely populated residential and commercial areas.

According to a study conducted by Akande Tanimola *et al*, more than 73.2% of Nigerians own and use generators for

---

[186] B. IBRAHIM, "Strategic approach to reducing vehicle emissions in Nigeria: role of fleet operators, Op. Cit.

domestic, commercial and industrial purposes.[187] This has made Nigeria one of the biggest markets for electricity generators in the world. Each building in our cities is usually serviced by a number of generators waiting to roar into life as often as PHCN light fails. In the statistics made available by the National Electricity Regulatory Commission (NERC) Nigerians spend about N796.4 billion on fuel to generate electric power from their generators every year. This figure is strikingly close to the federal budget of 796.7 billion Naira, for capital expenditure for the fiscal year, 2009. In 2009, the Federal Government that is responsible for the generation and distribution of electricity has come under heavy criticism for budgeting 2 billion Naira to buy, maintain and fuel its own generators.[188] This trend of Government budgeting huge sums each year to generators has continued till date. In my nuclear family alone, for example, we have five generators (two big, two medium and one small) serving the household just to ensure the availability of electricity for household chores. This does not include the extended family. Given the average utilization factor of these generators in Nigeria, we can only shudder at the amount of environmental degradation caused by green house gasses (GHG) emissions released into the atmosphere on every street and neighbourhood, in the cities and in the countryside of Nigeria, and the adverse environmental and health impacts.[189]

Generator fumes can be very dangerous to healthy human living. In both residential and industrial areas, instances of generator fumes spewing into the streets and even the living rooms are quite common. Unfortunately, these fumes known to be primary air pollutants, since they are emitted directly into the air, are inimical to human health. But

[187] Cf. T. AKANDE et all (eds.). "Awareness and Attitude to Social and Health Hazards from Generators Use in Nigeria" in Medwell research journal of Medical sciences 2,4 2008, 186, http://www.medwelljournals.com/fulltext/rjms/2008/185-189.pdf (accessed 25/10/09).
[188] Cf. P. UGEH Patrick, "Citizens Spend N796 Billion to Fuel Generators Yearly", 28 September 2009, http://allafrica.com/stories/200909281059.html (accessed 25/10/09).
[189] Cf. A. ADACHABA, "Climate Change and Power Supply Solutions: LFGE / MSWE Project development in Nigeria", June 2009, http://www.cdmbazzar.net/UserManagement/FileStorage/JLB7TU1RKOPQHNFVGX84MSC62YW5DZ (accessed 25/10/09).

residents and passers-by inhale them daily thus breathing in unhealthy air. According to Stella Odueme, "Apart from air pollution, they also generate noise pollution, which has been said to result in hearing loss for some 7.2 million Nigerians representing 17.9 per cent of the population aside other health implications. According to research, prolonged exposures to intense noise lead to permanent hearing loss, hinder mental efforts, induce stress, cause inefficiency at work, prevent sleep, cause irritability and generally degrade the quality of life".[190] One only hopes that the current move by the Nigerian Government under its Nigerian Integrated Power Projects (NIPPS) will provide electricity to Nigerians and thus reduce the pollution menace from generators in the country.

- **Bush Burning and Fire-wooding**
These traditional practices of agriculture and domestic cooking respectively send thick gaseous smokes into the atmosphere and contaminate the air waves. More conventional ways of farming and cooking are gradually gaining ground. But they still remain largely elitist while the predominant countryside poor still go by the traditional ways.

- **Agricultural Practices:**
Agricultural Waste e.g. pesticides (herbicides and fungicides), and pesticide and agro-chemical residue levels in our air, soil and water are significantly on the high side due to unsupervised agricultural and farming practices. The Church in Africa has opted for an agricultural development (production and practices) which respects the environment.[191]

- **The Construction Industry**
In Nigeria today, if a census of the completed and the uncompleted buildings are to be done, the number of the uncompleted structures and buildings may most likely be more than the completed ones. This

[190] S.ODUEME, "On dangers of Generator fumes, noise pollution, 21 January 2009, http://allafrica.com/stories/200901220469.html (accessed 25/10/09).
[191] SECOND SPECIAL ASSEMBLY FOR AFRICA OF THE SYNOD OF BISHOPS, The 57 propositions, op. cit. 30.

creates poor scenery. And the rate at which buildings are collapsing is another dimension to it. The noise generated at building sites, the unwarranted vibrations created, the dust pollution, the provocation of erosion, flooding and landslides due to poor building plans, and the habitat destruction of local environmental resources and natural beautiful contours under the guise of development - these also constitute a serious source of environmental degradation and pollution in Nigeria. This situation raises questions as to Government approved standards, quality control mechanisms, monitoring and aesthetics in the construction industry.

- **Domestic, Commercial and Industrial waste**
  Domestic waste are those generated from household activities. They occur in different forms: water-borne waste from households, including sewage and sullage water, rubbish, human and animal remains. Commercial waste are those generated from commercial establishments as they do business daily. Industrial waste are generated from industrial activities such as chemicals, pesticides, paints, grease, inorganic materials, oil sludge, and so on. Domestic waste production is increasing and is compounded by a cycle of poverty, population increase, decreasing standards of living, bad governance, and the low level of environmental awareness. Slums and shanty neighborhoods receive least attention in regard to waste collection and disposal services. Commercial waste generation is also on the increase because of increased commercial activities due to growing industrialization and consequent development. According to Dr. Akindeji Falaki, electronic wastes (e-waste) in the form of outdated electronics could be toxic and could affect the health of people when exposed to them or disposed indiscriminately. According to him, some of them contain mercury and lead. Lead can lead to deformity and neurological challenges; mercury can poison the blood, and shut down the kidney and the liver[192]

These waste materials may be gaseous, liquid, or solid. Whereas gaseous and liquid wastes are free flowing and can easily migrate from

---

[192] http://tribune.com.ng/news/community-news/item/15860-environmental ist-warns-against-indiscriminate-dumping-of-e-waste

one place to another, solid wastes are not free flowing.[193] According to Olanike Adeyemo: "Disposal and management of wastes in Nigeria present serious environmental problems. The usual methods of waste disposal in the country are: land filling, dumpsites, land spreads, water disposal, and incineration. Each of these methods has serious environmental implications because of their potential to pollute and contaminate underground and surface water bodies in the country."[194]

Most of the waste dumps are located close to residential areas, markets, farms, roadsides, and creeks. The composition of waste dumps varies widely, with many human activities located close to dump sites. The situation gets complicated again as often the dumped waste are burnt in the open.

Environmental scientists and managers have identified some major techniques of waste management and disposal: Traditional landfill, Incineration, Recycling, Avoidance and composting.[195] We examine them briefly to see what is on ground in Nigeria.

Traditional Landfill: Landfills are the most widely utilized solid waste management option. This is the method of burying waste to dispose of it. A properly designed and well-managed landfill can be a hygienic and relatively inexpensive method of disposing waste materials. Improved modern landfill method can contain such waste in a gas engine and burn them to generate electricity.

In Nigeria, the common type of landfill generally used is the "Burrow Pit". Some are natural. Some are created (conventional) to serve as "Dumps". To an extent, this is helpful in waste disposal. But because most of them are located in habitable areas because of improper urban planning, they often add to environmental degradation by creating odour problems and killing surface vegetation. Burning of waste inside the Burrow Pits further creates air pollution.

Incineration: Incineration is a common method of waste disposal. This is a disposal method that involves combustion of solid, liquid and

---

[193] Cf. D. OGBONNA et al, "Waste management: a tool for environmental protection in Nigeria" in *Ambio journal of the* human environment 31, 1 (2002), 55.
[194] A. OLANIKE, " Consequences of pollution and degradation of Nigerian aquatic environment on fisheries resources," in *The Environment* 23 (2003), 297.
[195] Cf. P. HAFFNER, op. cit. 22.

gaseous waste. This is also called 'thermal treatment'. This is generally used in areas that are short of land space. Initially, incinerators were simply used to reduce the volume of waste. Now, most are waste-to-energy facilities, which use the combustion process to also generate useful by-products, including heat, steam and electricity.

High temperature incineration can also destroy many pathogens and toxic materials, which is why incinerators are often used in the disposal of biomedical waste. Incinerators reduce the volume of waste by up to 90 percent, a significant reduction that would otherwise likely go into a landfill. Yet, some believe that this option reduces the incentive to recycle, since communities can often save more money by burning trash to generate electricity than by recovering materials for later sale. In Nigeria, this method is scarcely available only in the big cities where they are also grossly inadequate.

Recycling: Recycling is the collection, processing, and usage of materials. The recycled materials can be used in the manufacturing of other products. This is the process of recycling waste materials in order to extract resources or value from waste. Recycling turns the waste into raw materials or converts them to energy. The waste are categorised into recyclable groups depending on the type of materials. This appears to be the most effective and hygienic method of waste disposal with readily available technology and manpower. But due to lack of political will on the part of Government, Government monopoly in providing social services and unfavourable conditions for private participation, recycling facilities which could have eased drastically the menace of waste/refuse are pre-eminently not available in greater parts of the country. Where they are available, they are either not efficient or non functional.

Avoidance: This method of waste management prevents waste materials from being generated *ab initio* or reduces its generation drastically. Avoidance methods include re-use (of second branded products), repair (of faulty items instead of buying new ones), and refill (design of products that are refillable or re-usable to encourage consumers to avoid the use of disposable products).

In Nigeria today, because a greater percentage of the population are struggling to survive in the midst of plenty, the re-use and repair strategy is already a way of life as materials are used for a very long time. On the other hand, because considerations of issues are more on the economic side than on the side of personal and environment health, disposable products have today flooded and taken over the Nigerian markets and even the psyche of many Nigerians. This weakens the Refill Avoidance method as a strategy for waste management.

Composting: This is a biochemical process in which organic materials are biodegraded and decomposed to useful humus-like materials. Compost is a rich organic material that can be used to supplement soil for growing plants by providing additional nutrients and minerals. The process can be natural, through the ordinary process of biological decomposition, or created by combining organic wastes with other materials in order to accelerate breakdown. The composting process, unlike natural decomposition, can produce temperatures that will destroy pathogens and stabilize the material.

Food residue and yard trimmings make up a handsome part of all rural and municipal solid waste in Nigeria, a large amount that can be useful as composted organic waste. But it is practiced on a small scale in some rural areas of Nigeria. This technique of waste disposal is particularly useful especially in those areas where land for arable farming is decreasing and bush fallowing is no longer tenable. The demand for compost manure, as a better and less harmful alternative to artificial fertilizers for sustainable agriculture, boosts this practice.

Nigeria is a developing and industrialising nation. But she is yet to acquire the required technology for handling safely domestic, commercial and industrial waste. In recognition of the hazards the waste poses to the environment and human life, past governments in Nigeria have attempted to tackle waste-management issues through the "task force" approach. This approach has been counterproductive in the long run as it created more problems due to lack of proper coordination and technological know-how on the side of the responsible agencies.

Indiscriminate disposal, dumping and improper management of waste have thus become common phenomena in Nigeria. This situation constitutes one of the main causes of environmental degradation and pollution in Nigeria. Though there are many waste disposal regulations, there is gross inadequacy of proper disposal facilities. Where these facilities are minimally available in the cities, their activities of waste disposal often concentrate more around the "elitist sections" in town. Worse still, even when municipal waste dumping sites are designated for waste disposal, both the citizens and the disposal agents dump such wastes in an uncontrolled manner. The poor handling and disposal of waste thus leads to environmental degradation, destruction of the environment, and poses great risks to public health. Everywhere in the country, one can observe that the environment of the average Nigerian is not decent and can be inimical to health. Apart from various diseases and toxic conditions inherent in and derivable from these waste products, the presence of such heaps of waste degenerates the aesthetic value of the environment.

Besides, another disturbing dimension of the issue of waste in Nigeria is its connection to Flooding. This brings to the fore the whole issue of illegal waste dumping and flooding. Environmental degradation induced flooding in Nigeria is assuming a disturbing dimension due to blatant blockage of drainages through illegal dumping of refuse. An increase in the volume of rainfall during the rainy season in some regions of Nigeria due to change in global temperatures exposes the vulnerability of the Nigerian environment. Extensive flooding due to blocked drainages in recent times in Nigeria has led to loss of lives and properties, and total displacement of millions of Nigerians who have become home-made refugees. This brings to question the undesirability of the surface gutters and open drainage system prevalent in Nigeria and which increases for the environmentally unenlightened majority of Nigerians the temptation to dump waste into drainage lines. The Government has to rethink this area, not only to avert destructive flooding but to also checkmate the health hazards associated with the surface drainage system.

Talking of political will on the part of government, Nigerians are worried that there is not much on ground in the country to justify the approximately six billion naira spent by government on waste management in Nigeria annually.[196] Nigeria must involve an Integrated Environmental Management Strategy (IEMS). This integrated strategy must be clear that waste management and disposal involves the government, civil society and the private sector in tackling the issues

---

[196] Nta Tuesday Life, "Environment in Nigeria 11pm, 17 may 2011.

of domestic or primary, industrial and nuclear waste. This integrated strategy must be committed to all the four most important ladders of effective waste management: generation (producing waste), collection (getting waste out), transportation and disposal (harnessing waste and finding where to dump it), and management (waste to wealth).

The Federal Ministry of Environment in Nigeria through the Environmental Health Registration and Regulatory Council must ensure proper monitoring of waste management from point of generation to point of disposal and management. Countries with the technology generate electricity from waste. It is pertinent to state here that the government of Nigeria must encourage the private sector to invest in waste management by restoring confidence to the citizens and investors. A critical issue in waste management in developing countries and economies is the technology. Because waste management is contextual, developing appropriate waste disposal technology for Nigeria has to take into consideration the culture of the people and their level of development.

In sum, the motto of waste management strategies for waste minimization in Nigeria according to their desirability ought to revisit vigorously the "3R" formula – reduce, re-use, and reclaim/recycle[197]. Rethinking waste and redesigning processes in ways that more closely mimic natural processes is an emerging field. Industrial ecologists look at product design and the manufacturing process to discover how to prevent waste from occurring, and to develop methods of utilizing waste products as raw materials for other industries. They also attempt to analyze the flow of materials and energy in the industrial process to identify other ways to reduce the environmental and economic costs of production, use, and disposal.

Being a nation of more than 170 million people, no matter the number of policies put in place, without the proper education, techniques and political will, Nigeria will continue to rank among the environmentally dirty and deadly countries in Africa. Nigerians dump domestic and commercial waste indiscriminately because the government has failed to provide Nigerians with a functional alternative

---

[197] ENVIRONMENT AND SOCIETY, http://www.enviroliteracy.org/category.php/5. html (accessed 08/28/11)

that can effectively checkmate the poor waste management culture in the country. D. Ogbonna captures the situation this way:

> In 1985, the Federal Government of Nigeria introduced a major initiative, the Environmental Sanitation (clean-up campaign). All resident Nigerians were mandated to carry out compulsory environmental clean-up every last Saturday in the month. The initiative was good, but its implementation generated more problems. Garbages/ waste from the exercise were dumped along roadsides instead of at the dump sites designated by the local authorities for the purpose. The waste was left to decompose naturally (micro-organisms), to be eaten by animals, picked by scavengers, or washed away by rainwater/floods. In the estuarine environment, these wastes are carried away by the tidal floods into the larger creeks and rivers and thus, will affect surface-water quality. When the dump sites are eventually cleared, the waste materials end up somewhere on the outskirts of town in, e.g. abandoned excavation pits, river channels, ravines, and even open spaces; basically a transfer of waste from locations where some people feel inconvenienced by its presence to other locations where its nuisance value is believed to be lower. However, there is little or no consideration given to the ecological consequences. This type of "waste transfer" practice can not be considered as an appropriate environmental management option, as it simply appeases one environmental segment at the expense of another.[198]

---

[198] D. OGBONNA et al, "Waste management: a tool for environmental protection in Nigeria", op. cit. 56.

CHAPTER EIGHT

CONSEQUENCES OF ENVIRONMENTAL DEGRADATION IN NIGERIA

In this chapter, I have x-rayed the consequences of environmental degradation in Nigeria, in order to expose the magnitude of environmental hazards to which Nigerians are exposed and the degree of decay of a hitherto beautiful environment. The question is: given the situation of the Nigerian environment as x-rayed above, what are the human prizes? It is often said that degradation/pollution has a cost. And that cost must be borne by the polluter. In Nigeria, the victims bear more of the burden of environmental degradation, and the ethical-spiritual, economic, political, socio- cultural and health tolls are incalculable.

Ethical-spiritual

People today usually talk about "environmental spirituality". Though spirituality and religiosity are not synonymous, both influence and are influenced by natural environment. Permit me a deeper analysis of these terms. The issue of spirituality is hydra-headed in the sense that almost everybody speaks of it from different perspectives, yet no one seems to have complete meaning of it. According to Smith cited by A. Nwachukwu: "Spirituality is an elusive term and has as many definitions as people who write about it".[199] In the religious circles, those who belong to certain sodalities or religious bodies claim to be spiritual

---

[199] A. Nwachukwu, *Keeping Human relationships Together: Self-Guide to Healthy Living (Studies in Spiritual Psychology vis-à-vis Human values*, 163.

in scope and content. For instances, those who belong to some secret societies are by that singular association seen as spiritual people with some cosmic powers and knowledge. Even, among the ministers of the Gospel message, to disentangle them from being spiritual is an insult to their person. Spirituality is synonymous with the sacred priesthood or religious professions. These are the subtle misgivings that create problem in discussing this topic. It is pertinent to ask certain questions such as: "Who is spiritual? Is being spiritual limited in its scope and content? Is spirituality heaven-bound or has it any worldly or material implication? There can be no end to such questions. In order to remain focused on this issue of spirituality and environment, we take a deeper analysis.

Spirituality involves ".... the little daily decisions and choices we make, what kind of food we eat, how we talk to the clerk in the store, how much time (if any) we devote in prayer. Our spirituality also includes the big choices we make; whom we decide to marry or befriend, the kind of home we live in, the type of work we choose to do. When life presents us with few options, our spirituality influences the way we accept and work within the confines of such restrictions"[200] Spirituality is, therefore, life. Spirituality may include religiosity. But religiosity does not necessarily indicate spirituality. This is to say that one can be spiritual but not religious, or one can be religious without being spiritual, or one can be both.

A spiritual person is he who sees the world around him clearly, understands his limits and cultivates his strengths. He is one who, when faced with good and evil in real life, uses one's positive energies to evolve for good in all relationships whether human or environmental. A spiritual person is that individual who lives out his transcendental ideals and ultimate concerns within his historical and existential context: religion, politics, economics, culture and environment. Spirituality here represents that intrinsic quality of the individual in response to existence. Here, religion could become an ethical pathway or container for spirituality. So, a basic quality of a spiritual person is ability for positive sensitivity and positive involvement to the world around him. So spirituality has to do with

---

[200] A. NWACHUKWU, Op. Cit. (Svoboda in Nwachukwu), 163.

the environment. Spirituality is about life, and life is environmental. Environment is the basis for any advancement and achievement. He is spiritual whose life objective begins from there because spirituality draws from the motivational energies within the environment as the place of experience, understanding and action. And the interplay of experience, understanding and action shape spirituality's direction. Environment as the place of "residence" and "culture" becomes the grounding point of spirituality. Hence, spirituality and environment are allies in a common cause. That is why in his existential perspective, Karl Rahner holds that the future in which God comes does not frustrate the present in which man lives. Man realizes openness to the absolute future through a relation to the present, i.e. the future is realized in responsible availability to the present.[201]

In this connection, G. Kaufman also holds that the divine future in which God comes does not negate or frustrate the human future towards which humanity goes.[202] A spiritual person is not one who has and practises a body of systematically formulated religious beliefs/creeds whether revealed or natural. A spiritual person is one who incorporates good works and good behaviour with religion (theology) in a spirit of stewardship, which leads to best application of one's talents and resources for the good of oneself, others and the environment. This spiritual person might have no formal religion but has positive human values and virtues to share with others.

However, from the foregoing, one can be religious and pietistic but totally lacks a spirituality that promotes ethical values and virtues. On the other hand, another can have a spirituality bent that strongly

---

[201] Cf. K. RAHNER, "The eternal significance of the humanity of Jesus for our salvation" in K. RAHNER, Theological investigations 3, Seabury (NY) 1974, 43-44; cf. also K. RAHNER, "The theological problems entailed in the idea of 'the new earth'" in K. RAHNER, Theological investigations 10, Darton, Longmann and Todd, London 1973, 270; cf. also K. RAHNER, "Resurrection" in RAHNER Karl (ed.), Encyclopedia of theology: a concise sacramentum mundi, Burns & Oats, London 1975, 1438-1442.
[202] Cf. G. KAUFMAN, "The human niche in earth's ecological order" in RAY Kathleen (ed.), Ecology, economy, and God, theology that matters, Fortress Press Minneapolis (MN) 2006, 119.

upholds ethical values and virtues without having any formal religion. But one can be both spiritual and religious when one's spirituality (values and virtues) strongly build upon one's religious views or affirms them. This is where our religion flows into spirituality when a spiritual person spells out where he stands on any given issue influenced by his religious views.

So, in practice, to be religious is not strictly to be spiritual. Thus, A. Nwachukwu asserts that nobody should claim to be spiritual who cannot relate well with others and do things that are good for the overall well being of society[203] because spirituality "is holistic when it acknowledges that all aspects of a person's life must be subjected to the transforming influence of the incarnation"[204]

In sum, Spirituality is action-oriented. It does not matter how one rationalizes one's actions spirituality is the test. As rational beings, each of us is expected to behave true to type befitting of our nature. Therefore, whenever our actions synchronize with our thoughts as human beings, there must be elements of spirituality there. This means that spirituality is "a form of socialization". In the view of A. Nwachukwu, spirituality is both human and divine oriented[205]. A spiritual person does not allow his religion to become an obstacle to his human relationships with people who equally share those human values and virtues that promote society. A Spiritual individual can relate and live together with others despite their religions because his spirit is emancipated.

It has become necessary; therefore, we distinguish where spirituality resembles religion and where they differ. While Spirituality could be described as the quality or fact of being spiritual as shown in character and quality of thought and life, Religion is a body of systematically formulated religious beliefs/creeds whether revealed or natural practised by a group. The relationship between Spirituality and Religion has been a heated debate. In this debate, I identify three currents of thought: Those who argue that the two concepts have same meaning; those

---

[203] .http://www.emergentuk.org/resources/alan_jamieson/churchless_faith/faith_stageseminar_notes.doc (accessed 04/20/2011).
[204] A. Nwachukwu, Op. Cit. 163.
[205] http://www.emergentuk.org/resources/alan_jamieson/churchless_faith/faith_stageseminar_notes.doc (accessed 04/20/2011).

who see the concepts as completely different and unrelated; and those who see the concepts as different but related and complimentary. This paper will agree with the last current of thought, i.e. that Spirituality and Religion are not synonymous but complimentary.

Religion promotes a set of exclusive belief systems held and practiced by a group or community. On the other hand, Spirituality deals with inner spiritual attitudes, dispositions and abilities of individuals to adapt to the world around them in a way that is expected to enhance relationships. While Religion emphasises community, group and is tied to and actualised in a community that has shared traditions, Spirituality deals with the individual and operates in the first person singular and has to do with a sense of peace, purpose and connection to others in order to give creative activity to received and abstract ideas as they rise to the surface of the concrete world – thus spirituality is generative. This could be why A Nwachukwu sees Spirituality as holistic as it tries to subject all aspects of a person's life to the transforming influence of the incarnation[206]. So Spirituality as a natural human disposition transcends religious-secular boundaries. While Religion can be dogmatic, Spirituality is a process, i.e. while Spirituality deals with how the individual person is progressively guided to view reality; Religion has its view of reality impressed on the individual person because it has its own truths to be believed, worship to be carried out, and rules to guide conduct[207].

However, because Religion is the travelling path of the group to fulfilment and meaning as perceived by them, and Spirituality is the travelling path of the individual to fulfilment and meaning, each compliments the other in this area of fulfilment and meaning despite their seemingly different paths. This is where Spirituality and Religion have always shared values, which impact on meaning, disposition and strategies for personal accompaniment and accomplishment. And this is where "spiritual people" have certain fundamental things in common with "religious people". A person's spiritual disposition may include elements of the person's Religion. In fact, both Spirituality and Religion express a desire for meaning and belongingness in life.

---

[206] A. NWACHUKWU, Op. Cit. 163.
[207] Cf. A. NWACHUKWU, Op. Cit. 168.

This is where the spiritual flows into the religious and vice versa. As Religion deals with the belief system of a group, Spirituality deals with the overall inner attitudes of the person in response to the world outside him in search for this fulfilment and meaning. In this search, the individual can appeal to tools of Religion. This is because even though Spirituality may not necessarily root the search for meaning in some transcendent Being as Religion does, yet Spirituality has to do with quest or search of some kind, which transcends the individual. Thus, A. Nwachukwu asserts, "...the human person, the apogee of existence, the summary and climax of all living things and life, is purposeful and meaningful. This meaning goes beyond any human imagination and ultimately traceable to a source whose existence is permanence and beauty itself"[208]. This is where Spirituality appeals to Religion because in its nature, the phenomenon of Spirituality points to the existence of fundamental interior needs in humans that yearn for an outlet. But as we have observed above, Spirituality does this taking a holistic approach that involves real life and positive models of response to concrete life issues, i.e. it incorporates the whole of life vicissitudes.

In sum, there is substantive difference between Spirituality and Religion[209], and yet they need each other to be life giving and redeeming. Salvation (in the sense of wholeness) is what Religion promises its adherents. And because Spirituality is also holistic (incorporates whole life vicissitudes), both touch on the great desires each person holds in his/her heart. In this connection and sense, however, one can say that Spirituality gives a practical and concrete expression to Religion in real life situations. This is what A. Nwachukwu is alluding to when he affirms: "Of what significance are religious beliefs, practices, services, concepts of Church, heaven and the efforts millions make to worship God if religious practices have no effects in individual lives"[210]. Thus, "wholeness" of Religion translates into "holistic-ness" of Spirituality. And "holistic" spirituality (in the sense of total and concrete life situation of the individual person) enriches

---

[208] A. NWACHUKWU, Op. Cit. 196.
[209] Cf. COUSINS, Ewert, http://www.emergentuk.org/resources/alan_jamieson/churchless_faith/faith_stageseminar_notes.doc (accessed 06/24/2010).
[210] A. NWACHUKWU, Op. Cit. 170.

"wholeness" (in the sense of peace with the divine and fellow humans) of Religion. This is where Spirituality as a process of transformation, de-formation and reformation of the individual person ought to belong to all Religions and ought to be relevant for all Religions since all Religions accept that each individual person must develop via the inner spiritual way. So, Religion is spiritually earth-bound.[211] Thus A. Nwachukwu states: "...any religious belief that has no practical application to individual concerns and problems on the moment is misleading...religion and spiritual psychology have such unique and enormous roles in the life of the individual"[212]. The concern now is for both to effectively work together to realise this common agenda. This is because Religion without Spirituality is fundamentalism, and Spirituality without Religion could also lead to mere sentimentalism. Spirituality is the embodiment and synthesis of Religion in action. Authentic Spirituality affects the whole structure of society for good and thus assists Religion to become a practical instrument of positive change in society as it (spirituality) connects individual persons to both the transcendent and the immanent. Thus, Religion devoid of Spirituality could become shallow and impotent. It becomes then true that whenever any Religion gets out of touch with the basic essence of Spirituality (holistically), it (religion) runs the risk of loosing identity, value and meaning for its adherents. But when Spirituality is married to Religion, a humane community can be generated. Religion should be nourished and animated by beliefs that are concretised in action. Spirituality, rather than being the death of Religion, can become a means of its rejuvenation as the spiritual person discovers fundamental interior needs that Religion can satisfy or has answers to. Moreover, the special nature of Spirituality as an innovative instrument can benefit Religion by helping the individual to understand religious values and virtues in a more positive light.

Spirituality has broad implications for a wide spectrum of human life – psychological, physical, socio-cultural as well as religious – all these impart on the general well being of the individual person. Spirituality tries to network all these to serve the individual's and humanity's needs.

[211] Cf. A. NWACHUKWU, Op. Cit. 169.
[212] A. NWACHUKWU, Op. Cit. 209.

Hence, Spirituality has broad implications for Psychology in the overall well being of individuals.

According to A Nwachukwu, "...relationships are basically psychological in nature"[213]. And "...there is nothing human beings do that is not psychological including religious practices"[214]. While Psychology has to deal primarily with the state of the mind (cognitive activities and actions) and how it translates into behavioural patterns, Spirituality has to deal with how a person tries to reconcile and harmonize these inner mental and emotional drives, attitudes and behavioural patterns to other external factors. In line with the above, A. Nwachukwu observes that what the human brain is to human cognitive activities and actions, spirituality is to human social and ethical consciousness and behaviours[215]. Spirituality, thus, evaluates the mental, emotional and physical states of the person in relation to factors around him using the findings of Psychology in a way that the overall human behaviour imparts positively on the well being of all. In this way, Spirituality employs psychological findings for spiritual growth. This is why it has been said that Spirituality relates to some Psychological experience of the individual that is primordial in nature.

This shows that both have the human person and the human mind as subject in factoring human behaviour. Hence, John Welwood affirms that both Psychology and spirituality deal with three major dimensions of human existence: personal, interpersonal and supra personal, and that both take us to the heart of what it means to be human[216]. So, while Psychology offers Spirituality an anatomy of human behaviour and workings of the human mind, Spirituality helps to proffer solutions to Psychological problems as Psychologists are also intensely interested in Spirituality and would want to introduce the later into their practices.. In line with the above premise, both apply a holistic approach – incorporate all aspects of human life. And to combine Psychology and Spirituality effectively for the good of

---

[213] A. Nwachukwu, Op. Cit. 158.

[214] A. Nwachukwu, Op. Cit. 160.

[215] Cf. A. Nwachukwu, Op. Cit. 159.

[216] Cf. Welwood John, "Integrating Psychology and Spirituality" quoted in http://www.emergentuk.org/resources/alan_jamieson/churchless_faith/faith_stageseminar_notes.doc.(accessed 06/24/2010).

society, there is need for Spiritual Psychologists who can guide human relationships, especially in the young.

To guide the holistic objectives of Spirituality, therefore, the importance of Psychological findings cannot be underestimated. Since we live and reflect our "psychologies" as individuals in our actions as we relate and interact with others, there is need for a Spirituality that addresses burning issues of human relationships. Thus, Spiritual Psychology offers an inclusive guide for creating, maintaining and constructing fulfilling relationships. Religion *per se* cannot offer this since it is exclusive in nature.

This is why "Spiritual Psychology" is the psychological practice that functionally guides the individual persons to self-supervise their relationships in order to become both "changed and change agents" in themselves, their environment, community, organisation, profession, and interaction with others irrespective of religion, race, sex, culture and language in expectation for better life.[217] It incorporates both basic and applied psychology in its pursuit for a holistic personality[218].

A. Nwachukwu puts it this way: "Spiritual psychology...tries to throw light on the mysteries that surround individuals in their interpersonal relationships"[219]. The human activities of believing and doing have to flow from the human activity of relating. In this way, the individual begins to visualise and unwind his assignment of life influenced by his relationships to others and the environment in which he lives, and religion becomes for him, not just a set of formulas, dogmas and creeds, but solution and accompaniment in his journey through life. This approach strikes also a balance between pure individualism or self-sufficiency and commitment to relationships, to community and to society.

As stated earlier, spirituality has to do with the environment too. Spirituality is about life, and life is environmental. Environment is the basis for any advancement and achievement. He is spiritual whose life objective begins from there because spirituality draws from the motivational energies within the environment as the place of

---

[217] Cf. A. Nwachukwu, Op. Cit. 158.
[218] Cf. A. Nwachukwu, Op. Cit. 159, 158.
[219] A. Nwachukwu, Op. Cit. 163.

experience, understanding and action. And the interplay of experience, understanding and action shape spirituality's direction. Environment as the place of "residence" and of "culture" becomes the grounding point of spirituality. This means that spirituality and environment are allies in a common cause. The analysis made above on the interconnectivity between the environment and human spirituality exposes the ethical-spiritual damage environmental degradation in Nigeria has done to the psyche of the average Nigerian. Nigerians are very religious and spiritual people. They believe that in the serenity of nature, man can contemplate transcendence. But through the massive environmental devastations, there is already a seeming rupture of human harmony with nature and all the serenity that nature offers to human spirituality and religiosity and link with transcendence as the sacred groves, forests, trees and places of worship come under attack under either under the guise of economic development or under the illusion of misguided practice of religion.

Economic

The environmental problem is intimately connected to justice for the poor. The Church's teachings make us aware that the poor suffer most directly from environmental degradation. They are its victims.

In the words of St. Pope John Paul II: "It must also be said that the proper ecological balance will not be found without directly addressing the structural forms of poverty. In the fact of such situations it would be wrong to assign the responsibility to the poor alone for the negative environmental consequences of their actions. This will require a courageous reform of structures."[220]

It is a fact that both rich and poor can devastate the environment, the former from greed and the latter from need. But in the opinion of John Hart, "...while rich and poor people harm their environment, the poor do so out of their desperation to survive, and so the social and structural conditions that provoke this should be changed".[221] Environment and

---

[220] POPE JOHN PAUL II, *Message for the Celebration of the World Day of Peace*, Op. cit. n. 11.
[221] J. HART, op. cit. 26.

economics are linked, for a proper environmental balance will not be found without directly addressing the structural forms of poverty. Thus, Johannes Nissen asserts: "...the link between the economic debt of the poor and the moral debt of the rich. If the basic rights of the poor are neglected, a moral guilt on the part of the rich will arise. In other words, the relationship between the rich and the poor is not just an economic problem. It has to be seen within the context of guilt and blame....Each generation must take responsibility for responding to God's decree of liberty, and for doing justice in its own circumstances and for its children."[222]

In Nigeria, the crisis of the environment is not separate from the crisis of the poor. Both are a single crisis of community. It is the poor and powerless who most directly bear the burden of current environmental recklessness. Poisoning of land, air and water in areas in which they live and work creates unemployment, as their habitat becomes an economically non-sustainable environment. One consequence of these various forms of degradation is the regular occurrence of *acid rain* in Nigeria induced from pollutants from vehicles, industries and power-generating outfits. This has seriously devastated vegetation and compromised the aquatic environment in Nigeria. It has had adverse impacts on forests, fresh waters and soils, decimating aquatic life forms as well as causing damage to buildings and human life. Acid rain not only deprives people of healthy drinkable rainwater and stunts crop growth; it is also affecting people's homes.

Subsistence farming and fishing are the mainstay of the over 27 million people living in the oil-exploited regions of Nigeria. For decades, oil spills from oil installations and pipelines have affected local people. Oil spills often destroy crops, farmlands, aquatic life, and the flora and fauna of the entire region. For the farmers and fishermen in the region who depend essentially upon these for their sustenance, the situation often spells doom. In most cases, those who suffer loss from these oil production activities are not usually adequately compensated or not compensated at all, even when they are robbed of the sources of livelihood (agriculture, fishing, transportation, their homes, etc.)

---

[222] J. NISSEN, *New Testament and mission: historical and hermeneutical perspectives*, Peter Lang GmbH, Frankfort 1999, 68.

Moreover, the cleaning-up of oil spills is often done superficially, leaving much poisonous oil in soil and water. In sum, this land degradation, which manifests in the forms of soil erosion, nutrient depletion, salinity and disruption of natural cycles, is a fundamental and persistent problem in Nigeria. These diminish productivity, undermine food security and consequently increase the cycle of poverty. Why is it that the thoroughness with which Mobil handled the oil spillage in the Mexican Gulf of the United States in 2010, for example, cannot be applied by the same Mobil when there is oil spillage in the oil producing areas of Nigeria? This is, to say the least, environmental racism.

The nonchalant attitude of the oil producers and government have led to frequent agitations by irate youths, unending chaos, hostilities, rift and anarchy, which are being witnessed over the years, especially in the oil rich regions of Nigeria, but which has now spread all over the country. Many of the poor people in Nigeria, and in fact in all developing countries, live in degrading and desperate situations that often lead them to adopt environmentally harmful practices. There is no doubt that some ethnic conflicts in Nigeria today are environmental degradation related. This has resulted in an intensified struggle for increase resource control by ethnic nationalities in Nigeria, a struggle which has fanned the embers of militancy and armed conflict. The struggle can be over economic opportunities, as well as political and civil rights violations, among other contestable factors. According to S. Mansoob Murshed, Grievances play a major part in contemporary conflict. He notes that ultimately, open warfare cannot emerge inside a society with a functioning social contract, as greed and grievances are managed and conflict is contained when countries have properly operating institutions[223].

While there are debates currently about the extent to which the availability or distribution of natural resources contributes to conflicts[224], environmental degradation experienced in the process of exploitation of these natural resources, coupled with the failure to protect the rights

---

[223] S. MANHOOB MURSHED, "Conflict, Civil War and underdevelopment" in http://jpr.sagepub.com/content/39/4/387.short (accessed 08/27/11).
[224] ENVIRONMENTAL LITERACY COUNCIL, http://www.enviroliteracy.org/subcategory.php/222.html, (accessed 08/28/11),

of minorities, greed (the desire to control resources and capture rents) and unstable corrupt political institutions contribute in greater part to the conflicts in the country. Consequently, resolution of environmental conflicts in Nigeria will require the just reconstitution of the social contract.

Political

Politics in Nigeria has become the tool of the minority against the majority. Parochial and selfish motivations obscure and impede efforts at real solution to environmental problems in Nigeria as such negotiations become political tools in the hands of few Elites who feed on the ignorance of the majority poor masses. Groups are influenced and pitched against one another by those who want to connive in evil and reap from the phenomenon of environmental degradation. Bishop Matthew Kukah of the Catholic Archdiocese of Sokoto in Nigeria made this striking assertion, in an interview with *NTA international* just after his Episcopal ordination and installation. that Nigeria is being systematically destroyed, not by Christianity or Islam, not by Housa or Yoruba or Igbo or any other ethnic group, but by people who have decided to be evil[225]. This is why a struggle for the environment becomes a war of one brother or sister against another. This turns politics into a game of deceit and manipulation rather than an art and instrument of good governance and public well-being.

Socio-cultural

In some places, especially in the oil prospecting zones, their artefacts, roads, recreational and historical sites, even homes, are lost to environmental degradation. There is the more painful decimation of social and cultural harmony with nature and all the serenity that nature offers to human development and wellbeing through disturbances and displacements of the local inhabitants. There is also breakdown of social relationships as pollution outfits in connivance with some greedy individuals try to employ the policy of divide and rule to split the

---
[225] NTA INTERNATIONAL NEWS, September 8, 2011.

communities by using money to entice a section of the people against others, thereby destroying effective social cohesion. This breakdown of social relationships and socio-cultural cohesions has produced environmental refugees especially in the oil-rich regions - people who are forced by the degradation of their natural habitat to forsake it, and often their possessions as well, to face the dangers and uncertainties of forced displacement.

Health

Just as we can talk of health in different perspectives, psychological health, emotional health, social health, spiritual health et cetera, there also exists environmental health. Environmental health is the health with reference to the general life-style of the members of a particular society in relation to their environment. It includes the ability to effectively cope with ones environment. No wonder the popular aphorism, "As one makes one's bed, so will one lie on it". Our environment creates, re-creates and can lead to life or death, depending on individual dynamics and mannerisms. For instance, public health extends to environmental sanitation and waste disposal, prevention and control of epidemics and communicable diseases, general health education and enlightened campaigns. It also involves prevention of air, soil and water pollutions and enforcement of health regulations and standards in public places.[226] Hence, the saying, "Cleanness is next to Godliness". We are our own environments. All activities cease outside the environment.

The World Health Organization (WHO) estimates that about a quarter of the diseases facing mankind today occur due to prolonged exposure to environmental degradation. Health hazards due to poor environment and sanitation management can cripple a population's productive energies; and there cannot be a healthy nation without a healthy environment.

From the principle of chain of life, it is not an overstatement that environmental degradation in Nigeria corrodes the health of Nigerians. Apart from their economic mainstay that is badly affected, the health of

---

[226] Cf. S. KALAGBOR, *Health administration in Nigeria*, Horizon Concepts, Port Harcourt (Nigeria) 2004, 12.

the inhabitants also tends to plummet because once food and drinking water are contaminated, the consumers contact various infectious diseases such as typhoid, cholera, amoebic infections, bacillary dysentery, diarrhoea, guinea worm, hepatitis, hook worm infestation, skin diseases, malaria, etc. These often lead to death. The citizens are also exposed to a host of other sicknesses and malfunctioning: respiratory abnormalities, abdominal and intestinal problems, dental disorders, ear infections, skeletal and muscular pain, central nervous system disorders, eye infections, and blood disorders. Others include chicken pox, septic wounds and congenital abnormalities, cardiovascular diseases and lung cancer, etc. The toxicants which can be found in air, water and soil are routed into the human system through *inhalation* (movement of air from the external environment through the body airways during breathing), *ingestion* (the consumption of a substance by an organism either man or animals), *absorption* (the movement and uptake of substances into cells or across tissues such as skin by way of diffusion or osmosis).

Particularly in the oil producing regions, the inhabitants experience respiratory problems, skin rashes, tumours, gastrointestinal problems, cancers and malnourishment. Many children have been observed with distended bellies and light hair, which are evidence of *kwashiorkor*, a protein deficiency syndrome. The spread of *kwashiorkor* in these communities are attributed to decline in fish catch and reduced agricultural productivity as a result of the contamination of rivers, ponds, seawaters and land by oil spills.

In 2004, Nigerian Health System was accessed by WHO to be 187th in the world. In 2014, the World Health Organization ranked the Nigerian Health System in the 197th place out of WHO's 200 nations evaluated with Nigeria allocating less than five percent of its annual budget to the health sector as against 15 percent recommended by the World Health Organization[227] This is worsened by the fact that with well over 167[228] million people, 774 local government areas, vast area of land covering 923,768km sq. and bordering Benin, Niger, Chad and

---

[227] Cf. FEDERAL MINISTRY OF HEALTH (FHOH), *Revised national health policy*, Abuja FMOH 2004, 4, 7. See http://www.vanguardngr.com/2010/10/nigerias-health-system-ranks-197-of-whos-200-nations-nhis/#sthash.YHZely5g.dpuf
[228] NTAI, NTA24 News, October 27, 2011.

Cameroon, it looks cumbersome for Government to adequately fund the Public Health System in Nigeria. In all these consequences, we find a common thread: that environmental degradation and pollution ultimately impact negatively on the common good of the Nigerian human family, and ultimately on human dignity. The ranking could get worse by day if no urgent steps are taken to revamp Health delivery in Nigeria. The Government in Nigeria must have the political will to invest massively in the health sector. Any investment to secure the health of the citizenry of any Nation that also guarantees clean environment ought not to be considered a waste; such investment guarantees overall peace, progress and enhanced development. Reintroduction of aggressive sanitation inspectorate at all levels of Government is a *sine qua non*. The inspectorate must ensure that Waste bags and domestic Waste disposal bins are made big issues in sanitation inspection.

In sum, we have tried to x-ray summarily the environmental picture of Nigeria from the degradation angle catalysed by human activities. Distributive justice becomes idealistic and a mirage in a country as Nigeria where the environment is devastated. This is because, according to John Hart:

> Ideally, distributive justice would ensure that everyone's need (but not everyone's greed) would be met, in property, in land, in basic food, clothing, shelter, energy and medicine. When the environment is devastated by adverse human practices (such as dumping harmful effluents into rivers, releasing harmful emissions into air, and pouring chemical wastes onto the land), the needs of the entire human family cannot be met. If people care for the environment, Earth will be able to produce what humanity needs.[229]

This is exactly the present picture of the Nigerian environment. The question is: Who can help to change the tide? Is it the Government, the civil society, the polluting outfits, and the pro-environment groups, the Church? There is need for concrete practical steps on the part of

---

[229] J. HART, op. cit. 113.

all Nigerians. The issue of the abhorred environmental degradation and the much desired environmental health is a concern for entire communities irrespective of creed. And the Catholic Church in Nigeria is also a stakeholder here.

In Nigeria, The Federal Environmental Protection Agency (FEPA) is one of the umbrella organs empowered to ensure healthy environmental practices in Nigeria. Decree 58 of 1988, by the Federal Government of Nigeria, created this.

The FEPA has statutory responsibility for overall protection of the environment, and its initial functions and priorities include:

- Co-ordinating all environmental activities and programmes within the country.
- Serving as the national environmental focal point and the co-ordinating body for all bilateral and multilateral activities on the environment with other countries and international organisations.
- Setting and enforcing ambient and emission standards for air, water and noise pollution.
- Controlling substances, which may affect the stratosphere, especially the ozone layer.
- Preventing and controlling discharges to air, water or soil of harmful and hazardous substances.

Since then, FEPA has developed the following instruments for combating environmental degradation in Nigeria:

(i) The National Policy on the Environment.
Launched by Government on 27th November 1989, this document describes guidelines and strategies for achieving the Policy Goal of Sustainable Development.

(ii) National guidelines and Standards for environmental pollution Control in Nigeria
This was launched on March 12th 1991 and represents the basic instrument for monitoring and controlling industrial and urban pollution.

(iii) National Effluence Limitation Regulations S.I.8 of 1991

This instrument makes it mandatory that industrial facilities install anti-pollution equipment, make provision for further effluent treatment, prescribe maximum limit of effluent parameters allowed for discharge, and spell out penalties for contravention.

(iv) Pollution Abatement in Industries facilities Generating Waste regulations S.I.9 of 1991

Restrictions are imposed hereunder on the release of toxic substances and requirement stipulated;

- Monitoring of pollution to ensure permissible limits are not exceeded;
- Unusual and accidental discharges;
- Contingency plans;
- Generator's liabilities
- Strategies of waste reduction and safety for workers.

(v) Waste Management regulation S.I.15 of 1991

These regulate the collection, treatment and disposal of solid and hazardous waste from municipal and industrial sources and give the comprehensive list of chemicals and chemical waste by toxicity categories.

(vi) Environmental Impact Assessment (EIA) Decree No 86 of 1992

This legislation makes EIA mandatory for any major developmental project likely to have adverse impact on the environment, and prescribes the procedure. (S.2 Decree No 86 of 1992).

(vii) The Sectoral for EIA

Pursuant to S.60 (1) (a) of Decree No 86 of 1992 prescribes the detailed guidelines for conducting EIA for projects on Industry-by-Industry basis.

The National Environmental Standards and Regulations Enforcement Agency (NESREA) is another organ of the then

Federal Ministry of Environment, Housing and Urban Development put in place to oversee environmental matters. The NESREA Act 2007 saw its establishment.

Vision: The vision of the Agency is to ensure a cleaner and healthier environment for Nigerians.

Mission: To inspire personal and collective responsibility in building an environmentally conscious society for the achievement of sustainable development in Nigeria.

Functions: NESREA has responsibility for the protection and development of the environment, biodiversity conservation and sustainable development of Nigeria's natural resources in general and environmental technology including coordination, and liaison with relevant stakeholders within and outside Nigeria on matters of enforcement of environmental standards, regulations, rules, laws, policies and guidelines.

Some functions of the Agency, amongst others include to:

- Enforce compliance with laws, guidelines, policies and standards on environmental matters;
- Coordinate and liaise with, stakeholders, within and outside Nigeria on matters of environmental standards, regulations and enforcement;
- Enforce compliance with the provisions of international agreements, protocols, conventions and treaties on the environment including climate change, biodiversity conservation, desertification, forestry, oil and gas, chemicals, hazardous wastes, ozone depletion, marine and wild life, pollution, sanitation and such other environmental agreements as may from time to time come into force;
- Enforce compliance with policies, standards,, legislation and guidelines on water quality, environmental health and sanitation, including pollution abatement;

- enforce compliance with guidelines, and legislation on sustainable management of the ecosystem, biodiversity conservation and the development of Nigeria's natural resources;
- Enforce compliance with any legislation on sound chemical management, safe use of pesticides and disposal of spent packages thereof;
    o enforce compliance with regulations on the importation, exportation, production, distribution, storage, sale, use, handling and disposal of hazardous chemicals
    o and waste, other than in the oil and gas sector;
- Enforce through compliance monitoring, the environmental regulations and standards on noise, air, land, seas, oceans and other water bodies other than in the oil and gas sector;
- Ensure that environmental projects funded by donor organizations and external support agencies adhere to regulations in environmental safety and protection;
- Enforce environmental control measures through registration, licensing and permitting systems other than in the oil and gas sector;
- Conduct environmental audit and establish data bank on regulatory and enforcement mechanisms of environmental standards other than in the oil and gas sector;
- Create public awareness and provide environmental education on sustainable environmental management, promote private sector compliance with environmental regulations other than in the oil and gas sector and publish general scientific or other data resulting from the performance of its functions; and carry out such activities as are necessary or expedient for the performance of its functions.

These two umbrella instruments contain positive and realistic planning that balances human needs against the carrying capacity of the environment. There are also a number of complementary policies, strategies and management approaches being put in place, which should ensure, among others, that:

- environmental concerns are integrated into major economic decision- making process;
- environmental remediation costs are built into major development projects;
- economic instruments are employed in the management of natural resources;
- environmentally friendly technologies are applied;
- Environmental Impact Assessment is mandatorily carried out before any major development project is embarked on.
- The principle of *intergenerational equity*, which requires that the needs of the present generation be met without compromising the ability of future generations to meet their own needs;
- The principle of *intra-generational equity* which requires that different groups of people within the country and within the present generation have the right to benefit equally from the exploitation of resources and that they have an equal right to a clean and healthy environment.

Nonetheless, the picture painted above about the Nigerian environment is not abating but seems to worsen by day despite all instruments put in place by Government. The question would be: why is it so? Nigeria is almost becoming a country where well thought-out programmes and policies rarely work, and where useful recommendations hardly survive the light of day. This is because the greatest problem today facing Nigeria and setting the country backwards is that its citizens to a greater extent feel above the law, do not obey the law, do not keep the law. In this case, both the rich and the poor are culpable. Though we have all this policies in place to safeguard the environment, though we have well thought-out legal framework to tackle environmental concerns like FEPA and NASREA under the Federal Ministry of Environment, there is a great lack of conscientious and patriotic supervision, control, steady surveillance, and responsible and efficacious planning on the part of public authorities. In short, there is a lack of leadership. This situation, perhaps, is not unconnected with corruption. The situation is worsened by a lack of vigilance and sensitivity on the part of civil society to what is happening to their hitherto beautiful environment.

Commitment to a national environmental policy that will ensure sustainable development based on proper management of the environment is called for. Let us hope that the newly created Federal Ministry for Environment and its subordinate Environmental Health Registration and Regulatory Council will really have the vision and will to tackle environmental issues in Nigeria headlong. Until the civil society, men and women of goodwill in Nigeria rise up and ask Government to account for the decaying environment; Nigeria may remain in it for a long time to come. We shall come back to this in Chapter five.

Summarily in this chapter, I have tried to ex-ray how much human induced activities have contributed to a decaying environment in Nigeria and the consequences of this to both human life and the overall environment. I have also tried to show what the Government has put in place as policies and strategies to tackle environmental issues in Nigeria. However, I have opined that they are not working effectively yet due to some factors mentioned on the sides of the civil society, multi-national corporations and Government. From the foregoing, therefore, it is obvious that Nigeria has neither measured up to the principles of the Church's environmental stewardship nor complied fully with international standards concerning environmental management whether at the level of hygiene consciousness of its citizens, or at the level of her developmental strides, or at the level of the exploitation of her natural resources. The principle of responsible stewardship over creation does not govern, to a large extent, Nigeria's environmental practices. Her developmental strides and exploitation of natural resources, to a large extent, violate the principle of respect for human life and integrity of creation. There is an overriding primacy of economic and political interests over that of ethics and values. The Nigerian Government is not in environmental solidarity with its citizens because its projects are economically propelled but not people oriented. This leads one to conclude that the fundamental principles of authentic development upon which a sound environmental ethos ought to be based, as enunciated vividly by the Church's theology of environment, is yet to enjoy adequate acceptance and commitment in Nigeria. To a greater extent, ignorance about environmental issues is responsible.

In the next chapter, we turn attention to the Catholic Church in Nigeria and how she can, through her environmental initiatives, abate this environmental ignorance and augment the efforts of State in this direction by using the Church's environmental principles to assist in an environmental education that can reverse this grim picture of the Nigerian environment. This will be in line with the incessant calls today by the Church's *Magisterium* that "Local and Particular Churches should get really involved in environmental issues within their own contexts in the spirit of "think globally and act locally".

CHAPTER NINE

THE ENVIRONMENTAL CHALLENGE IN NIGERIA: PROPOSALS FOR PASTORAL ACTION

In this chapter, I summarily examine the Catholic Church in Nigeria and how she has responded and can still respond to the incessant calls today by the Church's *Magisterium* that Local or Particular Churches get really involved in environmental issues within their own contexts. What are the challenges? This work, here, offers some proposals as its own contribution to an unfolding environmental debate, awareness and engagement in Nigeria.

In the Post-synodal exhortation *Ecclesia in Africa*,[230] the Church in Africa holds that integral human development — the development of every person and of the whole person, especially of the poorest and most neglected in the community — is at the very heart of evangelisation. This is because between evangelisation and human advancement, development and liberation, there are in fact profound links. These include links of an anthropological order, because the man who is to be evangelised is not an abstract being but is subject to social and economic questions. They also include links of the theological order, since one cannot dissociate the plan of creation from the plan of Redemption. The latter plan touches the very concrete situations of injustice to be combated and of justice to be restored. They also include links of the

---

[230] JOHN PAUL II, Post-synodal exhortation *Ecclesia in Africa* (14 September 1995), AAS 88 (1996), Op. cit. n. 68.

eminently prophetic order, which is that of charity: how in fact can we proclaim the new commandment of love without promoting in justice and peace the true, authentic advancement of peoples especially as the voice of the voiceless?

For us as for all, Jesus began his public ministry in the synagogue at Nazareth; the Lord thus considers himself as sent to relieve human misery and combat every kind of neglect. He came to *liberate* humanity. It is, therefore, impossible to accept that in evangelisation one could or should ignore the importance of the problems so much discussed today, concerning justice, liberation, the environment, development and peace in the world.

The liberation that evangelisation proclaims cannot be contained in the simple and restricted dimension of economics, politics, social or cultural life; it must envisage the whole humanity, in all aspects, right up to and including openness to the absolute, even the Divine Absolute. Thus the Kingdom is the source of full liberation and total salvation for all people: with this in mind then, the Church walks and lives intimately bound in a real sense to the world and to history.

Human history finds its true meaning in the Incarnation of the Word of God, who is the foundation of restored human dignity. Endowed with this extraordinary dignity, people should not live in sub-human religious, social, economic, cultural and political conditions. This is the theological foundation of the struggle for the defence of personal dignity, for justice and social peace, for the promotion, liberation and integral human development of all people and of every individual in solidarity.

The Church, the document declares, must continue to exercise her prophetic role and be the voice of the voiceless, so that everywhere the human dignity of every individual will be acknowledged, and that people will always be at the centre of all government programmes. This is the only option to ensure lasting peace in Africa where structural injustices are largely responsible for armed conflicts and wars. The Church must only not identify with structures and laws that promote oppression and violate the dignity of the human person. It must also encourage responsible activities that confront unjust social, economic, political and environmental structures.

The Synod document challenges the consciences of Heads of State and those responsible for the public domain and for moulding public opinion to guarantee ever more the liberation and development of their peoples.

Finally, the document emphasises that evangelisation must denounce and combat all that degrades and destroys the person. The condemnation of evils and injustices is also part of that ministry of evangelisation in the social field, which is an aspect of the Church's prophetic role. But it makes clear that proclamation (education) is always more important than condemnation, and the latter cannot ignore the former.

In line, therefore, the Catholic Church in its National, Provincial, Regional and Diocesan communities, has to be challenged to evaluate her responsibility to the issues of development, human promotion, peace and justice. This is part of the motivation for this dissertation and what it intends to accomplish.

Pastoral Response by the Church in Nigeria before now

In his message for the 1990 World Day of Peace, St. Pope John Paul II asserts that an education in environmental responsibility is urgent: a true education in which Churches and religious bodies, non-governmental and governmental organizations, indeed all members of society have a precise role to play, ought to motivate people to care for their environment.[231] The document asked that the new environmental awareness rooted in the Church's theology of environment be translated into concrete programs and initiatives based on an ethically coherent worldview.[232]

In his inaugural speech as the 266th Pope, Benedict XVI noted: "The external deserts in the world are growing because the internal deserts have become so vast….The Church as a whole and all her

---

[231] Cf. JOHN PAUL II, Message for world Day of Peace, *Peace with God the Creator, Peace with all of Creation*, Op. Cit. no. 13.
[232] Cf. JOHN PAUL II, Message for world Day of Peace, *Peace with God the Creator, Peace with all of Creation*, Op. Cit. nn.1&2

pastors, like Christ, must set out to lead people out of the desert, towards the place of life, towards friendship with the Son of God, towards the one who gives us life, and life in abundance."[233]

Again, in his closing Homily of the Second Synod for Africa, Pope Benedict XVI tells the Church in Africa to promote "...living the Gospel in the first person, trying to translate it into projects and undertakings that are consistent with its principle dynamic foundation in love".[234] This is in line with the affirmation of the Church in Africa that "integral human development...is at the very heart of evangelization...there are in fact profound links. These include links of an anthropological order, because the man who is to be evangelized is not an abstract being but is subject to social and economic questions".[235]

How has the Church in Nigeria responded to these invitations? How has she confronted the issues of the environment that face the people in the present times as one way to make the gospel relevant to their environment, connect with their lives, and as part of her quest to realise a holistic and integral ministry? This is necessary because people today are much on the frontier of advanced consumerism, worship of wealth and technology, and selfish individualism. And unless the Church is encouraged to meet the new challenges where they are being felt, society and the Church will be the looser. David Bosch's assertion is instructive for all local Churches:

> Christian ethics may not be based only 'protologically' in what Christ has already done, but also 'eschatologically' in what God will still do...So Christians can combat the oppressive structures of the powers of sin and death, which in our world cry out for God's world of justice and peace, as well as the false apocalypses of power politics which assert themselves on both the left and the right,

---

[233] BENEDICT XVI, *Mass for the inauguration of the pontificate of his holiness Benedict XVI*, (24 April 2005) http://www.vatican.va/holy_father/benedict_xvi/homilies/2005/documents/hf_ben_xvi_hom_20050424_initio-pontificato_en.html (accessed 17/01/2010).
[234] L'OSSERVATORE Romano, Final message of the second special assembly for Africa of the synod of bishops, 43 (2117), op. cit. 12.
[235] JOHN PAUL II, Post-synodal exhortation *Ecclesia in Africa*, Op. cit. n. 68.

> only by accounting for the hope that is in them…and by being agitators for God's coming reign; they must erect, in the here and now and in the teeth of those structures, signs of God's new world.[236]

In one of their joint pastoral letters, the Catholic Bishops of Nigeria said:

> God has blessed us with a beautiful country, endowed with a mild climate, rich vegetation and abundant sources of water. It is however regrettable that our environment has been subjected to mindless abuse through oil spillage resulting from careless exploration and exploitation of the nations oil reserves, urban pollution characterised by mountains of uncleared refuse, clogged drains and badly disposed industrial waste and depletion of forest resources, among others. We would therefore want to sound a note of warning that if the situation is not redressed…Nigeria may soon be faced with health and ecological disasters.[237]

They went further to say that such problems derive from the abuse of chemicals and fertilizers, the destruction of forests trees for industrial purpose, air pollution, and in general the destruction of the natural environment. They called for more appreciation of the gift of the natural environment by caring and protecting it with significant dedication.[238] The above and such other statements now and again, in an effort to link mission and environmental concerns by the Catholic Church in Nigeria, represent some humble beginnings and only point towards the concrete responses that the Church can make in this direction. It also underscores the truth that environmental involvement in the Nigerian Church is just at the germinal stage. Indeed, not much is on ground. A lot remain to be done by the Church in the specific and concrete role of educating the

---

[236] D. BOSCH, *Transforming mission, paradigm shifts in theology*, Orbit Books, MaryKnoll (NY) 2005, 176.

[237] CBCN, Joint Pastoral Letter, *The church in Nigeria: family of God on mission*, Catholic Secretariat of Nigeria, Lagos Nigeria 2004, 98.

[238] Cf. Ibidem 99.

people in environmental responsibility and injecting ethical values into environmental considerations. This matter involves not only context and consciousness (awareness) but, also and very importantly too, conscience. And conscience formation is the privileged role of the Church. The truth is that for now, even if there are scattered responses here and there, environmental pollution and degradation as a social menace in Nigeria has not received the deserved attention from the Catholic Church leadership, and in fact from all Christian Confessions in Nigeria. It does not seem an overstatement to even say that the Church in Nigeria shares part of the blame for the bad governance and environmental degradation in the country for lack of significant action to reduce environmental ignorance. As the Church condemns the unpatriotic actions of a good number of our politicians in the country, as the Church condemns the lion-like vulgarity with which industries and multinational corporations devastate our environment in search of wealth and natural resources, the same Church must pause to ask herself the following questions: How much has the Church in Nigeria been concretely involved in forming the political conscience of Christian politicians according to the principles of the Social Teachings of the Church? How much has the Church in Nigeria been concretely involved in forming the environmental conscience of major pollution outfits in Nigeria in line with the Church's theology of environment? How much has the various Catholic Dioceses in Nigeria been involved in doing the above for their local politicians and pollution outfits in their Particular Churches and areas? Teaching is always more important than condemnation. The former gives the later true solidity and force of higher motivation.[239] The Church must continue to enlighten the civic and environmental conscience of the people to the social exigencies of the Gospel.

A Sample Study: Church and Environment in Asia.

I have decided to do this sample study because of my conviction that countries in Asia have a lot in common with Nigeria: they are still

---

[239] Cf. JOHN PAUL II, Post-synodal exhortation *Ecclesia in Africa* (14 September 1995), AAS 88 (1996), Op. Cit. n. 70.

developing; they have large population indices; their Youth population is very vibrant; they exhibit high degree of cultural awareness; they are victims of the impact of Western technology. A sample study of how the Church in Asia is gradually but progressively responding to the clarion call by the Church's *Magisterium*, that local and regional Churches address specific and peculiar environmental issues and inspire positive political and pastoral efforts to transform perspectives and practices towards the environment among communities of faith throughout the world, is surely an impetus to the Church in Nigeria.

In line with the spirit of the Universal Church and her *Magisterium*, The Church in the continent of Asia is deep into environmental concerns. Among their most enlightened documents on the environment are:

- Pastoral Letter on Ecology, *What is happening to our Beautiful Land?* (29 January 1988).[240]
- Council Act of the Second Plenary council of the Philippines 1991.
- *Love for Creation: An Asian Response to the Ecological crisis* (February 1993).[241]
- Post-Synodal Apostolic Exhortation, *Ecclesia in Asia* (6 November 1999).[242]

In line with the Church's theology of the Environment, these four documents have articulated the concerns of the Church in Asia on the environment:

The Philippines Bishops' pastoral letter of 1988 on ecology outlined the following points:[243]

---

[240] CATHOLIC BISHOPS CONFERENCE OF THE PHILIPPINES, Pastoral letter on ecology, *What is Happening to our Beautiful Land?* (29 January 1988).

[241] FEDERATION OF ASIAN BISHOPS' CONFERENCE, *Love for creation: An Asian response to the ecological crisis* (February 1993).

[242] JOHN PAUL II, Post-synodal Apostolic Exhortation *Ecclesia in Asia* (6 November 1999).

[243] Cf. M. RAMIREZ, *"Ecology and inculturation"* in M.S. DIAS (ed.), *Rooting the faith in Asia, source book for inculturation*, Claritian Publications, Bangalore 2005, 285-289.

- Environmental consciousness: remaining aware of what is happening in one's area.
- Ecological conversion: remaining pro-life in all environmental considerations.
- Filipino theology of creation: sensitivity to their living world, diverse cultures and religious heritage.
- Authentic development: Going beyond mere economic and demographic considerations when dealing with issues concerning the human person and his environment.
- NGO's: Collaboration with those ones that are pro-life.

In 1991, the Council Act of the Second Plenary Council of the Philippines affirmed:[244]

- Christians are called by faith to practice stewardship of God's creation.
- This stewardship granted by the creator is not a licence to misuse God's creation.
- Moral issues are, therefore, involved for adequate safeguards for environmental integrity.

The Federation of Asian Bishops Conference (hereafter referred to as FABC) document on *Ecology, Love for Creation: an Asian response to the Ecological crisis* highlights the moral nature of environmental issues and proposes the following solutions:[245]

- Good education.
- Integration of science and faith: Scientific solutions to environmental issues must recognise faith dimensions.
- Harmonising mastership of creation with responsible stewardship.
- Integration of culture, science and technology: the efforts of science and technology must be permeated by authentic human and cultural values, in order to put them at the service

---

[244] IBIDEM.
[245] Cf. P. HAFFNER, *Towards a theology of the environment*, Lightning Source uk Ltd, Leominster (UK) 2008, 157.

of humanity and in the protection and stewardship of our fragile environment.

• Pursuance of authentic human development: The development of the whole person and, of every human being refers also to the correct relationship of individual persons with God, with nature and with society.

The necessity for the above stipulations arises from the urgency of the subject matter of environment in the messages of the Catholic Bishops' conference of the Philippines in 1988, the Sixth Plenary Assembly of the FABC in 1995, as well as *Ecclesia in Asia* in 1999.

The Philippines Bishops state: "The Philippines is now at a critical point in its history…. One does not need to be an expert to see what is happening and to be profoundly troubled by it….At this point in the history of our country, it is crucial that people motivated by religious faith develop a deep appreciation for the fragility of our Islands life-systems and to take steps to defend the Earth. It is a matter of life and death."[246]

What is true of the Philippines is most probably equally true of any other nation in Asia and the world. Again in 1995, the document of the sixth Plenary Assembly of the FABC states: "The Lord, the giver of life, calls our discipleship in Asia into question on the time bomb issue of ecology. Choosing life requires our discipleship to discern and act with other faiths and groups against the forces of ecological destruction."[247] The post-synodal exhortation, *Ecclesia in Asia*, affirms: "The protection of the Environment is not only a technical question; it is also and above all an ethical issue. All have a moral duty to care for the environment, not only for their own good but also for the good of future generations."[248]

In the area of inculturated environmental engagements by the Church in Asia, M. Ramirez calls for an Asian involvement that would touch base with her original philosophies and her indigenous religious traditions that speak of harmony with creation; one that must rediscover

[246] Quoted in M. RAMIREZ, op. cit., 287.
[247] Sixth Plenary Assembly of the Federation of Asian Bishops' Conference, quoted from http://www.ucanews.com/htm/fabc-papers/fabc-92r.htm (accessed 03/25/09).
[248] JOHN PAUL II, Post-Synodal Apostolic Exhortation *Ecclesia in Asia* (1999), no. 41.

that basic character of oriental socio-religious culture which addresses a concern for the environment, as for example, *aikodo* from Japan, *tai-chi* from China, and *yoga* from India, among others.[249]

Soosai Arokiasamy, along the line of this inculturated environmental initiative speaks of the concept of *ecosophy* in a working paper for the FABC: "For an adequate response to the eco-crisis, we need to develop an ecosophy of religious and cultural traditions of peoples... This ecosophy will challenge and correct the lop-sided and dominant techno-rationality guiding the present models of development....The Church is called to be prophetic in its option and commitment.... Deeply aware of the interrelatedness of human beings and nature, the Church stands for and promotes a sacramental vision of nature and a caring attitude of reverence and responsibility."[250]

Hence, the Asiatic vision of FABC in confronting problems that face the peoples and continent of Asia as well as the Church in the present times is contextual, concrete, and born out of a desire to make the gospel truly part of the local cultures, i.e., the gospel taking the forms of expression of the local communities. This inculturating vision envelops pluralism in Asia, the great Asiatic religions, the great number of their youths and their vitality, massive poverty, women movement issues, agitations for cultural identity, environmental issues, etc.[251]

Thus the FABC theology of harmony, which builds on the Asian approach to reality rooted in the foundations of a cosmic harmony and unity within the Asian religio-cultural traditions is understandable. But they do not stop there. This theology of harmony stretches further to a Trinitarian perspective. This Cosmo Trinitarian harmony acknowledges the integrity of nature and invites humanity to live in harmony with the environment and to foster its growth. Thus environmental harmony and balance of the natural environment in relation to human life is inextricably bound up with the way humans cultivate the earth and manage its resources. This is why, as we said earlier, the Philippines

---

[249] Cf. M. RAMIREZ, op. cit., 288.
[250] S. AROKIASAMY, http://www.ucanews.com/htm/fabc-papers/fabc-90.htm (accessed 21/03/09).
[251] Cf. P.B. STEFFEN, Dispense M. 108, *teologia pastorale missionaria* 2007-2008, 15.

Bishops advocate for a Filipino theology of creation which is sensitive to their living world, diverse cultures and religious heritage. And the FABC document on ecology envisions the integration of culture, science and technology in such a way that scientific and technological efforts in environmental matters must be permeated by authentic human and cultural values.

In response, therefore, to the call for inculturated environmental concerns by the Church in Asia in line with the spirit of the universal Church, certain concrete and practical initiatives are noted by M. Ramirez.[252] The six short accounts of Church involvement in efforts to link mission and environmental concerns represent some humble beginnings towards concrete responses that Christians can make in this area. Though the narratives emerge from Philippine experience, they are characteristic of similar efforts throughout the local Churches of Asia:

- Sister Marimil S. Lobregat, FMM, a Filipina religious, under the auspices of the Religious of the Good Shepherd in Manila, teaches socially involved religious and laity a bio-spiritual exercise, known as *Shibashi*. The goal of this activity is to assist socio-pastoral workers to sustain and generate even more environment- friendly energy for their mission.
- Asia is home to many ashrams and Zen meditation centres. In the Philippines, for example, there are eco-sites that become retreat or learning centres for developing a sacred relationship with the environment. One's environmental consciousness may be awakened in the cosmic garden of the Maryknoll Sisters in *Baguio*, in the Ecozolic Center of the Columban Fathers in Silang, Cavite, in the Ecological Garden of the Benedictine Sisters in Tagaytay City, or in the eco-life-style site of the Sisters of the Immaculate Heart of Mary, an indigenous group of religious sisters in the Cordilleras region.
- Gatherings of inter-university and inter-sectoral youths such as the *Kilusan para sa Kinabukasan ng Kanata* have an ecological focus. The youth gather to plant trees and to celebrate through rituals

---

[252] Cf. M. RAMIREZ, op. cit., 285-286.

their connectedness with all elements of life—earth, fire, water, and air. After such encounters, young people become highly creative.

- The Sisters of the Immaculate Heart of Mary have established a bio-gas system. This effort heals the earth and causes organic herbal plants, flowers and vegetables to grow. They also produce honey. As one lives with them, one gets a sense of the natural flow of the cycle of life. As an expression of ecological and cosmic consciousness, their novitiate gives evidence of nature's abundance, of creativity, and of communion. Their liturgies are replete with their own arts and crafts, their chants and dances, their own unique expressions of God's presence among His people. Their ecological life-style is healing the consumerist and materialistic attitude of today's world of economic globalisation.

- A young Redemptorist priest inspired people in a remote village of Surigao del Norte, Mindanao, Philippines to organize themselves to protect, conserve, manage and develop their environment. They have planted the sturdiest trees of the Philippines, and these have become magnificent forests, where springs provide cool, clear and refreshing waters whose sounds create a symphony with the songs of birds, insects and the rustling of leaves. Sustained by an eco-spirituality, the people have been able to apprehend powerful illegal loggers who are a threat to their forests and their lives. Fortunately, they have been able to secure the support of their town mayor and an ecumenical group.

- On the level of graduate education, the Asian Social Institute in Manila offers a Doctoral program in Applied Cosmic Anthropology; its curriculum employs elements from the physical, human, and social sciences as well as from creation spirituality. It aims to foster a holistic approach to social transformation. It considers both the intangible and tangible elements for a life geared to transformative approaches. Courses such as "Introduction to Creation Spirituality," "Asian Values and Creation Spirituality," "Harmonizing Ecology and Technology" and "Spiritual Expressions of Cosmic Consciousness" all make up the subject cluster for this Creation Spirituality Course.

In as much as I applaud the ecological efforts of the Church in the Asian soil in creating awareness, there are a lot to be done by the Church in the specific and concrete role of educating the people in environmental responsibility and injecting ethical values into environmental considerations. This "matter of life and death" (Philippines Bishops 1988), this "time bomb" (FABC 1995), as stated earlier, involves not only context and consciousness (awareness), but also and very importantly too, conscience. And conscience formation is the privileged role of the Church.

Indeed, I have intended the above survey to act as a proper tonic for the Church in Nigeria. There is need for the Church in Nigeria to give clear ethical guidance on the environment. This means that the Church in Nigeria herself is called to *ecological conversion* – in terms of commitment, in terms of structures needed, in terms of personnel, in terms of environmental initiatives and in terms of funds. The crucial questions for an inquiring mind like me include:

- How does the Church evolve an engaging pastoral catechesis of the environment?
- How does the Church embark on public education and sensitisation?
- How does the Church come to the rescue of victims of the man-made environmental hazards?
- How does the Church dialogue and form the environmental conscience of Governments?
- How does the Church form the environmental conscience of the operators of major pollution outfits?
- How does the Church co-operate with pro-environment N.G.O's?
- What of the Church's ownership of Radio/Television Station in Nigeria?

The real challenge begins now. This is so because the role of the Church in Nigeria in the area under investigation has been more on the side of posing of the problem than suggesting or proffering solutions. The Church in our country will become capable of greater response through continuous and concrete commitment to the work of developing an inculturated environmental catechesis, through an appropriate implementation of the principal demands of the Church's theology of environment, through an appropriate fortification of the JDPC at all level, through providing specialisation opportunities in environmental studies for her clergy and laity, and above all through a balanced and holistic formation (including environmental formation) of her future ministers.

Developing a Pastoral Catechesis of the Environment

Because of poor leadership and lack of sincerity on the part of government, there is great lack of enthusiasm and trust on the part of the citizenry in governance and utter suspicion built around every government programme, policy and apparatus even when the operators mean well for the citizenry. This could be one reason for the citizens' poor environmental behavior, apathy, and poor responsiveness to environmental initiatives. Since the Church is still credible and commands followership[253], her role in helping Nigerians imbibe positive environmental performance becomes crucial. The Church is, therefore, called to be prophetic in its option and commitment. In this context, therefore, the Catholic Faith has an important contribution to make to environmental behaviour.[254] It can give meaning and motivation, build an environmental ethos, and contribute to the foundations of an environmental ethics. This is in line with the recommendation of the Second Special Assembly for Africa of the Synod of Bishops that every National and Regional Episcopal Conference revise all catechetical materials at every level (children, youth, young couples, families) to include elements of the Church's Social Teaching.

The fundamental task of the Catechesis of the environment that must be developed from the background of the Catholic theology of

---

[253] Cf. LINEAMENTA, II Special Assembly for Africa of the Synod of Bishops, op cit. n. 6.
[254] SECOND SPECIAL ASSEMBLY FOR AFRICA OF THE SYNOD OF BISHOPS, The 57 propositions, op. cit. 18.

environment will be to show the inner relationship between faith in Jesus of Nazareth and environmental commitment .It must also tap into our peoples' native spiritualities, which embody much of respect for creation and the environment. This will be in line with Pope Benedict XVI call, in his homily for the conclusion of the Second Synod for Africa, that the Church in particular promotes a model of development "that respects local cultures and the environment"[255], as well as his call for a profound cultural renewal which has need to rediscover those values in people's culture which constitute a solid foundation for constructing a better future for all.[256]

Such a pastoral catechesis of the environment will stimulate a transformation in the way people perceive and treat their environment; help people to assess more objectively their patterns of consumption and environmental degradation and their responsibilities to humanity, to environmental resources and to God; lead to enhanced spiritual sense of the presence of God-immanent; translate such stimulation, assessment and enhanced spiritual sense into concrete historical projects of social and environmental transformation which will lead to a renewed environment consensus.

The *task* of developing this Catechesis concerning the environment will rest on the Catholic Bishops Conference of Nigeria. Its *target* will be to recall the meaning and religious significance of safeguarding the environment. And its *implementation* will be intimately connected to the work of Pastors. Its important *impact* would be a renewed perception of the value itself of life and a significant solution to social and environmental problems, and to offer the society a credible witness of their sense of responsibility in safeguarding the environment.

I must, therefore, emphasise here the importance of developing and producing a Nigerian "Catechism" handbook or "manual" for environmental education which will incorporate systematically in its contents the core principal themes of the Church's theology

---

[255] L'OSSERVATORE Romano, *Homily for the conclusion of the Second Assembly for Africa of the Synod of Bishops*, 12.
[256] Cf. POPE BENEDICT XVI, Message for world day of peace, *If you want to cultivate peace, protect creation* (1 January 2010), Op. Cit. n. 5.

of environment as set out in the forth chapter of my work. Such a catechism handbook on the environment will now become the reference material on environmental education in our families, in our schools and institutions, and in our parishes. This will begin to have more concrete impact on the society as people begin to internalise the theologically rich environmental principles of the Church that would guide concrete contextual projects in their various communities.

Sensitization and Education

As already highlighted, many of the poor people in Nigeria, and in fact in all developing countries, live in degrading and desperate situations that often lead them to adopt environmentally harmful practices. While veracious consumerism in the industrialised countries might be a major cause of environmental degradation, it is mostly poverty in those still developing and industrialising. Part of the solution is improved education and enhanced social conditions. Education is a dynamic instrument of change. The "propositions" 22 of the Second Special Assembly for Africa of the Synod of Bishops accepted that to guarantee sustainable and responsible care of the earth, there is need for all particular Churches in Africa "to promote environmental education and awareness".[257]

As at today in Nigeria, the level of awareness and environmental education about potential hazards relating to a degraded and polluted environment is still abysmally low. Greater percentages of the people (who are ironically poor in the midst of plenty) are more concerned with daily survival and would not even be bothered with what they consider as "elitist" concepts, like waste management.

In this circumstance, the Church has a fundamental role to play as regards the conservation of God's creation and the promotion of a sound and secure environment for the good of all. She has an important mission of educating the people regarding the ethical or moral implications of the way they live in relation to the other members of the human family and to the rest of creation.

---

[257] SECOND SPECIAL ASSEMBLY FOR AFRICA OF THE SYNOD OF BISHOPS, The 57 propositions op. cit. 22.

In his submission at the Second Special Assembly for Africa of the Synod of Bishops in Rome from 4 to 25 October 2009, Bishop Lucius Ugorji of Umuahia Diocese Nigeria said:

> The Church in Africa is to stimulate 'ecological conversion' through intensive education. She is to educate people in Africa to be more sensitive to the increasing disaster caused by environmental damage and the need to minimise it. All are to be made ever conscious that future generations have a right to live in an environment that is intact and healthy and to enjoy its resources.[258]

This educative process must not overlook the fundamental role of Catholic parents in the education of their children to respect the environment and to care for the environment as God's gift to all. It is also in the family that a child can develop a sense of beauty, can learn to contemplate the wonders of God's creation and recognize the need to restore it when damaged, to preserve it when it is made whole and to respect its rhythms in our lives. Catholic schools and educational institutions have to include instructions on the environment in their curriculum from the very first years to instill in future generations a profound love and respect for morality and for nature, making them aware that morality extends to this. The Church is to develop their social sense of attentiveness, and to guide the young into an appreciation rather than an exploitation of their environment. They must be sensitised to this need. The respectful enjoyment of nature should be considered an important part of their educational development.

Parishes and Church groups are to be involved in this education, and to be encouraged to organise and participate in community activities aimed at developing environmental awareness at the local level.

Summarily, the educational and sensitisation targets can be reached if the Church in Nigeria can,

---

[258] Vatican: Second Special Assembly for Africa of the Synod of Bishops, Rome, 4 to 25 October 2009.

a) Develop blueprint manual for environmental education and public awareness as indicated earlier.

b) Ensure that environmental education is a core ingredient of the educational system at all levels of her education outfit.

c) Involve school children in local studies on environmental health, and the environmental impacts of life styles.

d) Use sensitisation campaigns through the mass media to encourage all sectors of society, including industries, universities, and community organisations to healthy environmental habits.

e) Conscientise the media, theatre groups, entertainment and advertising outfits to promote the culture of healthy environmental habits in their programmes.

f) Open up this area of the apostolate by offering specialisation training on Environmental Studies and Management to some of her ministers and laity.

The Church must continue to educate in order to influence the overall ethical tenor of society, which is of primary importance, without which all incentives at development will become a farce.

JDPC and Victims of Environmental Degradation

Social justice and proper respect for the environment are related issues in Nigeria. The volume of tension, revolt and armed conflict environmental degradation and pollution have generated in Nigeria in recent times attests to this claim. An issue which greatly stares on our human and Christian conscience in Nigeria today is the human inflicted poverty on millions of men and women whose environments have been decapitated by a travesty of true development and progress in the country.

In line with her overall Social concerns, the Catholic Church, in its national, provincial and regional communities, has begun to evaluate her responsibility to the issues of human promotion and development so that the world might meet humanity's needs. Encouraged by the Church's social teachings, and as a principal agent in the promotion of human development, Peace and justice in Nigeria, the Catholic Bishops

Conference of Nigeria (CBCN) set up the Justice, Development and Peace Commission (JDPC) as one of the organs of the Department of Church and Society of the CBCN to address social issues and concerns. The JDPC has done a good job so far. At various levels (national, provincial, diocesan, parochial), this commission has engaged in public media enlightenment, conscience formation, developmental projects, election/political monitoring, societal bridge-building, education of the less privileged, youth empowerment (through computer literacy, agriculture, economic initiatives, capacity development), Aids mitigation programs, etc. But it is yet to flex its muscles in the all important area of the environment, concrete defense of the poor and civic education. It is yet to become an advocate of the environment and a defender of victims of environmental abuse and injustice. It is yet to make environmental issues a visible aspect of its agenda, media enlightenment and conscience formation. It is yet to speak out eloquently and enlighten citizens on environmental rights and obligations.

The Biblical story of Naboth's Vineyard[259] involving three *dramatis personae* - King Ahab, Naboth and the Prophet of God, Elijah - is informing. It reminds us of how *top-down power game*[260] can legitimize illegitimacy and make it appear just under the guise of law. Naboth's sentencing to death points today to the so many in our country who suffer the ultimate consequences of degradation and even death through the loss of their God-given lands. In the figure of Naboth, they cry out to the society and to the Church. Therefore, in the figure of Prophet Elijah, the Church in our land is summoned to her prophetic and evangelical role of coming to the aid of those who suffer injustice. Or can the Church remain impassive in the face of actual and potential conflicts these situations generate? All these are issues with a profound impact on the exercise of human rights such as the right to life, food, health and authentic human development.

The Church in Nigeria through her appropriate legal organs need to listen to the angry and pleading voices of people in Nigeria whose God-given natural habitats are been destroyed, and respond to them. She

---

[259] 1Kings 21:1-29.
[260] Cf. J. RIEGER, "*God, power, prophets, and native lands*" in RAY Kathleen (ed.), *Ecology, economy, and God: theology that matters*, op. cit. 58-71.

will do this by committing resources and personnel to assist them, by writing statements to the faithful and presenting concrete testimonies of this devastation to Governmental bodies and the world in order to alter the unjust structures and circumstances. She will also by concrete social action eliminate environmental injustices that are often ignored or not noticed, especially when the people harmed are in the minority, or they have not the financial resources or political guts to pressure for change. They are those most vulnerable to environmental degradation, and their opinions and ideas are rarely heard in environmental discussions and decision-making. The Church in Nigeria must only not identify with the structures and laws that promote oppression and violate the dignity of the human person; she must also encourage responsible activities that confront unjust social, economic, political and environmental structures. Violence as it concerns environmental degradation will not be eradicated, until we change the social structures, which cause the growing impoverishment of people and the scandalous enrichment of the few at the expense of the poor majority.

The fight for the environment cannot be segregated from the fight for life and the option for the poor. This becomes more pertinent in Nigeria where victims of crimes against humanity are fearful of seeking justice for crimes committed against them because of procedural bureaucracies in prosecuting those guilty of serious human right abuses, a situation which perpetuates a cycle of conflict and violence. In this situation, the Church becomes "the voice of the voiceless"[261]

In what seemed a serious soul-searching, the Federal Government of Nigeria has reappraised the hydra-headed crisis in the oil producing regions and submitted that negligence on the part of oil companies operating in the area led to severe environmental problems like oil spillage, gas flaring, water and air pollution, which in turn engendered the current youth restiveness in the region. The Niger Delta region is made up of 9 States of the Nigerian Federation namely Abia, Akwa Ibom, Bayelsa, Cross River, Delta, Edo, Imo, Ondo and Rivers States. The Niger Delta has diverse ethnic group speaking about 250 dialects spreading about 5,000 communities. About 90% of Nigerian earning is from oil and gas, which come from the Niger Delta region. The region also accounts

---

[261] JOHN PAUL II, Post-synodal exhortation *Ecclesia in Africa*, Op. cit. n. 70.

for oil reserves of about 30 billion barrels. But the region is ranked one of the most poverty-stricken in the world despite its abundant natural resources. In many of the oil communities, the activities of exploration and exploitation have killed fishes, destroyed the ecosystem, and made agriculture and economic activities almost impossible. Who bears the pains and burdens of this exploitation and degradation?

People need land for life and livelihood. The *Ogoni* Environmental Pollution saga in Nigeria and the agitation by the *Ogonis* against the degradation and pollution of their land by the oil companies operating in Nigeria need special mention here. Their struggle to save their environment led to the unjust execution of the *"Ogoni 10"*. Picturing the situation in the Niger Delta Region of Nigeria, Romanus Ejim said:

> The Niger Delta area has become Africa's biggest reservoir of petroleum, with many oil wells. Some 2 million barrels a day are extracted in the Niger Delta. Since 1975, the region has accounted for more than 75% of Nigeria's export earnings. Much of the natural gas extracted in oil wells in the Niger Delta is immediately burned, or flared, into the air at a rate of approximately 70 million m³ per day. This is equivalent to 40% of Africa natural gas consumption, and forms the single largest source of greenhouse gas emissions on the planet. The environmental devastation associated with the industry and the lack of distribution of oil wealth have been the source and the key aggravating factors of numerous environmental movements and inter-ethnic conflicts in the region, including recent guerrilla activity by the Movement for the Emancipation of the Niger Delta (MEND).[262]

The absence of a sincere dialogue on these issues, both on the part of Government and the operators of major pollution outfits in the oil industry, has in no small measure prompted armed struggle (militancy) in the Niger Delta regions of Nigeria. The activities in Nigeria of some armed ethnic groups – such as the Odua Peoples Congress (OPC) in

---

[262] R. EJIM, *Self-determination of the indigenous peoples through peaceful means: the Nigerian experience*, Snaap Press Ltd., Enugu 2008, 80.

the West, the Arewa Peoples Front (APF) in the North, the Movement for the Actualisation of the Sovereign State of Biafra (MASSOB) in the East, the Movement for the Survival of the Ogoni People (MOSOP) in the South-South, and currently the notorious Boko Haram terrorists - are to some degree traceable to and motivated by unheard grievances. This situation neither helps in the realisation of the just interests and goals of each group nor favours national progress. According to *Nigeriawatch* in its *"Second Report on Violence 2007-2008"*, environmental related issues connected to oil and land account for the third highest level of conflicts, violence and deaths in Nigeria after road accidents and religious conflicts.[263] Martin Luther King Jr. is always quoted as having said that "violence is the language of the unheard". Yet, the use of violence is not the best option to seek redress and reparation. It is not the best alternative for redressing the ills of oil prospecting in the Niger Delta region for more than 35 years that has left their environment plundered, looted, destroyed. An ideological war is never won by bickering but by subtle and sound reasoning together.

The once legal action that ensued for more than fifteen years against the oil giant Royal Dutch Shell which forced the later to chose the part of compensation underscores two points: one, moral imputability for actions is as much binding on individuals as it is binding on groups and corporations; and two, the power of the non-violent process in seeking justice – this is creative resistance.

For the victims of Environmental degradation, liberation begins when the goods of the earth cease to be instruments of human rivalry and exploitation in order to become a means of friendship and communion where justice is at home. Only a commitment to sincere dialogue aimed at the welfare of all can guarantee this.

On furthering the cause of permanent peace through freedom from environmental restiveness, the Church in Nigeria must initiate responsive dialogue between the parties as choosing the part of dialogue rather than the part of unilateral decisions will enhance responsible cooperation. The Church has to ensure that this dialogue is based on real understanding of the issues involved on both sides of the divide

---

[263] Cf. NIGERIAWATCH.ORG, *http://www.nigeriawatch.org/media/htm/NGA-watch-Report08.pdf* (accessed 22/01/2010).

(and not on parochial interests) and a commitment to work for a just and peaceful society. Only sincere dialogues, open to the legitimate claims of all parties involved, can create an environment of real justice and peace and generate development. Nigerians are hoping that the Amnesty deal brokered by the late President Yar'Adua Administration and implemented by subsequent administrations between Government, the Oil Companies and the Niger Delta regions will be able to redress decades of environmental injustice meted out on a section of the country.

The encyclical *Redemptoris Missio* captures constructive dialogue this way: "The Church's social concern is always guided by the word of God. Hence it is a noble struggle for justice which is neither the struggle of one brother against another nor of one group against another, but which on the contrary must always take its inspiration from the Gospel principles of collaboration and dialogue, fostering integral development and liberation from all forms of oppression."[264]

The Church in Dialogue with Government

Speaking at a "Red Mass" in the Archdiocese of Boston on September 19, 2011, Cardinal Seán O'Malley said: "When Satan tempted Jesus in the desert he based his arguments on passages from the Old Testament, which has given rise to the saying that even the devil can quote Scripture. Ironically those who advocate a strict separation of Church and State often quote Jesus words: "Render therefore unto Caesar the things that are Caesar's and to God the things that are God's". What they often mean by that is "Let's lock God in the sacristy and let Caesar call all the shots." That can be very perilous, especially if Caesar happens to be a blood thirsty ideologue who likes to throw people to the lions."[265] This is why Pope Benedict XVI affirms that the ethical foundation for political choices must be found, not in the role of Religion as to supply the norms (since supplying concrete political solutions would be all together outside the competence of Religion), but in the role of Religion to help purify and shed light upon the application of reason to the discovery

---

[264] JOHN PAUL II, Enciclical Letter, *Redemptoris Missio*, op. cit. No. 58
[265] CARDINAL SEÁN O'MALLEY, Red Mass, Archdiocese of Boston, 19 September 2011.

of objective moral principles. He maintains that without the corrective supplied by religion, reason too can fall prey to distortions, as when it is manipulated by ideology or applied in a partial way that fails to take full account of the dignity of the human person.[266]

Thus, the "propositions" 22 of the Second Special Assembly for Africa of the Synod of Bishops calls on all particular (local) Churches in Africa to engage their Governments; especially in the area of the environment, the Particular (local) Churches are: "To persuade their local and national governments to adopt policies and binding legal regulations for the protection of the environment and promote alternative and renewable sources of energy."[267]

In the spirit of this engagement, the Catholic Church in Nigeria has the responsibility to examine, in the light of Gospel principles and authentic environmental stewardship, government's environmental policies and programs.[268] She is to facilitate, through dialogue between her own environmental specialists and Government, that environmental strategies and programs of Government are in line with ethically acceptable standards and that Government adopts a clean development mechanism that has people always at the center of Government initiatives.

The duty of Government is not only to share wealth, but also to preserve and promote the values and institutions that generate wealth: economic freedom, political liberty, private property, the rule of law, and respect for human life and environmental rights. No amount of handout (aid) can ever be enough if the leaders of Nigeria are not conscientised to respect the people, invest in better health and education, conserve the natural environment, and abide by a legal system that is fair and consistent and above all protect the poor and defenceless. Efforts at the control of environmental degradation by Government must include: conservation of natural resources (to restore the balance upset by natural phenomenon or human mismanagement), sanitary engineering (water

---

[266] POPE BENEDICT XVI, Address to Parliament, Westminster Hall, England 2010.
[267] SECOND ASSEMBLY FOR AFRICA OF THE SYNOD OF BISHOPS, *The 57 propositions of the Second Africa Synod*, Op. Cit. 22.
[268] Cf. JOHN PAUL II, Post-synodal exhortation *Ecclesia in Africa, op. cit.* n. 70; Cf. Benedict XVI, Post synodal exhortation *Africae Munus*, Libreria Editrice Vaticana (2011). n. 80.

purity and waste water disposal), electronic precipitation (to control air pollution), solid waste disposal (garbage generated by society), atomic waste disposal (radioactive wastes), street cleaning, public health service and reforestation.[269]

Political corruption and greed that subject citizens to conditions of extreme poverty contribute to the deteriorating environment. Their elimination is part of the solution. It is true that official corruption exists in every continent and in every country. But while people elsewhere are empowered and emboldened by existing legal instruments in their countries to confront this virus, in greater parts of Africa especially in Nigeria, the people seem helpless in the face of corruption despite the existing legal framework against it. This is the more reasons the Church as liberator must help conscientise the people to become instruments of their own liberation. She plays this role through a more concrete engagement in social matters. Hence, the Church in Nigeria must get more involved in governance and politics by creating and supporting structures that engage government in meaningful dialogue for development, justice and peace, and protection of the environment.

The Church and Operators of Major Pollution Outfits

Pollution has a cost. And that cost has to be borne by the polluter. And every economic decision has an ethical consequence. The Church in Nigeria has an obligation to teach the major pollution outfits that economic activity also involves a grave ethical obligation both to repair and restitute for damage already inflicted on the environment, and to prevent any negative effects, which may arise. In doing this, the Church will be playing a significant role in ameliorating the incessant conflicts between these outfits and the communities in which they operate, and will be creating a more conducive atmosphere for fruitful dialogue between them. This is because conflict management is more creative when it is preventive than when it is curative. The cost will entail a reduced profit than would have been possible on the side of the pollution outfits, as well as the acknowledgment of new costs deriving

---

[269] Cf. E. HUMPHREY et al (eds.), *New age encyclopedia* vol. 14, op. cit. 497.

from environmental degradation. But the gain will be a more peaceful and conducive atmosphere for doing business.

According to Paul Haffner, determining the penance to be done for environmental sin includes restitution, as every grave act which does harm to another person or to the common good demands not only penance but also a certain form of reparation.[270] A more careful control of possible consequences on the natural environment is required in the wake of industrialization, especially in regard to toxic residue, and in those areas marked by an excessive use of chemicals. The relationship between issues of development and environment demands that economic activity projects accept the expenses entailed by environmental degradation as demanded by the community in which those activities take place. Such expenses must not be accounted as an incidental surcharge, but rather as an essential element of the actual cost of doing business within that particular environment. The expense is considered "rent" for the land hired from the communities to the companies. This is called in business "Corporate Social Responsibility". The involved communities need the money for their pains and sufferings as a result of the destruction of their means of livelihood, and their environment through environmental pollution. The Church in Nigeria has to bring this ethics of doing business home to the major polluting outfits in Nigeria, as they do not seem to get it.

The Church and Pro-environment N.G.O's

Choosing life requires our discipleship to discern and act with other faiths and groups against the forces of environmental destruction. In the event of a gradual growing awareness on environmental matters in the country, the Catholic Church in Nigeria must seek the collaboration of other environmental groups whose visions and modes of operation agree with the Church's environmental principles.

In this way, a greater, more penetrating and diffusing impact will be made on the larger society, the Government and the major pollution outfits. There is need for a coordinated, consistent and persistent crusade to save our environment in Nigeria.

---

[270] Cf. P. HAFFNER, op. cit., 252.

An Option for Radio/Television Apostolate

One of the vibrant means through which the Church in Nigeria can realise the above objectives for a safe environment is through the Mass Media. The Mass Media, this modern *Areopagus*, controls the mode of thinking of individuals, families and cultures. The Mass Media today is the principal informative and formative instrument that guides and inspires the behaviour of individuals, families and societies. The new generations, above all, grow in modes conditioned from it, and they depend on it for information, guidance, education and motivation.[271] In his intervention at the Second Special Assembly for Africa of the Synod of Bishops, Bishop Emmanuel Adetoyese Badejo, Coadjutor Bishop of Oyo, Nigeria, strongly affirmed that in today's audiovisual world, far too many opportunities of such communicative presence whereby the Church and her agents in Africa could reach the otherwise unreachable members of the human community are missed.[272]

Presently, most of the Dioceses in Nigeria own Catholic Newspapers, and some own Catholic Printing Press. But their impact on society would be little when compared to the influence of Radio and Television. The question many still ask is why the CBCN has up till now not considered setting up a national Radio and Television Station in Nigeria. Of the over 163 Catholic Radio Stations today in 32 of the 53 nations in Africa[273], I do not know of any of the about 54 Dioceses in Nigeria which owns a radio or television station. This work believes that to realise its proposals, ownership of radio and television stations by the Church in Nigeria ought to be considered strategic. The Church in Nigeria has to put in place the personnel, resources and the structures to realise this in the near future as a veritable avenue to pursue her projects devoid of censorship and stifling bureaucracies that have often characterised the use by the Church of Government-owned and other private Media outfits. Any Government inhibition on the way of the realization of

---

[271] Cf. JOHN PAUL II, Encyclical letter *Redemptoris Missio* (7 December 1990), n. 37c.
[272] BISHOP E. BADEJO, Social Communication and the African Synod, Intervention at the Second Special Assembly for Africa of the Synod of Bishops Rome October 4 – 24 2009.
[273] Cf. L'OSSERVATORE Romano, Final message of the second special assembly for Africa of the synod of bishops, op. cit. n. 18.

this project has to be revisited. This means that the Church in Nigeria ought to, as a matter of urgency, engage in dialogue with the Nigerian Communication Commission to relax its laws on Religious bodies and ownership of Broadcast houses. There is really no justification for excluding Religious bodies from the nation's communication outfit. This is against International best practices.

CHAPTER TEN

NIGERIA (AFRICA) AND THE REST OF THE WORLD

Countries with 1% emissions are the greatest victims of Environmental degradation. This is unjust. Environmental Conversion and International solidarity calls for a total elimination of Eco-racism in all its dimensions in international relations. A sincere fight against eco-racism must incorporate in it a disciplined and sustained fight against the capitalist greed of the world's strongest economies. This is because, according to John Hart, this phenomenon of eco-racism has led to the

> ...diminution of the goods of the earth such as land, water, plants used for food and medicine, and the habitat because of the insatiable quest for land resources and effluence in the dominant cultures, and the military and industrial measures used to acquire them; and the loss of basic earth goods such as soil, water, and air to polluting effluents and emissions.[274]

Toxic waste dumps, toxic waste landfills, toxic waste burning plants, unguarded oil explorations and their consequent oil spills in countries in Africa by the world's powerful economies has been described by James H. Cone as a "contemporary version of lynching a whole people and destroying their environment".[275] Lending a voice to this, the Church in

---

[274] J. HART, op. cit. 114.
[275] J. CONE, "*Whose earth is it anyway*" in HESSEL Dieter and RASMUSSEN Larry (eds.), *Earth habitat: eco-justice and the church's response*, Fortress Press, Minneapolis (MN) 2001, 26.

Africa through the final message of the Second Synod for Africa cries out to the world:

> Multinationals have to stop their criminal devastation of the environment in their greedy exploitation of natural resources. It is short-sighted policy to foment wars in order to make fast gains from chaos, at the cost of human lives and blood.[276]

Foreign nations and the multinational corporations of the industrialized countries may not exercise a monopoly on the exploitation of the nonrenewable resources of the developing countries, an attitude which has often not been sensitive to the intergenerational responsibility that ought to be built around those resources on the side of the host countries. In line with this, Pope Benedict observes and warns:

> The stockpiling of natural resources, which in many cases are found in the poor countries themselves, gives rise to exploitation and frequent conflicts between and within nations. These conflicts are often fought on the soil of those same countries, with a heavy toll of death, destruction and further decay. The international community has an urgent duty to find institutional means of regulating the exploitation of non-renewable resources, involving poor countries in the process, in order to plan together for the future.[277]

Another heart burgling dimension of this eco-racism is the incessant exportation of hazardous waste from European countries into Africa. Africa, especially Nigeria, may have become a dumping ground for the incessant dumping of hazardous waste and used electronic gadgets from Europe, with their disastrous consequences to the environment and to health. This phenomenon is assuming a disturbing dimension.

Not long ago, a Nigerian newspaper, *The Daily Sun*, reported that between March and May 2009, more than 30,000 tons and 1,500 pieces of illegal hazardous waste from Europe to various African countries were made in 57

---

[276] L'OSSERVATORE Romano, *Final message of the second special assembly for Africa of the synod of bishops* n. 33, op. cit. 6
[277] POPE BENEDICT XVI, Encyclical letter *Caritas in Veritate* no. 49.

seizures. The contraband included household wastes such as used refrigerators, old computers, old television screens, iron scraps, metals, discarded electronic goods and used vehicle parts. These seizures were made possible through a cooperation pact between African Customs officials at over 300 seaports and other selected points, supported by their national environmental agencies, the Secretariat of the Basel Convention, the EU Network for Implementation and Enforcement of Environmental Law (IMPEL), and the WCO Regional Intelligence Liaison Offices (RILO) located in the participating regions.[278] This type of incident is recurrent. This in not part of the unnoticed hazardous shipments that foreign multinational companies make to the continent under the guise of needed raw materials. How and where they dispose of them is the imagination of any person. Of recent, such hazardous waste have started making their way to Africa from some countries in Asia as China and from the United States of America.

Certainly, these illegal shipments cannot be possible without the knowledge and cooperation of corrupt insiders. Both 'generators' and 'disposers' are equally culpable in this case. The deadly toxic Waste exportation from Italy to Gboko in Nigeria in 1987 and its impact on humans and the environment is still fresh in the memory. All nations of the world must grow to a universal horizon of perspectives and come to a clear understanding that we are so closely knit to one another. Renato Gaglianone captures this idea succinctly when he asserts: "It is myopic to export pollution deluding oneself to be free of it, or to introduce carbon dioxide into the atmosphere thinking that it will be lost elsewhere. It is not only egoistic but also senseless…. The evils that overhung us, both economically and ecologically, concern all the countries of the earth. There is need, therefore, that all begin to think with universal perimeters."[279]

---

[278] Cf. A. Aĸao, "*Dumping ground! World Customs Organisation raises alarm over used hazardous electronics flooding Nigeria, Intercepts Lagos-bound container*" in *Daily Sun Newspaper Nigeria*, Wednesday, July 22, 2009.
[279] R. Gaglianone, Dispensa Corso MLE 1005 "Evangelizzazione e promozione umana: pastorale della promozione umana e dello sviluppo", 11: "È da miopi espotare inquinamento illudendosi di esserne liberi, o immetere anidride carbonica nell' atmosfera pensando che essa sarà dispersa altrove. È da egoisti, ma anche da insensati….I mali che ci sovrastano, sia economici che ecologici, riguardano tutti i paesi della terra. Occorre dunque che tutti comincino a pensare con parametri universali".

The Basel Convention,[280] an instrument of the United Nations which regulates the trans-boundary movement of hazardous wastes and their disposal, decrees that parties to the convention have the right to prohibit the import of waste, and parties are also prohibited from exporting waste without pre-consent from importing countries. Where this occurs without consent it is regarded as illegal trafficking and criminal, and exporting countries are obligated to take back the waste or dispose of it properly in accordance with the terms of the Basel Convention.[281] Nigeria is a party to it.

Based on the different dimensions of this eco-racism in the African continent, the African Union prepared an intervention in 2009 for the Copenhagen climate conference (COP 15) in which Africa made a case for reparation:

> Africa, in the context of environmental justice, seeks to be equitably compensated for environmental, social and economic losses…based on the priorities determined by the continent, including food security, poverty alleviation and climate risk management.[282]

In this chapter I have made my proposals for the Church in Nigeria which will involve more of action than condemnation in tackling our environmental issues: to provide an environmental manual for teaching at family, school and parish levels, to conscientise the Civil Society, Government, major pollution outfits on environmental ethical standards, to come to the aid of powerless victims of environmental degradation, and to participate in ecumenical environmental projects.

But it must be summarily said that environmental degradation in Nigeria and all its solutions is not the responsibility only of the fossil

---

[280] The *Basel Convention* is global, while the *Bamako Convention* is regional: They try to regulate and checkmate trans-border illegal hazardous importations/shipments.

[281] Cf. BASEL CONVENTION, on the control of trans-boundary movements of hazardous wastes and their disposal (22 March 1989), Articles 4&9.

[282] AFRICAN UNION, "Concept note for the conference of African heads of state and government on climate change and African lead experts on climate change", Addis Ababa Ethiopia (24 August 2009), Appendix 1.

fuel companies in Nigeria, or only of the multinational companies in Nigeria, or only of the industries in Nigeria, or only of the international community, or only of the Church. All consumers, businesses, government, labour and civil society must be made aware of their roles in the growth of the problem and their responsibility in helping to solve it. Respect for the common good of humanity and the integrity of creation demands that we take urgent steps to move away from the harmful practices and behaviours that impact too negatively on the environment, and instead begin to observe healthy environmental habits which will ensure wellbeing and harmonious co-existence in our abundantly blessed country.

However, the Catholic Church, having been a pacesetter in many other sectors of Nigerian life (e.g. in schools, hospitals, etc.), also has a stake in this crusade to salvage the Nigerian environment which cuts across various strata of society. The Nigerian environment is redeemable if all stakeholders can get down to work. And the author believes strongly that we in the Church might be the instruments of change that Nigeria needs in this area of desperate need. This is the optimism of the author in this book as one principal way to guarantee peace, justice and authentic development in the country.

CHAPTER ELEVEN

A CURSORY LOOK AT THE CHURCH IN NIGERIA (AFRICA) AS IT FACES THE FUTURE

In line with the above, I will here move beyond the first Synod for Africa, to analyse and evaluate current challenges facing the Church today in Nigeria and the whole of Africa from the point of view of the Second Synod for Africa. The focus here is to investigate and capture in a nutshell these challenges to the Church in Nigeria and Africa. This scholarly assessment and evaluation of the Second Synod for Africa will help to discern the theological and pastoral orientations for ministry in Nigeria and Africa today in view of the socio-cultural and spiritual resources available in the African continent for the Church in this millennium.

From October 4 – 25 2009, Africa made up of 53 countries and 36 Episcopal conferences, Bishops from 17 countries, Episcopal representatives from other 4 continents, 244 members of the Synod, fraternal delegates from 6 Churches and Ecclesial Communities, 29 experts and 49 auditors[283] gathered in prayer, reflection and listening. This meeting, at the instance of the Second Special Assembly for Africa of the Synod of Bishops convoked by Pope Benedict XVI in the Vatican City with the theme *"The Church in Africa in Service to Reconciliation,*

---

[283] Cf. L'OSSERVATORE Romano, Report by General Secretary of the Synod of Bishops, First General Congregation, in L'OSSERVATORE Romano English Edition, 41 (2115), 9.

Justice and Peace: 'You Are the Salt of the Earth...You Are the Light of the World' (Mt 5:13, 14)" was to review the situation in Africa since the first Synod in 1994, strengthen the resolutions made then and update, in the face of recent changes that have brought considerable challenges to and created opportunities for evangelisation in this vast continent.[284] It was a time of Pastoral rethinking and evangelical renewal.

We can indeed talk of Nigeria and Africa today in terms of the *Good*, the *Bad* and the *Challenge*. The "*Good*" of Africa, and indeed of Nigeria, from the First Synod to present include: Success of evangelisation and growth of local churches, emergence of democracies and social, cultural, economic and political reawakening. The "*Bad*" of Africa, and indeed of Nigeria, from the First Synod to present include: syncretistic tendencies, proliferation of religious movements and sects, politicisation and intolerance of Islam, despotic and dictatorial regimes, bad governance, war and violence, illegal trades, widespread corruption, unacceptable poverty, the scarce presence of the church in Africa north of the equator, etc.

The Synod asserts: "In a continent part of which live under the shadow of conflict and death, the Church must sow seeds of life: life-giving initiatives. She must preserve the continent and its people from the putrefying effects of hatred, violence, injustice and ethnocentrism. The Church must purify and heal minds and hearts of corrupt and evil ways; and administer her life-giving Gospel message to keep the continent and its people alive, preserving them in the part of virtue and gospel values".[285] The "*Challenge*" lies in the question: How best can the Church in Africa, and indeed Nigeria, accompany its people in the circumstances? How can the Church achieve reconciliation, justice and peace in Africa, and indeed Nigeria, and with which means or resources? In answering the above questions, the optimism of the Synod Fathers lay in the conviction that the socio-cultural and spiritual riches of the vast continent are ready tools for the realisation of the transforming ministry of the church in Africa in showing Africa the road

---

[284] Cf. L'OSSERVATORE Romano, Preface to Lineamenta; Cf. also *Relatio post Disceptationem*, in L'OSSERVATORE Romano English Edition, 42 (2116), 26.
[285] Cf. L'OSSERVATORE Romano, *Relatio Ante Disceptationem*, in L'OSSERVATORE Romano English Edition, 41 (2115), 18.

to self-actualisation.[286] How can the Church in Africa re-invent Africa in view of present African challenges?[287]

In particular, the above Second Special Assembly will like to inspire structures and forms of pastoral ministry in the Church-Family of God in Africa and renew the continents apostolic commitment to making reconciliation, justice and peace prevail in Africa. This is the urgent face and form of the apostolic ministry of the Church-Family of God in Africa and its Islands.[288] It is articulated this way in the "Final Message" of the Synod: "...to celebrate the blessings of the Lord on our continent, to assess our stewardship as pastors of God's flock, and to seek fresh inspiration and encouragement for the tasks and challenges that lie ahead...to concentrate on a theme of the greatest urgency for Africa: our service to reconciliation, justice and peace in a continent that is very much in dire need of these graces and virtues."[289]

For the Synod, *Reconciliation* is the dynamic process and task to re-establish through love and mercy broken relationships, fraternal bonds, trust and confidence.[290] *Justice* is the right order of things and the fulfilment of the just demands of relationships.[291] *Peace* is the tranquillity of order and the respect for and development of what human life requires.[292] The central idea is to develop and strengthen the concept of "Church-Family of God" in Africa, which was a central idea in the First Special Assembly for Africa of the Synod of Bishops in 1994. This concept, "a new paradigm" in African Catholic Theology and one of the unique contributions of Africa to the universal Church

---

[286] Cf. L'OSSERVATORE Romano, *Relatio Ante Disceptationem*, in L'OSSERVATORE Romano English Edition, 41 (2115), 14.

[287] L'OSSERVATORE Romano English Edition, 41 (2115), 9 and 13)

[288] Cf. Second Synod Proposition nos. 2 and 41.

[289] L'OSSERVATORE Romano, Final message of the second special assembly for Africa of the synod of bishops, *Message to the people of God*, in L'OSSERVATORE Romano English Edition, 43 (2117), 3.

[290] Cf. L'OSSERVATORE Romano, *Relatio Ante Disceptationem*, in L'OSSERVATORE Romano English Edition, 41 (2115), 16.

[291] Cf. L'OSSERVATORE Romano, *Relatio Ante Disceptationem*, in L'OSSERVATORE Romano English Edition, 41 (2115), 17.

[292] Cf. L'OSSERVATORE Romano, *Relatio Ante Disceptationem*, in L'OSSERVATORE Romano English Edition, 41 (2115), 17.

and her ecclesiology, "...underlie the unity and the communion of all despite differences."[293]

The Synod affirms strongly:

> The imagery of *Church-Family of God* evoked such values as care for others, solidarity, dialogue, and trust, acceptance and warmth in relationship. But it also evoked the socio-cultural realities of parenthood, generation and filiation, kinship and fraternity, as well as networks of relationship which are generated by these social realities and in which the members stand. The relationships build the life of communion of the family; but they also make their demands on the members, the fulfilment of which both constitute their justice and make the relationship harmonious and peaceful. When, however, the demands of the relationship are not fulfilled, justice is infringed upon, relationships are broken and the life of communion is hurt, damaged and impaired... The restoration of communion and just order in such cases is what reconciliation stands for; and it takes the form of the re-establishment of justice, which only restores peace and harmony to the Church-Family of God and the family of society.[294]

This work will, therefore, examine the *Lineamenta*, the *Instrumentum laboris*, the reports *ante* and *post disceptationem*, the texts of the interventions and the reports on the deliberations in the small groups, the closing message of the Synod, the opening and closing messages and reflections by Pope Benedict XVI during the synod, and the concrete "Propositions" made by the Synod Fathers, in order to glean out the African pastoral resources to accomplish this task of reconciliation, justice and peace in Africa within the Church's pastoral priorities. For the Synod Fathers, Africans must accept the responsibility of taking

---

[293] Cf. L'Osservatore Romano, *Relatio post Disceptationem*, in L'Osservatore Romano English Edition, 42 (2116), 25; Cf. also *Relatio Ante Disceptationem*, in L'Osservatore Romano English Edition, 41 (2115), 14, Cf. also Report by Archbishop Laurent Monsengwo Pasinya on 'Ecclesia in Africa', in L'Osservatore Romano English Edition, 41 (2115) 22 and 23.

[294] L'Osservatore Romano *Relatio Ante Disceptationem*, in L'Osservatore Romano English Edition, 41 (2115), 16.

their destiny in their hands as instruments of reconciliation, justice and peace in their communities throughout Africa.

The big question is, "What are the socio-cultural and spiritual resources Africa has that can enrich theologically and pastorally this concept of "Church-Family of God" and contribute to the reconstruction of Africa?" The "Socio-Cultural and Spiritual Resources" is to be understood in this context as those human and Christian values necessary to reach and realise reconciliation, justice and peace in Africa.

The Socio-Cultural Resources of Africa for the Promotion of Reconciliation, Justice and Peace (RJP): African Traditional Values/Inculturation

Traditional Cultural values represent a number of principles and life perimeters, which a people or a group hold sacrosanct as determinant patterns of their relationships and social behaviour. The minister in Africa today must recognise the true, the good and the holy in the African cultures and religions. This means recognizing, preserving and promoting the good things, spiritual and moral, as well as the socio-cultural values found in Africa. This means making African values which include the sense of the primacy of God, of sense of the sacred, religion and morality, of community and solidarity, of generosity/hospitality and common good, of sacredness of and respect for life, of family and familial pride, of honesty, truth and honour, of harmony with nature, both known and loved. But how, for example, does one reconcile "African Hospitality/Solidarity" with ethnicism, tribalism and discrimination in society and Church in Africa? And how does one, for example, reconcile "sacredness of life" with the genocide Africans commit against their brothers?

Concerning the richness of the African values at the service of reconciliation, justice and peace (RJP), Pope Benedict has this to say in his homily at the solemn inauguration of the synod: "Africa is the depository of a priceless treasure for the whole world...Africa's treasures...the abundant riches...the spiritual and cultural heritage which humanity needs even more than raw materials."[295] He called

---

[295] L'OSSERVATORE Romano English Edition, 40 (2114), 8.

Africa the "Spiritual lung" for humanity, but a lung that is about to be infected by two viruses or toxic waste from the West – practical materialism and religious fundamentalism.[296]

The way out is for the Church in Africa to urgently re-visit the rich religious and cultural values of Africa in view of inculturation.[297]

- But this must be preceded by qualified and profound study to discern the strength and possible weakness of each value[298], to enrich, to set aside contrary aspects, to animate and evangelise cultures;
- This involves in practical terms: to identify those aspects of culture which promote and those which hinder the inculturation of Gospel values;
- Positive cultural values be promoted and inculcated in all its institutions of learning and training;
- The work of authentic African theologians be encouraged and promoted;
- Positive elements of African traditional cultures be incorporated into the Church's rites;
- Pastoral agents learn the local languages and cultures, so that Gospel values can touch people's hearts and help them towards a genuine reconciliation, which leads to lasting peace.[299]
- "Culture study centres" to be set up.[300]
- Call for adequate inculturation of the sacraments.

This is important because the teaching of culture conditions the integral development of individuals and groups. Hence, Churches in Africa should promote the cultural heritage of their regions. Africans should cherish their good cultural values, avoiding "anthropological alienation" but, at the same time, open them to an encounter with the gospel.

---

[296] Ibidem.

[297] Cf. L'OSSERVATORE Romano, "Intervention" of Bishop Edward Gabriel Risi of South Africa, in L'OSSERVATORE Romano English Edition, 42 (2116), 9.

[298] Cf. Synod Proposition no. 13.

[299] Cf. Synod Propositions no. 33.

[300] Cf. L'OSSERVATORE Romano, *Relatio post Disceptationem*, in L'OSSERVATORE Romano English Edition, 42 (2116), 27.

I want to stress a little on the African sense of harmony with nature. Africans are very religious people. They believe that in the serenity of nature, man can contemplate transcendence. But through the massive environmental devastations, there is already a seeming rupture of human harmony with nature and all the serenity that nature offers to human religiosity and link with transcendence as the sacred groves, forests, trees and places of worship come under attack under the guise of economic development. In some places, especially in the oil prospecting zones, their artefacts, roads, recreational and historical sites, even homes, are lost to environmental pollution. There is the more painful decimation of social and cultural harmony with nature and all the serenity that nature offers to human development and wellbeing through disturbances and displacements of the local inhabitants. There is also breakdown of social relationships as pollution outfits in connivance with some greedy individuals try to employ the policy of divide and rule to split the communities by using money to entice a section of the people against others, thereby destroying effective social cohesion.

Eventually, this breakdown of social relationships and socio-cultural cohesions has caused armed conflicts and wars which have produced environmental refugees especially in the oil-rich regions - people who are forced by the degradation of their natural habitat to forsake it, and often their possessions as well, to face the dangers and uncertainties of forced displacement. For example in Nigeria, environmental related issues account for the third highest level of conflicts, violence and deaths after religious conflicts and road accidents.[301] This threatens the prospects of living in peace in Africa.[302]

The Synod calls on ministry in Africa today to positively alter environmental behaviour at all levels – individual, government, pollution outfits. To guarantee reconciliation, justice and peace, therefore, particular Churches must promote environmental education and awareness and persuade their local and national governments to adopt policies and binding legal regulations for the protection of the

[301] Cf. NIGERIAWATCH.ORG, Second Report on Violence 2007-2008, in _http://www.nigeriawatch.org/media/htm/NGA-watch-Report08.pdf_, (accessed 01/22/2011).
[302] Cf. "Intervention" Bishop Lucius Ugorji of Nigeria, in L'OSSERVATORE Romano English Edition, 41 (2115), 31.

environment.[303] On inculturation of the sacraments, a serious and in-depth study should be done on the traditional African ceremonies of reconciliation and arbitration of conflicts.[304]

Ethnic Diversity: Though the Synod decried the colonial boundaries imposed on African Nations, it, however, opts for "a corresponding development of a sense of nationalism that makes ethnic diversity mutually enriching, and that extols the common national good over parochial ethnic interests"[305] by ministers in Africa. If Africa is being threatened by a false nationalism and exaltation of race, Pastoral ministry in Africa now needs to emphasise the "meeting/encounter of cultures" in Africa rather than the "conflict of cultures" This will de-emphasise ethnicity which is exclusive and which destroys community living and becomes intolerant to other cultures and ethnic groups and fratricidal even to one's own people.[306] Thus, the Synod sees the rich ethnic, cultural, political and religious diversities of the African peoples as an asset than a liability, a unity in diversity or diversity in unity in which ministry ought to tap the positive values of these diversities as a source of strength to forge social harmony, peace and progress.[307] Formation in Africa should be intercultural, international and inter-ethnic.[308]

Means of Social Communication: The means of social communication, Mass Media (visual, audio, web and print) are indispensable for the promotion of reconciliation, justice and peace in Africa.[309] This is more so to help Africa, which has been burdened for too long from outside

---

[303] Cf. Synod propositions no. 22; Cf. also *Relatio Ante Disceptationem*, in L'OSSERVATORE Romano English Edition, 41 (2115), 15; Cf. also *Relatio post Disceptationem*, in L'OSSERVATORE Romano English Edition, 42 (2116), 29.

[304] Cf. Synod Proposition no. 7.

[305] L'OSSERVATORE Romano, *Relatio Ante Disceptationem*, in L'OSSERVATORE Romano English Edition, 41 (2115), 15.

[306] Cf. L'OSSERVATORE Romano, *Relatio post Disceptationem*, in L'OSSERVATORE Romano English Edition, 42 (2116), 5, 25 and 26.

[307] Cf. Synod Proposition no. 32; L'OSSERVATORE Romano English Edition, 40 (2114), 9.

[308] Cf. L'OSSERVATORE Romano English Edition, 41 (2115), 31.

[309] Cf. Synod Propositions no. 56; Cf. also "Intervention" of Archbishop Claudio Maria Celli, in L'OSSERVATORE Romano English Edition, 42 (2116), 10.

by everything that is loathsome about her destiny, to tell the world her own story.[310]

In line with this conviction, The Synod recommends:

- An increased presence of the Church in the media;
- The professional training and ethical formation of journalists to promote a culture of dialogue;
- Use of the modern media for the spread of the Gospel and the fruits of the present Synod, for the education of African peoples in truth, reconciliation, the promotion of justice and peace;
- Ensure educational and formative media which is ready to convey morally healthy cultural and Gospel virtues.
- Educating the entire faithful, especially youths, to have a proper critical spirit concerning mass media issues.[311]
- And readiness to invest and pay the cost.

J.D.P.C: In addition to its other functions, this organ of the Church has to:

- Create proper forum for increasing awareness and participation of young people and women towards empowerment and social transformation.
- Create proper forum to encourage lay society groups towards integrity in public life and care of the environment.
- Create solidarity out of people of different social classes and religious traditions to work together for a more just social order.
- Bring the values of the Kingdom of God into the new *areopaghi* of ministry.
- Help Christians to make informed decisions and interventions in social matters.
- Create spaces for dialogue and opportunities for collaboration.[312]

---

[310] Cf. L'OSSERVATORE Romano, *Relatio Ante Disceptationem*, in L'OSSERVATORE Romano English Edition, 41 (2115), 16.

[311] Cf. Synod Propositions no. 48; Cf. also *Relatio post Disceptationem*, in L'OSSERVATORE Romano English Edition, 42 (2116), 29 and 5.

[312] Cf. L'OSSERVATORE Romano, "Intervention" of Bishop Jose Bisign of Guinea-Bissau, in L'OSSERVATORE Romano English Edition, 43 (2117), 9.

Civic Education: To strengthen the African Family, condemnation is not the only response. Pastoral ministry needs positive initiatives in education to correct irregular situations. There is need for:

- o Promotion of multidimensional programmes of civic education to foster the formation of a social conscience at all levels.[313]
- o Civic education should cover the laws of the land, principles of sound democracy, rights and obligations of citizens, and also the demands of the Social Teachings of the Church.[314] It must co-opt Christian, human and African values.[315]
- The Church in Africa must educate the People of God and enable them to challenge unjust decisions and structures.[316]
- Formation in leadership for those who are engaged in directing political, economic and cultural affairs[317] especially laity for leadership for social transformation and to enable them in social dialogue to resist the advances of negative pressure groups.[318]
- Seminaries, schools, Institutes of higher education, nursery, primary and secondary schools – these still form privileged places for ministry and formation for RJP, inculturation, Church's Social Teaching and proper use of the Mass Media.[319]
- In the situation in Africa where over-politicisation of issues and "divide-and-conquer" mentality holds sway favouring a culture of violence, terrorism and wars, a civic education that implants love is an eloquent testimony of the church's

---

[313] Cf. Synod Proposition no. 25; Cf. also "Intervention" Bishop Jude Thaddeus Riwa'ichi, in L'Osservatore Romano English Edition, 42 (2116), 9; Cf. also "Intervention" by Dr. Pierre Titi Nwel, in L'Osservatore Romano English Edition, 42 (2116), 18.

[314] Cf. L'Osservatore Romano English Edition, 41 (2115), 27.

[315] Cf. L'Osservatore Romano English Edition, 42 (2116), 9.

[316] Cf. Synod Propositions no. 30.

[317] Cf. Synod Proposition no. 37; Cf. also "Intervention" of Rev. Franchesco Bartolomi, in L'Osservatore Romano English Edition, 42 (2116), 11.

[318] Cf. L'Osservatore Romano, "Intervention" by Archbishop Orlando B. Quevedo of FABC, in L'Osservatore Romano English Edition, 41 (2115), 20; Cf. L'Osservatore Romano English Edition, 41 (2115), 29.

[319] Cf. L'Osservatore Romano English Edition, 41 (2115), 27.

presence in society.[320] Pastors are to offer present and future leaders in political and economic life a fitting doctrinal, pastoral and practical formation capable of taking the best of ancestral traditions in Africa and integrating them with principles of good governance of modern societies as well as spiritual support and accompaniment by providing the stimuli for the gospel to challenge them based on the Social Teachings of the Church. In this way, politicians will learn to indulge in executive and legislative acts, which respect Christian ethical values. Not to give this accompaniment is disastrous.[321]

Dynamism of African Women and African Youths: If properly trained and given due opportunities, women and youths are indispensable instruments for the attainment of RJP in the continent of Africa rather than being used as instruments of strife.

On Women: The Synod sees women as among the "underdeveloped resources" of Africa.[322] It, therefore, recognizes;

o   their dignity, the many talents and resources of African women in the family, society and the Church and their natural disposition as ready instruments for RJP.
o   their rights must be upheld, their education and development enhanced, their
o   empowerment accelerated, and all acts of violence against them stopped

---

[320] Cf. L'OSSERVATORE Romano English Edition, 41 (2115), 31.
[321] Cf. Synod Propositions no. 25; Cf. also *Relatio Ante Disceptationem*, in L'OSSERVATORE Romano English Edition, 41 (2115), 15; Cf. also *Relatio post Disceptationem*, in L'OSSERVATORE Romano English Edition, 42 (2116), 25 and 29; Cf. also "Intervention" by Bishop Robert Patrick Ellison of Gambia, in L'OSSERVATORE Romano English Edition, 42 (2116), 16.
[322] Cf. L'OSSERVATORE Romano, *Relatio post Disceptationem*, in L'OSSERVATORE Romano English Edition, 42 (2116), 25.

o the Synod proposes a greater integration of women into Church structures and decision-making processes.[323]

o proposes empowerment through theological training, training in canon law and Social Teaching of the Church to enable them play better roles and enrich their choices in planning and implementing strategic actions for RJP in families, Christian communities, parishes, dioceses and beyond.[324]

o WUDCO (World Union of Catholic Women Organisation) organ in Africa, the ARCCWO (African Regional Conference of Catholic Women Organisations) is a force for RJP.

On Youths: The Synod observed that African youths who constitute the majority of the African population, and who are the future strength and hope of the Church and society, are particularly vulnerable.

Constituting a formidable force and great pastoral resource, they should be given an ongoing catechetical-biblical formation to educate them to be agents of reconciliation, justice and peace among themselves and in the larger society.[325] Making an intervention during the Synod, Bishop Ernesto Maguengue of Mozambique made a strong case for the Youths of Africa: Since they are exposed to violence, prostitution, drug trafficking and abuse, organised crime, political, ethnic and tribal strife, religious fundamentalism and satanic sects, only an aggressive pastoral response with updated pastoral strategies that respond to their needs and 'speak to their world' including active listening can upset this negative tide.[326] The Synod made

---

[323] Cf. L'OSSERVATORE Romano, Synod Proposition 47; Cf. also *Relatio post Disceptationem*, in L'OSSERVATORE Romano English Edition, 42 (2116), 25; Cf. also Interventions of Sr. Felicia Harry and Sr. Pauline Odia Bukasa, in L'OSSERVATORE Romano English Edition, 42 (2116), 12.

[324] Cf. L'OSSERVATORE Romano, "Intervention" by Bishop Abraham Desta of Ethiopia, in L'OSSERVATORE Romano English Edition, 43 (2117), 7.

[325] Cf. Synod Propositions no. 48.

[326] Cf. L'OSSERVATORE Romano English Edition, 43 (2117), 7.

o Recommendation to observe world Youths Day at all levels of Church life.

o Recommendation to consolidate structures for pastoral care of youths based on the Word of God, Prayer and the sacraments.

o Advice to inspire them through a witness of authentic Christian life.[327]

The Spiritual Resources of Africa for the Promotion of Reconciliation, Justice and Peace: Eucharist and Penance

The sacraments of the Eucharist and Penance are privileged moments for the realization of reconciliation, justice and peace in Africa, and inexhaustible sources of strength to build the Church, family of God.[328]

Eucharist and Penance liturgies should, therefore, become evangelising, i.e. we are to evolve an evangelising liturgy.

The synod affirms the centrality of the Eucharist in the Church-family of God as a symbol of unity and unique place for genuine reconciliation.[329] It is in the Eucharist that the Church recognises herself as the "Family of God" and it is where reconciliation and peace are best expressed.[330] In our differences, the Eucharistic Catechesis has to insist that the Eucharist is the bond and foundation of a new fellowship which opposes every hint of tribalism, racism, ethnicity, nepotism and hatred. It, therefore, remains the source and summit of reconciliation, justice and peace. The Synod urges a more thorough Catechesis on the

---

[327] Cf. L'Osservatore Romano, "Intervention" by Bishop Jean Claude Randrianarisoa of Madagascar, in L'Osservatore Romano English Edition, 43 (2117), 8.

[328] Cf. L'Osservatore Romano *Relatio post Disceptationem*, in L'Osservatore Romano English Edition, 42 (2116), 27 and 28; Cf. also "Intervention" by Archbishop Cornelius Esua of Cameroon, in L'Osservatore Romano English Edition, 42 (2116), 8.

[329] Cf. L'Osservatore Romano, *Relatio Ante Disceptationem*, in L'Osservatore Romano English Edition, 41 (2115), 14.

[330] Cf. L'Osservatore Romano, *Relatio post Disceptationem*, in L'Osservatore Romano English Edition, 42 (2116), 28; Cf. also "Intervention" Bishop Benedito Santos of Brasil, in L'Osservatore Romano English Edition, 42 (2116), 14.

Eucharist to help the faithful live it with greater dept in the life-realities of Africa.[331]

Reconciliation on the social level contributes to peace. It is both a way of life and a mission. The Synod proposed the celebration of the Sacrament of Penance in its dual aspects: personal and communal.[332] The Synod underscores the communitarian celebration of Penance/ Reconciliation to dress and heal the wounds of families and societies ripped apart by situations of violence, conflict and war: sin has a social dimension, so reconciliation should also engage the whole community.[333]

Practical Catechesis: Pastoral ministry must engage an ongoing practical catechesis: (transmission, education, formation) with improved pedagogy which guarantees adequate spiritual, biblical, doctrinal and moral formation of the Christian social conscience.[334] The Synod recommends that catechism must be vitally linked to social, political, economic and cultural life in order to become a lived reality and be able to checkmate Christians' involvement in social unrests, political corruption and occult practices.[335]

Holiness: From the beginning of Christianity, Africa has been a land of Saints from the great Doctor St. Augustine down to our time which today has a line-up of 13 "Blessed", 4 "Venerable" and 27 "Servants of God" cutting across all categories of the faithful. As their heroic witness to Christ's love brought forgiveness, justice and peace to their communities, holiness of life can today become a powerful resource for true reconciliation, justice and peace in Africa. There should be promotion of sanctification of priests, religious and lay faithful in Africa.[336]

---

[331] Cf. L'OSSERVATORE Romano, *Relatio post Disceptationem*, in L'OSSERVATORE Romano English Edition, 42 (2116), 28.
[332] Cf. Synod Proposition nos. 5 and 9.
[333] Cf. L'OSSERVATORE Romano, *Relatio post Disceptationem*, in L'OSSERVATORE Romano English Edition, 42 (2116), 28.
[334] Cf. Synod Proposition no. 37, Cf. L'OSSERVATORE Romano English Edition, 42 (2116), 4.
[335] Cf. L'OSSERVATORE Romano, "Intervention" Bishop Jude Thaddeus Riwa'ichi, in L'OSSERVATORE Romano English Edition, 42 (2116), 9.
[336] Cf. L'OSSERVATORE Romano English Edition, 42 (2116), 7.

Ecumenism: Here, the Churches are challenged to give our nations a model and an example of a reconciled, just and peaceful community.[337] Ecumenism among Churches should include theological ecumenism, spiritual ecumenism and ecumenism of life with Protestant traditions, Orthodox Churches, Evangelical, Charismatic and Pentecostal Movements.[338] An appropriate Catechesis must sharpen ecumenism and exploring in all Churches our common fatherhood, brotherhood and sisterhood should be relentlessly pursued.[339] In a pluralistic modern state/society, the ongoing efforts of the Pontifical Council for the Promotion of Christian Unity which initiate and sustain dialogue with other Churches and ecclesial communities (such as the Christian Association of Nigeria - CAN) could serve the cause of peace and reconciliation as the Catholic Church must join hands with other spiritual forces on the continent to achieve this.[340]

Dialogue: Dialogue and cooperation are treated at two levels – other religions (Islam and ATR) and Government/the Political Class.[341]

For the Synod Fathers, the issues of reconciliation, justice and peace generally are concerns for entire communities, irrespective of creed. Working on the many shared values between the faiths, Christians, Muslims and Traditional Religionists can contribute greatly towards restoring peace and reconciliation in our nations.[342] In the area of Interreligious Dialogue, the Synod made two strong affirmations: that Peace in Africa is very much determined by the relations among religions working together in associations dedicated to peace and justice, in a spirit of mutual respect, trust and support, and their families being taught the values of listening patiently and respecting one another. Dialogue with other religions, especially Islam and ATR, is an integral

---

[337] Cf. L'Osservatore Romano "Intervention" Bishop Rev. Francesco Bartolomi, in L'Osservatore Romano English Edition, 42 (2116), 11
[338] Cf. L'Osservatore Romano English Edition, 41 (2115), 29.
[339] Cf. L'Osservatore Romano English Edition, 41 (2115), 27.
[340] Cf. Synod Proposition no. 10; Cf. also "Intervention" by Archbishop John Onaiyekan of Nigeria, in L'Osservatore Romano English Edition, 42 (2116), 8 .
[341] Cf. L'Osservatore Romano, "Intervention" by Cardinal Tarcisio Bertone, in L'Osservatore Romano English Edition, 42 (2116), 10.
[342] Cf. L'Osservatore Romano English Edition, Final message, 43 (2117), 6..

part of the proclamation of the Gospel and the Church's pastoral activity on behalf of reconciliation, justice and peace.[343] The Synod urges pastoral ministers in Africa to actively engage in dialogue with, and a discussion about Islam and Traditional African Religion at all levels (both professional and day-to-day life) in order to eliminate the persistent politicisation of religion which has become the cause of conflicts, and to reduce religious intolerance which minimises/overcomes violence, forms of discrimination, intolerance and religious fundamentalism, promotes better knowledge and religious freedom, and dialogue of life through cooperative initiatives thus serving reconciliation, justice and peace.[344]

At the level of Dialogue with Government and the political Class: The Church should provide service of mediation between Government and resistant forces and ensure a meeting of sincere dialogue between the parties in dispute with a clear understanding of all that is at stake.[345] Dialogue with the political class and government appointees can create a laboratory for social analysis.[346] Also, the meeting of religious leaders and State for reflection on great societal questions, where they can exchange ideas and take decisions together on actions which favour reconciliation, justice and peace between their respective communities, the social groups and Government.[347]

Organic Pastoral Solidarity: Organic pastoral solidarity in Africa in all ecclesial structures and at all levels – diocesan, ecclesiastical provinces, at the national, regional, continental and international will assist the

[343] Cf. Synod Proposition no. 11; Cf. L'OSSERVATORE Romano English Edition, 42 (2116), 4.
[344] Cf. Synod Proposition nos. 11 and 12; Cf. also "Intervention" by Rev. Gerald Chabanon, in L'OSSERVATORE Romano English Edition, 42 (2116), 11.
[345] Cf. L'OSSERVATORE Romano English Edition, 41 (2115), 30; Cf. also "Intervention" by Bishop Edward Gabriel Risi of South Africa, in L'OSSERVATORE Romano English Edition, 42 (2116), 9.
[346] Cf. L'OSSERVATORE Romano, "Intervention" by Archbishop Marcel Utembi Tapa of DRC, in L'OSSERVATORE Romano English Edition, 42 (2116), 6.
[347] Cf L'OSSERVATORE Romano, "Intervention" by Bishop Jean-Baptiste Tiama of Mali, in L'OSSERVATORE Romano English Edition, 42 (2116), 10.

realisation of RJP.[348] SECAM has to foster an organic pastoral solidarity in the continent.[349] Missionary and formation exchange can enrich this pastoral Solidarity.[350]

Collaborative Ministry: In his intervention during the Third General Congregation, Archbishop Cardinal Angelo Sodano said that the Church in Africa would not be able to speak with one voice about reconciliation, justice and peace if there is a clear lack of adequate unity and communion.[351]

In order to explore and elaborate possible ways and means of ensuring unity and fruitful collaboration within the Church's structures, there is need for a continental council for the clergy, a continental council for the laity, and a continental council for Catholic women.[352] The Synod advocates stronger inter and intra collaboration between and among the members of SECAM, RECOWA, and COSMAM in Africa, and between SECAM and its equivalents in other regions of the world, as the CELAM, FABC and CCEE.[353]

Witness: According to Bishop Thomas Kabore of Burkina Faso, pastoral ministry is often more a question of witness than of methods and techniques.[354] To implement a spirituality of reconciliation, justice and peace, the Church needs witnesses deeply rooted in Christ, nourished by his Word and by the sacraments.[355] This means being architects of

---

[348] Cf. Synod Proposition no. 3; Cf also "Intervention" by Bishop Kiyus Nava Kianza of DRC, in L'OSSERVATORE Romano English Edition, 42 (2116), 19.

[349] Cf. L'OSSERVATORE Romano, *Relatio Ante Disceptationem*, in L'OSSERVATORE Romano English Edition, 41(2115), 15.

[350] Cf. L'OSSERVATORE Romano, "Intervention" by Archbishop Raymondo Damasceno Assis of Brasil, in L'OSSERVATORE Romano English Edition, 41 (2115), 20.

[351] Cf. L'OSSERVATORE Romano English Edition, 41 (2115), 26.

[352] Cf. Synod Proposition no. 4.

[353] Cf. L'OSSERVATORE Romano, *Relatio post Disceptationem*, in L'OSSERVATORE Romano English Edition, 42 (2116), 25.

[354] Cf. L'OSSERVATORE Romano, "Intervention", in L'OSSERVATORE Romano English Edition, 41 (2115), 28; Cf. L'OSSERVATORE Romano English Edition, 42 (2116), 4.

[355] Cf. Synod Proposition no. 9.

just structures in our societies[356], having a sense of sacrifice and service by all[357], an active witness that welcomes truth in all its dimensions: truth of facts, truth of commitments, and truth of the exercise of responsibilities.[358] The Synod notes with joy the gospel witness in Africa today to reconciliation, justice and peace made by persons of Consecrated Life who are often very near to victims of oppression, repression, discrimination, violence and sufferings of all kinds cutting across cultures, tribes and languages, and who live in religious communities characterized by racial, regional and ethnic mixings. By their life, they will continue to proclaim eloquently to Africans that God makes no distinctions between persons and that we are all his children, members of the same family, who ought to live in harmony and peace despite our diversity.[359]

Formation of Pastoral Agents: To enhance reconciliation, justice and peace in Africa, all pastoral agents are to receive integral formation which must include the intellectual, moral, spiritual, pastoral, human psychological and cultural aspects. Future pastoral agents are to be more firmly grounded in the understanding of their cultures.[360]

SCC/Lay Associations/New Ecclesial Movements: This Family of God extends beyond the bonds of blood, ethnicity, tribe, culture and race. The SCC, Lay Associations and New Ecclesial Movements are places for concretely living out reconciliation, justice and peace. They open paths to reconciliation with extended families, which have the tendency to close in on themselves. Pastoral is to promote in them a fraternal life of solidarity and spiritual listening in keeping with their faith.[361]

---

[356] Cf. Synod Proposition no. 14.
[357] Cf. Synod Proposition no. 16.
[358] Cf. L'OSSERVATORE Romano, "Intervention" by Prof. Raymond Ranjeva in L'OSSERVATORE Romano English Edition, 42 (2116), 14.
[359] Cf. Synod Proposition no. 42; Cf. "Intervention" by Rev. Guillermo Luis Basanes,Sdb, in L'OSSERVATORE Romano English Edition, 41 (2115), pg. 31; Cf. L'OSSERVATORE Romano English Edition, 42 (2116), pg. 6.
[360] Cf. Synod Proposition no. 40.
[361] Cf. Synod Proposition nos. 35, 36 and 37.

The Family: The Family, the "sanctuary of life" and the nucleus of society and the Church, is the first and proper place for learning and practicing the culture of reconciliation, pardon, justice, peace and harmony.[362] It is the first and indispensable teacher of peace because it enables its members in decisive ways to experience peace. All African cultures hold the family in great esteem, and for this reason, the Church in Africa defines herself as "Church-Family of God. But the African family and its dignity and esteem is under attack by enemies of the family and some cultural traditions.[363] Therefore, pastoral ministry in Africa must continue to confront all forms of ideological and clinical views which are modern day enemies of the traditional family, which are capable of diminishing human capital and endangering life.[364] Pastoral ministry must ensure adequate family catechesis, education of couples, pastoral support to parents, spiritual accompaniment for couples, celebration of jubilees, marriage counselling and institutes, and formation in marriage and family values through the media as pastoral priority.[365] Competent persons and lay movements must be trained and enabled to defend the family. Family apostolate must redefine the family as the "domestic church" and the primary and vibrant place for education in love, reconciliation, justice and peace, and become creative in responding to spiritual and ethical needs of families in an atmosphere of qualitative pastoral follow-up and continuous catechesis on Family and married life[366]

Caritas: There is need to establish a solidarity fund on the continental level through the *Caritas* network. Since a large part of the conflicts

---

[362] Cf. L'OSSERVATORE Romano, "Intervention" by Bishop Jan Ozga of Cameroon, in L'OSSERVATORE Romano English Edition, 42 (2116), 10.

[363] Cf. L'OSSERVATORE Romano, *Relatio post Disceptationem*, in L'OSSERVATORE Romano English Edition, 42 (2116), 28; Cf. L'OSSERVATORE Romano English Edition, 41 (2115), 29.

[364] Cf. L'OSSERVATORE Romano, *Relatio Ante Disceptationem*, in L'OSSERVATORE Romano English Edition, 41 (2115), 15; Cf. also *Relatio post Disceptationem*, in L'OSSERVATORE Romano English Edition, 42 (2116), 25.

[365] Cf. Synod Proposition no. 38.

[366] Cf. L'OSSERVATORE Romano, *Relatio post Disceptationem*, in L'OSSERVATORE Romano English Edition, 42 (2116), 5, and 28; also Cf. "Intervention" by Bishop Peter Musikuwa of Malawi, in L'OSSERVATORE Romano English Edition, 42 (2116), 7.

are as a result of dehumanising poverty, self-reliant initiatives such as micro-finance, agrarian and similar programmes would be the Church's concrete sign of solidarity with the poor and marginalized.[367] This organ is not only to intervene in situations of emergency and to provide assistance; *Caritas* has to contribute to the development of individuals and wellbeing of society: empowerment of communities, education and training for development in rural areas, health care, environmental stewardship, capacity building, life skills management training, psycho-social counselling, etc.[368]

Conversion: The Synod sees as "the remit of the evangelising mission of the Church on the continent and the islands" the conversion of hearts and the healing of eyes. This is because an affirmative response to the call for reconciliation, justice and peace would require that quantitative growth in the Church in Africa increasingly become qualitative.[369] This conversion is a resource because, the human heart, the citadel of love and peace, in Africa, which has become "wounded...the ultimate hiding place for the causes of everything destabilising the African continent"[370] now responds to a new impetus for healing and hope. Moreover, according to Bishop Sithembele Anton Sipuka of South Africa, change of external structures is impossible without change of mentality[371]; and for Rev. Edouard Tsimba, beautiful declarations and speeches are nothing without change of heart.[372]

---

[367] Cf. Synod Proposition no. 17; Cf. L'OSSERVATORE Romano English Edition, Final message, 43 (2117), 4.

[368] Cf. L'OSSERVATORE Romano "Intervention" by Archbishop Cyprain Kizito Lwanga of Uganda, in L'OSSERVATORE Romano English Edition, 42 (2116), 11.

[369] Cf. L'OSSERVATORE Romano, Report by General Secretary of the Synod of Bishops First General Congregation, in L'OSSERVATORE Romano English Edition, 41 (2115), 13.

[370] L'OSSERVATORE Romano, *Relatio post Disceptationem*, in L'OSSERVATORE Romano English Edition, 42 (2116), 26.

[371] Cf. L'OSSERVATORE Romano, "Intervention", in L'OSSERVATORE Romano English Edition, 41 (2115), 27; Cf. L'OSSERVATORE Romano English Edition, 42 (2116), 4; Cf. also "Intervention" by Bishop Jude Thaddeus Riwa'ichi, in L'OSSERVATORE Romano English Edition, 42 (2116), 9.

[372] Cf. L'OSSERVATORE Romano, "Intervention", in L'OSSERVATORE Romano English Edition, 42 (2116), 10.

Concrete experience of a Local
Church in Nigeria in the Promotion of
Reconciliation, Justice and Peace (RJP)

In line with the issues of reconciliation justice and peace, the Catholic Church in Nigeria is continuously evaluating her responsibility. The Pastoral resources outlined from the Second Special Assembly for Africa of the Synod of Bishops offer the light to mark out the part of man and of the Church in the heart of Africa today. It is now left for the Church in Nigeria to critically study these proposals in view of the prevailing situation in Nigeria, and coordinate efforts aimed at a harmonious cooperation between the family, the civil society, the Church, the school and the government to the obligation for reconciliation, justice and peace. The Church in Nigeria has been promoting RJP and must continue to stimulate a deeper knowledge and greater spreading of these human values: Christian Association of Nigeria (CAN) ensures RJP among Christians of various denominations; Nigerian Inter-religious Council (NIREC) ensures ongoing dialogue for RJP among various Religions in Nigeria, and between them and Government. These organs have to be reinforced for a more result-oriented performance.

These organs, however, are preoccupied more with religious issues. What of the so many other social issues cutting across societal and religious boundaries that generate tension, conflict and hatred among Nigerians? A major issue of development in Nigeria today which is generating enormous armed conflicts, injustice and oppression is the number of people whose environments are being destroyed by a travesty of progress and development. The crucial questions for an inquiring mind like me include:

- How does the Church in Africa evolve an engaging pastoral catechesis to realise RJP?
- How does the Church in Africa embark on public education and sensitization for RJP?
- How does the Church in Africa come to the rescue of victims of the man-made disasters which create conflicts and wars that often tear African communities and Nation-States apart?

- How does the Church in Africa bring conflicting parties to the dialogue table in search of RJP?
- And how does the Church in Africa more effectively co-operate with N.G.O's to realise RJP?

In the area of reconciliation, justice and peace, the Particular Church of Orlu Diocese of Nigeria, to which I belong, has some pastoral structures that respond to various other needs of sub-groups within and beyond the diocesan family and these structures promote peace and justice and enhance reconciliation. Among them are:

- The Justice, Development and Peace Commission (**JDPC**) undertake activities at assisting victims of injustice and dialogue with organs responsible for unjust structures. The JDPC has done a good job so far. At this level also (diocesan and parochial), this Committee has engaged in public media enlightenment, conscience formation, developmental projects, political education and election monitoring, societal bridge-building, education of the less privileged, youth empowerment (through computer literacy, agriculture, economic initiatives, capacity development), Aids mitigation programs, etc.
- The Human Development Resource Centre (**HUDSO**) coordinates concerns for skill acquisition especially among the youths..
- Nwannegadi Trust Fund (**NTF**) remits revolving loan to poor men, women and youths for petty businesses at an almost interest free rates to help them sustain themselves.
- Nwannegadi Football Club (**NFC**) for engaging budding youths who are talented to emerge professionals in the soccer arena.
- Nwannegadi Micro Finance Bank (**NMFB**) to provide more honest banking transactions for our people and to attract Government subsidies and grants directly to our people through this legally registered institution.
- *Aziona Verde* (***Associazione Don Bonifacio***) with headquarters in Italy takes care of children's development and empowerment through Medicare and education.

- **Kolping** Society handles youth development and employment through handcraft.
- Christian Foundation for Children and the Aged (**CFCA**) gives attention to the less privileged orphaned children, the childless and aging adults.
- **St. Monica** Association coordinates concerns for widows.

As already indicated above, from the challenges, opportunities and pastoral resources discussed in this work, the task for RJP goes beyond this in the particular environment of Orlu.

The Dioceses in Nigeria must now continue to do more than simply preach and teach about commitment to RJP. They must set examples by making all Diocesan activities and programs RJP friendly. The Catholic Diocese of Orlu has taken some of the right steps in the right direction. Much more needs to be done as these represent a humble beginning.

In conclusion, the effective utilisation of these pastoral resources in the Church-Family of God in Africa will lead to a Church transformed from within which in turn transforms the continent. The fruits will be: a continent liberated from fear; a conversion that is solid at all levels: Church and society; prevalence of mutual dialogue and respect; engraved respect for persons of all genders; changed attitudes and mentalities; a people positioned to resist the onslaught of globalisation, consumerism, fundamentalism and ethnocentrism. And with the resources fully mobilised, the Church in Africa will not only serve Africans, but in addition, will continue to be a blessing for the universal Church and the entire world.

In this posture, my dream of a third Synod for Africa of the future will be a harvest of the abundant fruits of "a new Pentecost" in a true African rebirth. How does the Church in Nigeria tap into this in the area of Environment?

CHAPTER TWELVE

GENERAL EVALUATION AND CONCLUSION

In the face of the so many conflicting voices and ideologies today on environmental issues which revolve between the economic and the power blocks, there is a high need to re-present the unmitigated Church's theology of environment to her members and to the world. *God and the Human Environment* presumes to have done that. Confronted with a decaying environment that seems to be the business of non due to a travesty of development in the face of a global crusade to save the environment which must be translated into concrete contextual projects in the spirit of "think globally and act locally", there is an urgent need to galvanise citizens to the fact that the safeguarding of our Earth is part of the divine plan for creation and an aspect of our Faith. *God and the Human Environment* believes to have done that. And in the face of the persistent calls by the *Magisterium* of the Church in recent times that Particular or Local Churches engage in environmental matters in line with her project of holistic evangelisation, the Catholic Church ought to be challenged to translate the Church's environmental principles into concrete contextual social engagements. *God and the Human Environment* hopes to have suggested some of the directions to follow to reach this goal.

Given the fact of a globalised environmental crisis that calls for a response along different cultural paths, the principles of the Church's theology of environment and her eco-voice, in God's name, invites humanity to pursue a culture of life which simultaneously enhances human life and especially that of the poor, cares ecologically for the earth, and proclaims the God of life. This Book is intended to act as guide and stimulus to Diocesan, Provincial, regional and even continental faith communities to help them engage in concrete and contextual environmental initiatives that would enhance the human person and promote the integrity of our environment. Thus doing, we move away from the temptation to follow a culture of death which degrades the earth to satisfy human greed and which worships the false idol of mammon. All are called to walk this part of authentic environmental concerns that thinks globally and acts locally.

In Nigeria where up till now environmental issues are considered "elitist" and seen as government "palaver" by a higher percentage of the population, this work enlarges the discussion base to the socio-political, economic and health realms and discovers the individual, corporate, government and church dimensions to the subject. This makes the subject matter one engaging for all. This work has tried to use the Church's theology of environment to give impetus to a practical engagement by the Catholic Church in Nigeria to assist in salvaging our environment from human induced degradation and reducing its human impacts. This is because commitment to reconciliation, justice and peace (which is the main trust of the Second Special Assembly for Africa of the Synod of Bishops) and the task of transforming social realities in Nigeria, especially in relation to environmental matters, cannot lead to concrete results without the inspiration that comes from the principles of the Church's theology of environment as outlined in this work. The Church's theology of environment continues to offer the light to mark out the part of man and of the Church in the heart of the world today. The Church in Nigeria must continue to stimulate a deeper knowledge and greater spreading of these principles within her own context.

It is now left for the Church in Nigeria to critically study these principles as well as the proposals made in this book in view of the prevailing condition of the Nigerian environment, and particularly in view of the proposition on the environment of the Second Special Assembly for Africa of the Synod of Bishops, and coordinate efforts aimed at a harmonious cooperation between the family, the Church, the school, local officials, and the government at the three levels of governance in the country to this environmental obligation. This is because a sincere engagement for environmental peace and harmony involves far-reaching decisions on the part of individuals, families, communities and States. We are all responsible for the protection and care of the environment. This responsibility knows no boundaries. Together in this way, we contribute to realise God's *Basilia* of life abundant in Christ for all.

This environmental project, though situated in the Nigerian environment, also addresses the global challenges facing the Church in different continents of the world in the area of the environment even if the dimensions of the problem may vary from place to place. This challenge can be more so in the developing and industrialising regions. Therefore, a broader perspective of analysis and judgement would certainly admit that the concerns addressed are of global and regional relevance and application. And the proposals made are equally of relevance everywhere – East, West, North and South.

It is my conviction that an inculturated environmental involvement by the Church can create environmental harmony, which is key to the peaceful co-existence of peoples, and further help countries still developing and industrialising to avoid the mistakes of the past and reduce drastically the incidents of environmental damage and the consequent hazards. According to Pope Benedict XVI, much comes tranquil and peaceful, renewed and rejuvenated, when humanity comes into contact with the serenity and harmony of nature.[373] "Therefore, in a coherent view, the human environment must include material, biological, intellectual, cultural, ethical and spiritual elements – all in relation to God the creator. It is therefore necessary to avoid cosmocentrism and exaggerated anthropocentrism. A Christological vision is fundamental in this regard".[374]

For Practical purposes, John Hart's twelve projects for environmental care are instructive and invite all to action individually and collectively:

---

[373] Cf. POPE BENEDICT XVI, Message for world day of peace, *If you want to cultivate peace, protect creation*, op. cit. no. 13.
[374] P. HAFFNER, op. cit., 93-94

- Develop environmental inventories.
- Use appropriate construction materials and alternative energy.
- Diminish or eliminate use of materials threatening life or health.
- Restore and conserve bio-regions.
- Develop restoration projects good for jobs, species and the environment.
- Recycle for the environment and for community programs.
- Actively promote justice for the poor and environmentally oppressed minorities.
- Analyse and alter unjust economic structures.
- Reduce and eliminate harmful chemical inputs.
- Evaluate the link between population, consumption and environmental issues.
- Form integrated and active environmental alliances and associations.[375]

Every Catholic as well as our structures - Bishops' Conferences, parish councils and schools etc. - have to make environment issues top priority. A large part of this struggle will be trying to persuade governments and industries that the needed changes are desirable for the good, happy, healthy and peaceful co-existence of all. The task is enormous but not impossible. Perhaps the biggest hurdle to be overcome is motivating and energizing people to tackle the problem. As mentioned in the introduction, mere knowledge of the situation is not enough. We must be prepared to join the crusade for a healthy environment through concrete actions.

In conclusion, the Dioceses in Nigeria must continue to do more than simply preach and teach about commitment to the environment. They must set examples by making all Diocesan activities and programs environment friendly.

Pope Benedict, who has been described as a "green Pope" more, I think, because of his concrete initiatives than his writings on the environment, was already leading in this practical example: In 2007, the Vatican became the World's first carbon-neutral country by offsetting greenhouse gas emissions through renewable energies and carbon

---

[375] Cf. J. HART, op. cit. 136-140.

credits; in the area of solar energy, the Vatican replaced the cement roof tiles of the Pope Paul VI auditorium with 2,400 solar panels that convert sunlight into some 300,000 kilowatts-hours of power each year – the panels are expected to reduce carbon dioxide emissions by 225 tons and save the equivalent of eighty tons of oil each year; other "green" projects are been planned by the Vatican City especially at *Castel Gandolfo* and at *Santa Maria di Galleria*, north of Rome.[376]

The five ethical imperatives of Jay McDaniel must confront the environmental conscience of each and of all in Nigeria in our struggle to save our environment: to live lovingly, to live self-critically, to live simply, to live ecologically, and to live religious diversity.[377] It is my conviction and remains the optimism of this work that the Nigerian environment is redeemable if all stakeholders can get down to work, and that this is one principal way to guarantee peace and harmonious co-existence in Nigeria. This work believes strongly that a healthy environmental practice by all in Nigeria is one of the routes to lasting peace and genuine progress.

[376] Cf. WOODEENE KOENIG-BRICKER, *Ten commandment for the environment, Pope Benedict XVI speaks out for creation and justice*, op. cit. 1-2.
[377] Cf. J. MCDANIEL, *"In the beginning is the listening"* in RAY Kathleen (ed.), *Ecology, economy, and God: theology that matters*, op. cit. (26-41), 38.

BIBLIOGRAPHY AND RESOURCES

ECCLESIASTICAL DOCUMENTS

THE NEW JERUSALEM BIBLE, Standard Edition, Darton, Longman and Todd Ltd, London 1985.

THE AFRICAN BIBLE, BIBLICAL TEXT OF THE NEW AMERICAN BIBLE, Artes Gráficas Carasa, Madrid 1999.

VATICAN II DOCUMENT, Pastoral Constitution on the Church in the Modern World, *Gaudium et Spes* (7 December 1965), AAS 58 (1966), 1025-1115.

THE CATECHISM OF THE CATHOLIC CHURCH, Paulines-Africa/Libreria Editrice Vaticana, Cittá Del Vaticano 1994.

PAUL VI, Encyclical letter *Populorum Progressio* (26 March 1967), AAS 59 (1967), 257- 299.

JOHN PAUL II, Encyclical letter *Redemptor Hominis* (4 March 1979), AAS 71 (1979), 257-324.

_____, Encyclical letter *Dominum et Vivificantem*, (18 May 1986).

_____, Encyclical letter *Sollicitudo Rei Socialis* (30 December 1987), AAS 80 (1987), 513-586.

_____, Apostolic exhortation *Christifideles Laici* (30 December 1988), AAS 81 (1989), 393-521.

_____, Message for world Day of Peace *Peace with God the Creator, Peace with all of Creation* (1 January 1990).

_____, Encyclical letter *Redemptoris Missio* (7 December 1990), AAS 83 (1991), 249-340.

_____, Encyclical letter *Centisimus Annus* (1 May 1991), AAS 83 (1991), 793-867.

_____, Encyclical letter *Evangelium Vitae*, (1995), AAS 87 (1995), 401-552

_____, Post-synodal exhortation *Ecclesia in Africa* (14 September 1995), AAS 88 (1996)

POPE BENEDICT XVI, *Message for the Celebration of the World Day of Peace*, 1 January 2007.

_____, Encyclical letter *Caritas in Veritate* (29 June 2009).

_____, Message for world day of peace, *If you want to cultivate peace, protect creation* (1 January 2010), Libreria Editrice Vaticana 2009.

_____, Post-synodal Apostolic Exhortation, *Africae Munus*, Libreria Editrice Vaticana (1January, 2011).

KOENIG-BRICKER Woodeene, *Ten commandments for the environment: pope Benedict XVI speaks out for creation and justice*, Ave Maria Press, Notre Dame (IN) 2009.

PONTIFICAL COUNCIL FOR CULTURE – PONTIFICAL COUNCIL FOR RELIGIOUS DIALOGUE, *Jesus Christ the bearer of the water of life, a christian reflection on the "new age"*, Libreria Editrice Vaticana, Vatican City 2003.

Pontifical Council for Justice and Peace, *Compendiun of the social doctrine of the church*, Libreria EditriceVaticana, Vatican City 2004.

Archbishop Renato Martino, Addresses at the *Earth Summit* in Rio De Janiero, Brazil, June 1992.

_____, *World Summit on Sustainable Development* in Johannesburg, South Africa, 2002.

Lineamenta, Synod of Bishops, II Special Assembly for Africa: *The Church in the Service of Reconciliation, Justice and Peace*, Vatican City 2006, n. 6.

Cbcn, Joint Pastoral Letter, *The church in Nigeria: family of God on mission*, Catholic Secretariat of Nigeria, Lagos Nigeria 2004.

Oseni Ogunu ed. *The African Enchiridion*, vol. I, Editrice Missionaria Italiana, Bologna 2005.

_____, *The African Enchiridion*, vol. II, Editrice Missionaria Italiana, Bologna 2006.

_____, *The African Enchiridion*, vol. III, Editrice Missionaria Italiana, Bologna 2006.

_____, *The African Enchiridion*, vol. IV, Editrice Missionaria Italiana, Bologna 2008.

II Special Assembly For Africa, Synod Propositions, *Elenchus Finalis Propositionum* (Vatican City: 2009).

II Special Assembly For Africa, *Instrumentum Laboris*, (Vatican City: 2009).

II Special Assembly For Africa, *Lineamenta*, (Vatican City: 2006).

L'Osservatore Romano English Edition, 41 (2115), (Vatican City: 2009).

L'Osservatore Romano English Edition, 42 (2116), (Vatican City: 2009).

L'Osservatore Romano English Edition, 43 (2117). (Vatican City: 2009).

L'Osservatore Romano, "Final message of the second special assembly for Africa of the synod of bishops", 43 (2117), Vatican City 28 October 2009.

Schineller Peter ed., *The Voice of the Voiceless: Pastoral Letters and Communiqués of the Catholic Bishops Conference of Nigeria* 1960-2002, Daily Graphics, Ibadan 2002.

Schineller Peter ed., *The Church Teaches: Stand of the Catholic Bishops of Nigeria on issues of Faith and Life*, Catholic Secretariat of Nigeria-Gaudium et Spes Institute, Abuja 2003.

BOOKS

Adaoti John, Technology and the environment in sub-saharan Africa: emerging trends in the *Nigerian manufacturing industry*, Ashgate Publishing, Aldershot (England) 2002.

Arthur Jones., *New Catholics for a new century*, an RCL Company, Texas 2000.

Auer J., *Etica dell'ambiente*, Queriniana, Brescia 1988.

Baringer T., *Africa bibliography 2006, works on Africa*, University Press, Edinburgh 2007.

BOFF Leonardo, *Cry of the earth, cry of the poor*, Orbis Books, MaryKnoll (NY) 1997.

BOFF Leonardo, *Ecology and liberation: a new paradigm*, Orbis Books, MaryKnoll (NY) 1996.

BOSCH David, *Transforming mission, paradigm shifts in theology*, Orbis Books, MaryKnoll (NY) 2005.

CLARK C., *The myth of over-population*, Advocate Press Pty Ltd, Melbourne 1973.

DIAS Mario (ed.), *Rooting faith in Asia, source book for inculturation*, Claritian Publications, Bangalore 2005.

DERRICK Christopher, *The delicate creation: towards a theology of the environment*, Devin Adair, Old Greenwich 1972.

DORR D., *The social justice agenda, justice, ecology, power and the church*, Grill and Macmillan, Dublin 1991.

EBOH Simeon, *Human rights and democratisation in Nigeria*, Snaap Press Ltd., Enugu 2003.

EDWARDS Denis, *Ecology at the heart of faith*, Orbis Books, MaryKnoll (NY) 2006.

EJIM Romanus, *Self-determination of the indigenous peoples through peaceful means: the Nigerian experience*, Snaap Press Ltd., Enugu 2008.

FOX MATTHEW, *Original blessings, a primer in creation spirituality*, Bear and Co, Santa Fe (NM) 1996.

FUELLENBACH John, *Church: community for the kingdom*, Orbis books MaryKnoll (N.Y.) 2001.

GANOCZY A., *Teologia della natura*, Queriniana, Brescia 1997.

GRAZIER Walter, *Catholics going green: a small guide for learning and living environmental justice*, Ave Maria Press, Notre Dame (IN) 2009.

HAFFNER Paul, *Mystery of creation*, Cromwell Press, Broughton Gifford 1995.

HAFFNER Paul, *Towards a theology of the environment*, Lightning Source uk Ltd., Leominster (UK) 2008.

HART John, *What they are saying about environmental theology?* Paulist Press, Mahwah (N.J.) 2004.

JENKINS Willis, *Ecologies of grace: environmental ethics and Christian theology*, Oxford University Press, New York (NY) 2008.

JONAS H., *The imperative of responsibility: in search of an ethics for the technological age*, The University of Chicago Press, Chicago 1984.

KALAGBOR Sam, *Health administration in Nigeria*, Horizon Concepts, Port Harcourt (Nigeria) 2004.

KEENAN Marjorie, *Care for creation: Human activity and the environment*, Libreria Editrice Vaticana, Città Del Vaticano 2000.

KULA E., *Economics of natural resources and the environment*, Chapman and Hall, London 1992

LEWIS C., *The abolition of man*, Geoffrey Bless, London 1962.

LEVINAS Emmanuel, *Of the God who comes to mind*, Palo Alto, Stanford University Press 1998.

MBAH Chike et al (eds.), *Management of environmental problems and hazards in Nigeria*, Antony Rowe Ltd., Chippenhen (GB) 2004

McGRATH Alister, *A scientific theology volume I: Nature*, Biddles Ltd., Norfork (GB) 2006.

MURPHY Charles, *At Home on Earth: Foundations for a Catholic Ethic of the Environment*, The Crossroad Publishing Company, Portland 1989.

NANNI C., *Pace, guisticia, salvaguardia del creato: impegno della chiesa, compito*

dell'educazione, LAS, Roma 1998.

NISSEN Johannes, *New Testament and mission: historical and hermeneutical perspectives*, Peter Lang GmbH, Frankfort 1999.

OGUNTOYIBO J. Et al (eds.), *A Geography of Nigerian Development*, Heinemann Educational Books Ltd., Ibadan 1987.

PASSMORE J., *La nostra responsabilità per la natura*, Feltrinelli, Milano 1986.

RAHNER Karl, *Theological investigations* 3, Seabury (NY) 1974, 35-46.

RAHNER Karl, *Theological investigations* 10, Darton, Longmann & Todd, London 1973, 260-272.

RAY Kathleen (ed.), *Ecology, economy, and God: theology that matters*, Fortress Press, Minneapolis (MN) 2006.

SIRICO Roberts et al (eds.), *Environmental Stewardship in the judeo-christian tradition*, Action Institute, Grand Rapids (MI) 2007.

UZOUKWU Samuel, *Peace through dialogue and solidarity*: the basis of true humanism, Snaap Press, Enugu 2004.

WOGAMAN Philip, *Christian perspectives on politics*, Westminster John Knox Press, Louisville 2000.

DICTIONARIES AND ENCYCLOPEDIAS

COULTER Michael et al (eds.), *Encyclopedia of catholic social thought, social science and social policy*, 1, The Scarecrow Press Inc, Lanham (Maryland) 2007, 360-361.

ELNELL Walter (ed.), *Evangelical dictionary of theology*, Baker Academic, Grand Rapids (MI) 2009, 181-182.

HUMPHREY Edward et al (eds.), *New age encyclopedia* vol. 6, Lexicon Publications 1963, 483-492.

HUMPHREY Edward et al (eds.), *New age encyclopedia* vol.14, Lexicon Publications 1963, 496-497.

KOMONCHAK J. (ed.), *The new dictionary of theology*, Macmillan, Dublin 1987.

MOREAU Scott et al (eds.), *Evangelical dictionary of world missions*, Baker Books, Grand Rapids, MI 2000, 296-297.

RAHNER Karl et al (eds.), *Encyclopedia of theology: sacramentum mundi* 5, Burns & Oats, London 1975, 1438-1442.

SHAW Russell (ed.), *Our Sunday visitor's encyclopaedia of catholic doctrine*, Our Sunday Visitor Publishing Inc, Huntington (IN) 1997.

REVIEWS IN JOURNALS AND ARTICLES

ADACHABA Achenyo Adachaba, "Climate Change and Power Supply Solutions: LFGE / MSWE Project development in Nigeria", June 2009,

ADENUGA Ade, "Petroleum, industry and environmental pollution: the Nigerian experience," in *Bullion* 23, 4 (December1999).

ADENUGA Ade et al (eds.), "Sustainability of the environment and water pollution in Nigeria: Problems, management and policy options," in *Bullion* 23, 4 (October 1999).

AINA E., "Nigeria's environmental balance sheet," in AINA E – ODEDIPE N eds., *The environmental consciousness for Nigerian national development*, monograph 3, Lagos1992.

AJOMO M., "An examination of federal environment laws in nigeria," in AJOMO M – ADEWALE O (eds.), *Environmental laws and sustainable development in nigeria*, NAILS conference series 5, 1994.

AKANDE Tanimola et all (eds.). "Awareness and Attitude to Social and Health Hazards from Generators Use in Nigeria" in *Medwell research journal of Medical sciences* 2, 4 2008, 185-189

AKAO Alex, "Dumping ground! World Customs Organisation raises alarm over used hazardous electronics flooding Nigeria, Intercepts Lagos-bound container" *in Daily Sun Newspaper Nigeria*, Wednesday, July 22, 2009.

CONE James, "Whose earth is it anyway" in HESSEL Dieter and RASMUSSEN Larry (eds.), *Earth habitat: eco-justice and the church's response*, Fortress Press, Minneapolis (MN) 2001.

GAGLIANONE Renato, Dispensa Corso MLE 1005 "Evangelizzazione e promozione umana: pastorale della promozione umana e dello sviluppo", PUU Rome 2009-2010.

IBRAHIM B, "Strategic approach to reducing vehicle emissions in Nigeria: role of fleet operators, Jos, 28 August 2009.

NWACHUKWU M.N., *et al* (eds), African Journal of Contextual Theology, Vol 2. Change Publications Ltd, Lagos 2010.

ODUEME Stelle, "On dangers of Generator fumes, noise pollution", 21 January 2009.

OGBONNA D. et al, "Waste management: a tool for environmental protection in Nigeria," in *Ambio journal of the human environment* 31, 1 (2002), 55-57.

OLANIKE Adeyemo, "Consequencies of pollution and degradation of Nigerian aquatic environment on fisheries resources," in *The Environment* 23 (2003), 297-306.

PONTIFICAL COUNCIL FOR JUSTICE AND PEACE, "Water, an essential element for life", The Fourth World Water Forum, Mexico City, 16-22 March 2006.

RAHNER Karl, "The theological problem entailed in the idea of 'the new earth" in *Theological investigation*, 10, Darton, Longmann & Todd, London (1973), 260-272.

UGEH Patrick, "Citizens Spend N796 Billion to Fuel Generators Yearly", 28 September 2009.

UNITED NATIONS DOCUMENTS
United Nations Environment Programme (UNEP), Global environment outlook (GEO), environment for development 4, Progress Press Ltd, Valletta 2007.

BASEL CONVENTION, on the control of trans-boundary movements of hazardous wastes and their *disposal* (22 March 1989).

AFRICAN UNION (AU) DOCUMENT
AFRICAN UNION, *Concept note for the conference of African heads of state and government on climate change and African lead experts on climate change*, Addis Ababa Ethiopia, 24 August 2009.

NIGERIAN GOVERNMENT DOCUMENTS

FEDERAL MINISTRY OF HEALTH (FHOH), *Revised national health policy,* Abuja FMOH 2004.

FEPA (Federal Environmental Protection Agency), *National guidelines and standards for* environmental pollution control in Nigeria, Federal Government Press, Lagos 1991

NESREA (National Environmental Standards and Regulations Enforcement Agency) Act 2007, *Environmental pollution in Nigeria.*

INTERNET SOURCES

http://www.vatican.va/holy_father/bebedict_xvi/speeches/2008/august/documents/hf_ben-xvi_spe_20080806_clero-bressanone_en.html.

http://www.vatican.va/holy_father/benedict_xvi/homilies/2005/documents/hf_ben_xvi_hom_20050424_initio-pontificato_en.html).

http://www.ecs.org.et/Doc/Propositions_Synod.htm.

FABC PAPERS: *http://www.ucanews.com/htm/fabc-papers.*

http://www.wcr.ab.ca/bin/eco-lett.htm.1998.

http://www.docstoc.com/docs/530426/ENVIRONMENTAL -POLLUTION-IN-NIGERIA.

http://www.thefreedictionary.com/pollution).

http://www.medwelljournals.com/fulltext/rjms/2008/185-189.pdf.

http://allafrica.com/stories/200909281059.html.

http://www.cdmbazzar.net/UserManagement/FileStorage/ JLB7TU1RKOPQHNFVGX84MSC62YW5DZ.

http://allafrica.com/stories/200901220469.html.

http://www.nigeriawatch.org/media/htm/NGA-watch-Report08.pdf.

http://dailymaverick.co.za/article/2011-08-05-a-brief-look-un-says-nigerian-oil-pollution-worse-than-first-thought.

http://jpr.sagepub.com/content/39/4/387.short.

http://www.enviroliteracy.org/subcategory.php/222.html.

http://www.enviroliteracy.org/category.php/5.html.

_http://www.emergentuk.org/resources/alan_jamieson/churchless_faith/faith_stageseminar_notes.doc._

_http://www.vatican.va/roman_curia/synod/index.htm._

_http://www.vatican.va/roman_curia/synod/documents/rc_synod_doc_20091023_elenco-prop-finali_en.html._

APPENDICES AND
GLOSSARY OF TERMS

Appendix 1
The Pontifical Council for Justice and Peace
Pontifical Council issues Ten Commandments (Principles) for the
Environment
The Bible lays out the fundamental moral principles of how to FACE
the ecological question.

1) The human person, made in God's image, is superior to all other earthly creatures, which should in turn be used responsibly. Christ's incarnation and his teachings testify to the value of nature: Nothing that exists in this world is outside the divine plan of creation and redemption.

2) The social teaching of the Church recalls two fundamental points. We should not reduce nature to a mere instrument to be manipulated and exploited. Nor should we make nature an absolute value, or put it above the dignity of the human person.

3) The question of the environment entails the whole planet, as it is a collective good. Our responsibility toward ecology extends to future generations.

4) It is necessary to confirm both the primacy of ethics and the rights of man over technology, thus preserving human dignity. The central point of reference for all scientific and technical applications must be respect for the human person, who in turn should treat the other created beings with respect.

5) Nature must not be regarded as a reality that is divine in itself; therefore, it is not removed from human action. It is, rather, a gift offered by our Creator to the human community, confided

to human intelligence and moral responsibility. It follows, then, that it is not illicit to modify the ecosystem, so long as this is done within the context of a respect for its order and beauty, and taking into consideration the utility of every creature.

6) Ecological questions highlight the need to achieve a greater harmony both between measures designed to foment economic development and those directed to preserving the ecology, and between national and international policies. Economic development, moreover, needs to take into consideration the integrity and rhythm of nature, because natural resources are limited. And all economic activity that uses natural resources should also include the costs of safeguarding the environment into the calculations of the overall costs of its activity.

7) Concern for the environment means that we should actively work for the integral development of the poorest regions. The goods of this world have been created by God to be wisely used by all. These goods should be shared, in a just and charitable manner. The principle of the universal destiny of goods offers a fundamental orientation to deal with the complex relationship between ecology and poverty.

8) Collaboration, by means of worldwide agreements, backed up by international law, is necessary to protect the environment. Responsibility toward the environment needs to be implemented in an adequate way at the juridical level. These laws and agreements should be guided by the demands of the common good.

9) Lifestyles should be oriented according to the principles of sobriety, temperance and self-discipline, both at the personal and social levels. People need to escape from the consumer mentality and promote methods of production that respect the created order, as well as satisfying the basic needs of all. This change of lifestyle would be helped by a greater awareness of the interdependence between all the inhabitants of the earth.

10) A spiritual response must be given to environmental questions, inspired by the conviction that creation is a gift that God has placed in the hands of mankind, to be used responsibly and with loving care. People's fundamental orientation toward the

created world should be one of gratitude and thankfulness. The world, in fact, leads people back to the mystery of God who has created it and continues to sustain it. If God is forgotten, nature is emptied of its deepest meaning and left impoverished. If, instead, nature is rediscovered in its role as something created, mankind can establish with it a relationship that takes into account its symbolic and mystical dimensions. This would open for mankind a path toward God, creator of the heavens and the earth.

Appendix II
Top 10 Reasons to Care for Creation!
1) God is the Creator of the Universe and maintains its existence through an ongoing creative will.
2) God has blessed and called "very good" all that is created.
3) God's plan for Creation is one of harmony and order. Creation forms a whole, a cosmos.
4) God loves the community of life.
5) God's creatures share a common home.
6) God's presence is discernable in all Creation.
7) God intends the Earth's goods to be equitably shared.
8) Within Creation, the human person enjoys a consummate dignity. Inherent to this dignity is that of exercising a wise and just stewardship over the rest of Creation.
9) In a mysterious way, Christ's redemptive mission extends to all of Creation.
10) Human greed devastates the environment; Ecological conversion and Solidarity can restore its dignity.

Appendix III
Some Stumbling Blocks:
1) Putting the human person on the same level as the rest of Creation, thereby actually reducing the responsibility of the person for his or her actions as regards the whole of Creation

2) A refusal to recognize that much of progress is good, that all is not bad in industrialization and in modern technology;
3) A certain "Garden of Eden" mentality that refuses all modern developments, rejecting them as evil;
4) A glorification of the goodness of nature that more or less romantically overlooks its harshness;
5) A demonisation of the First World and a refusal to consider that the Third World might have some part of responsibility for environmental degradation thereby blocking the needed common efforts;
6) A type of new paganism, fostering a form of nature worship.
7) Indifference, and/or trivializing of environmental problems.

Appendix IV
Cornwall Declaration on Environmental Stewardship
By the Interfaith Council for Environmental Stewardship

The past millennium brought unprecedented improvements in human health, nutrition, and life expectancy, especially among those most blessed by political and economic liberty and advances in science and technology. At the dawn of a new millennium, the opportunity exists to build on these advances and to extend them to more of the earth's people.

At the same time, many are concerned that liberty, science, and technology are more a threat to the environment than a blessing to humanity and nature. Out of shared reverence for God and His creation and love for our neighbours, we Jews, Catholics, and Protestants, speaking for ourselves and not officially on behalf of our respective communities, joined by others of good will, and committed to justice and compassion, unite in this declaration of our common concerns, beliefs, and aspirations.

Our Concerns
1) Human understanding and control of natural processes empower people not only to improve the human condition but also to do great harm to each other, to the earth, and to other

creatures. As concerns about the environment have grown in recent decades, the moral necessity of ecological stewardship has become increasingly clear. At the same time, however, certain misconceptions about nature and science, coupled with erroneous theological and anthropological positions, impede the advancement of a sound environmental ethic. In the midst of controversy over such matters, it is critically important to remember that while passion may energize environmental activism, it is reason – including sound theology and sound science – that must guide the decision-making process. We identify three areas of common misunderstanding:

2) Many people mistakenly view humans as principally consumers and polluters rather than producers and stewards. Consequently, they ignore our potential, as bearers of God's image, to add to the earth's abundance. The increasing realization of this potential has enabled people in societies blessed with an advanced economy not only to reduce pollution, while producing more of the goods and services responsible for the great improvements in the human condition, but also to alleviate the negative effects of much past pollution. A clean environment is a costly good; consequently, growing affluence, technological innovation, and the application of human and material capital are integral to environmental improvement. The tendency among some to oppose economic progress in the name of environmental stewardship is often sadly self-defeating.

3) Many people believe that "nature knows best," or that the earth–untouched by human hands–is the ideal. Such romanticism leads some to deify nature or oppose human dominion over creation. Our position, informed by revelation and confirmed by reason and experience, views human stewardship that unlocks the potential in creation for all the earth's inhabitants as good. Humanity alone of all the created order is capable of developing other resources and can thus enrich creation, so it can properly be said that the human person is the most valuable resource on earth. Human life, therefore, must be cherished and allowed to flourish. The alternative–denying the possibility of beneficial

human management of the earth—removes all rationale for environmental stewardship.

4) While some environmental concerns are well founded and serious, others are without foundation or greatly exaggerated. Some well-founded concerns focus on human health problems in the developing world arising from inadequate sanitation, widespread use of primitive biomass fuels like wood and dung, and primitive agricultural, industrial, and commercial practices; distorted resource consumption patterns driven by perverse economic incentives; and improper disposal of nuclear and other hazardous wastes in nations lacking adequate regulatory and legal safeguards. Some unfounded or undue concerns include fears of destructive manmade global warming, overpopulation, and rampant species loss. The real and merely alleged problems differ in the following ways:

    a. The former are proven and well understood, while the latter tend to be speculative.

    b. The former are often localized, while the latter are said to be global and cataclysmic in scope.

    c. The former are of concern to people in developing nations especially, while the latter are of concern mainly to environmentalists in wealthy nations.

    d. The former are of high and firmly established risk to human life and health, while the latter are of very low and largely hypothetical risk.

    e. Solutions proposed to the former are cost effective and maintain proven benefit, while solutions to the latter are unjustifiably costly and of dubious benefit.

Public policies to combat exaggerated risks can dangerously delay or reverse the economic development necessary to improve not only human life but also human stewardship of the environment. The poor, who are most often citizens of developing nations, are often forced to suffer longer in poverty with its attendant high rates of malnutrition, disease, and mortality; as a consequence, they are often the most injured by such misguided, though well-intended, policies.

Our Beliefs

1) Our common Judeo-Christian heritage teaches that the following theological and anthropological principles are the foundation of environmental stewardship:

2) God, the Creator of all things, rules over all and deserves our worship and adoration.

3) The earth, and with it all the cosmos, reveals its Creator's wisdom and is sustained and governed by His power and loving kindness.

4) Men and women were created in the image of God, given a privileged place among creatures, and commanded to exercise stewardship over the earth. Human persons are moral agents for whom freedom is an essential condition of responsible action. Sound environmental stewardship must attend both to the demands of human well being and to a divine call for human beings to exercise caring dominion over the earth. It affirms that human well being and the integrity of creation are not only compatible but also dynamically interdependent realities.

5) God's Law—summarized in the Decalogue and the two Great Commandments (to love God and neighbour), which are written on the human heart, thus revealing His own righteous character to the human person—represents God's design for shalom, or peace, and is the supreme rule of all conduct, for which personal or social prejudices must not be substituted.

6) By disobeying God's Law, humankind brought on itself moral and physical corruption as well as divine condemnation in the form of a curse on the earth. Since the fall into sin people have often ignored their Creator, harmed their neighbours, and defiled the good creation.

7) God in His mercy has not abandoned sinful people or the created order but has acted throughout history to restore men and women to fellowship with Him and through their stewardship to enhance the beauty and fertility of the earth.

8) Human beings are called to be fruitful, to bring forth good things from the earth, to join with God in making provision for our temporal well being, and to enhance the beauty and

fruitfulness of the rest of the earth. Our call to fruitfulness, therefore, is not contrary to but mutually complementary with our call to steward God's gifts. This call implies a serious commitment to fostering the intellectual, moral, and religious habits and practices needed for free economies and genuine care for the environment.

Our Aspirations

1) In light of these beliefs and concerns, we declare the following principled aspirations:

2) We aspire to a world in which human beings care wisely and humbly for all creatures, first and foremost for their fellow human beings, recognizing their proper place in the created order.

3) We aspire to a world in which objective moral principles—not personal prejudices—guide moral action.

4) We aspire to a world in which right reason (including sound theology and the careful use of scientific methods) guides the stewardship of human and ecological relationships.

5) We aspire to a world in which liberty as a condition of moral action is preferred over government-initiated management of the environment as a means to common goals.

6) We aspire to a world in which the relationships between stewardship and private property are fully appreciated, allowing people's natural incentive to care for their own property to reduce the need for collective ownership and control of resources and enterprises, and in which collective action, when deemed necessary, takes place at the most local level possible.

7) We aspire to a world in which widespread economic freedom—which is integral to private, market economies—makes sound ecological stewardship available to ever greater numbers.

8) We aspire to a world in which advancements in agriculture, industry, and commerce not only minimize pollution and transform most waste products into efficiently used resources but also improve the material conditions of life for people everywher

Appendix V
THE RIO DECLARATION ON ENVIRONMENT AND DEVELOPMENT.
Rio De Janiero (3-14 June, 1992)
The United Nations Conference on Environment and Development,
Having met at Rio de Janeiro from 3 to 14 June 1992,
Proclaims that:

PRINCIPLE 1
Human beings are at the centre of concerns for sustainable development. They are entitled to a healthy and productive life in harmony with nature.

PRINCIPLE 2
States have, in accordance with the Charter of the United Nations and the principles of international law, the sovereign right to exploit their own resources pursuant to their own environmental and developmental policies, and the responsibility to ensure that activities within their jurisdiction or control do not cause damage to the environment of other States or of areas beyond the limits of national jurisdiction.

PRINCIPLE 3
The right to development must be fulfilled so as to equitably meet developmental and environmental needs of present and future generations.

PRINCIPLE 4
In order to achieve sustainable development, environmental protection shall constitute an integral part of the development process and cannot be considered in isolation from it.

PRINCIPLE 5
All States and all people shall co-operate in the essential task of eradicating poverty as an indispensable requirement for sustainable development, in order to decrease the disparities in standards of living and better meet the needs of the majority of the people of the world.

PRINCIPLE 6

The special situation and needs of developing countries, particularly the least developed and those most environmentally vulnerable, shall be given special priority. International actions in the field of environment and development should also address the interests and needs of all countries.

PRINCIPLE 7

States shall co-operate in a spirit of global partnership to conserve, protect and restore the health and integrity of the Earth's ecosystem. In view of the different contributions to global environmental degradation, States have common but differentiated responsibilities. The developed countries acknowledge the responsibility that they bear in the international pursuit of sustainable development in view of the pressures their societies place on the global environment and of the technologies and financial resources they command.

PRINCIPLE 8

To achieve sustainable development and a higher quality of life for all people, States should reduce and eliminate unsustainable patterns of production and consumption and promote appropriate demographic policies.

PRINCIPLE 9

States should co-operate to strengthen endogenous capacity-building for sustainable development by improving scientific understanding through exchanges of scientific and technological knowledge, and by enhancing the development, adaptation, diffusion and transfer of technologies, including new and innovative technologies.

PRINCIPLE 10

Environmental issues are best handled with the participation of all concerned citizens, at the relevant level. At the national level, each individual shall have appropriate access to information concerning the environment that is held by public authorities, including information on hazardous materials and activities in their communities, and the opportunity to participate in decision-making processes. States shall facilitate and encourage public awareness and participation by making information widely available. Effective access to judicial and administrative proceedings, including redress and remedy, shall be provided.

PRINCIPLE 11
States shall enact effective environmental legislation. Environmental standards, management objectives and priorities should reflect the environmental and developmental context to which they apply. Standards applied by some countries may be inappropriate and of unwarranted economic and social cost to other countries, in particular developing countries.

PRINCIPLE 12
States should co-operate to promote a supportive and open international economic system that would lead to economic growth and sustainable development in all countries, to better address the problems of environmental degradation. Trade policy measures for environmental purposes should not constitute a means of arbitrary or unjustifiable discrimination or a disguised restriction on international trade. Unilateral actions to deal with environmental challenges outside the jurisdiction of the importing country should be avoided. Environmental measures addressing trans-boundary or global environmental problems should, as far as possible, be based on an international consensus.

PRINCIPLE 13
States shall develop national law regarding liability and compensation for the victims of pollution and other environmental damage. States shall also co-operate in an expeditious and more determined manner to develop further international law regarding liability and compensation for adverse effects of environmental damage caused by activities within their jurisdiction or control to areas beyond their jurisdiction.

PRINCIPLE 14

States should effectively co-operate to discourage or prevent the relocation and transfer to other States of any activities and substances that cause severe environmental degradation or are found to be harmful to human health.

PRINCIPLE 15

In order to protect the environment, the precautionary approach shall be widely applied by States according to their capabilities. Where there are threats of serious or irreversible damage, lack of full scientific certainty shall not be used as a reason for postponing cost-effective measures to prevent environmental degradation.

PRINCIPLE 16

National authorities should endeavour to promote the internalisation of environmental costs and the use of economic instruments, taking into account the approach that the polluter should, in principle, bear the cost of pollution, with due regard to the public interest and without distorting international trade and investment.

PRINCIPLE 17

Environmental impact assessment, as a national instrument, shall be undertaken for proposed activities that are likely to have a significant adverse impact on the environment and are subject to a decision of a competent national authority.

PRINCIPLE 18

States shall immediately notify other States of any natural disasters or other emergencies that are likely to produce sudden harmful effects on the environment of those States. Every effort shall be made by the international community to help States so afflicted.

PRINCIPLE 19

States shall provide prior and timely notification and relevant information to potentially affected States on activities that may have a significant adverse trans-boundary environmental effect and shall consult with those States at an early stage and in good faith.

PRINCIPLE 20

Women have a vital role in environmental management and development. Their full participation is therefore essential to achieve sustainable development.

PRINCIPLE 21

The creativity, ideals and courage of the youth of the world should be mobilized to forge a global partnership in order to achieve sustainable development and ensure a better future for all.

PRINCIPLE 22

Indigenous people and their communities, and other local communities, have a vital role in environmental management and development because of their knowledge and traditional practices.

States should recognize and duly support their identity, culture and interests and enable their effective participation in the achievement of sustainable development.

PRINCIPLE 23

The environment and natural resources of people under oppression, domination and occupation shall be protected.

PRINCIPLE 24

Warfare is inherently destructive of sustainable development. States shall therefore respect international law providing protection for the environment in times of armed conflict and co-operate in its further development, as necessary.

PRINCIPLE 25

Peace, development and environmental protection are interdependent and indivisible.

PRINCIPLE 26

States shall resolve all their environmental disputes peacefully and by appropriate means in accordance with the Charter of the United Nations.

PRINCIPLE 27

States and people shall co-operate in good faith and in a spirit of partnership in the fulfilment of the principles embodied in this Declaration and in the further development of international law in the field of sustainable development.

Appendix VI
THE EARTH SUMMIT AND AGENDA 21
INTRODUCTION

The United Nations Conference on Environment and Development (UNCED), which took place in Rio de Janeiro in June 1992, was a milestone event bringing together Heads of State and Chiefs of Government than any other meeting in the history of international relations, along with senior diplomats and government officials from around the globe, delegates from United Nations agencies, officials of international organizations, and many thousands of nongovernmental organization (NGO) representatives and journalists.

Agenda 21 is a unique step forward on the road toward sustainability, and offers a bold plan to mobilize local, national, and global action.

Overview of Agenda 21

SECTION ONE: SOCIAL AND ECONOMIC DIMENSIONS

The preamble and the following eight chapters consider the challenges that the adaptation of human behaviour to sustainable development poses to prevailing social and economic structures and institutions.

1. PREAMBLE

The preamble concludes, "Agenda 21 is a dynamic program. It will be carried out over time by the various actors according to the different situations, capacities and priorities of countries and regions involved.... The process marks the beginning of a new global partnership..."

2. ACCELERATING SUSTAINABLE DEVELOPMENT

Calls for a global partnership to provide a dynamic and growing world economy based on an "...open, equitable, secure, non-discriminatory, and predictable multilateral trading system," in which commodity exports of the developing countries can find markets at fair prices free of tariff and nontariff barriers.

3. COMBATING POVERTY

This poverty suggests that factors creating policies of development, resource management, and poverty be integrated. This objective is to be sought by improving access of the poor to education and health care, to safe water and sanitation, and to resources, especially land; by restoration of degraded resources; by empowerment of the disadvantaged, especially women, youth, and indigenous peoples; by ensuring that "women and men have the same right and the means to decide freely and responsibly on the number of spacing of their children."

4. CHANGING CONSUMPTION PATTERNS

"One of the most serious problems now facing the planet is that associated with historical patterns of unsustainable consumption, and production, particularly in the industrialized countries."

Social research and policy should bring forward new concepts of status and lifestyles, which are "less dependent on the Earth's finite resources and more in harmony with its carrying capacity." Greater efficiency in the use of energy and resources--for example, reducing wasteful packaging of products--must be sought by new technology and new social values.

Cost of implementation: The recommended measures are unlikely to require significant new financial resources.

5. POPULATION AND SUSTAINABILITY

This urges governments to develop and implement population policies integral with their economic development programs. Health services should "include women-centred, women-managed, safe and effective reproductive health care and affordable, accessible services, as appropriate, for the responsible planning of family size..." Health services are to emphasize reduction of infant death rates, which converge with low birth rates to stabilize world population at a sustainable number at the end of the century.

6. PROTECTING AND PROMOTING HUMAN HEALTH
Calls for meeting basic health needs of all populations; provide necessary specialized environmental health services; co-ordinate involvement of citizens, and the health sector, in solutions to health problems. Health service coverage should be achieved for population groups in greatest need, particularly those living in rural areas. The preventative measures urged include reckoning with urban health hazards and risks from environmental pollution.

7. SUSTAINABLE HUMAN SETTLEMENTS
Addresses the full range of issues facing urban-rural settlements, including: access to land, credit, and low-cost building materials by homeless poor and unemployed; upgrading of slums to ease the deficit in urban shelter; access to basic services of clean water, sanitation, and waste collection; use of appropriate construction materials, designs, and technologies; increased use of high-occupancy public transportation and bicycle and foot paths; reduction of long-distance commuting; support for the informal economic sector; development of urban renewal projects in partnership with non-governmental organizations; improved rural living conditions and land-use planning to prevent urban sprawl onto agricultural land and fragile regions.

8. MAKING DECISIONS FOR SUSTAINABLE DEVELOPMENT
Calls on governments to create sustainable development strategies to integrate social and environmental policies in all ministries and at all levels, including fiscal measures and the budget are expedient.

Encourages nations and corporate enterprises to integrate environmental protection, degradation, and restoration costs in decision-making at the outset, and to mount without delay the research necessary to reckon such costs, to develop protocols bringing these considerations into procedures at all levels of decision-making.

SECTION TWO: CONSERVATION AND MANAGEMENT OF RESOURCES

The environment itself is the subject of chapters 9 through 22, dealing with the conservation and management of resources for development.

9. PROTECTING THE ATMOSPHERE

This system urges constraint and efficiency in energy production and consumption, development of renewable energy sources; and promotion of mass transit technology and access thereto for developing countries. Conservation and expansion of "all sinks for greenhouse gases" is extolled, and trans-boundary pollution recognized as "subject to international controls." Governments need to develop more precise ways of predicting levels of atmospheric pollutants; modernize existing power systems to gain energy efficiency; and increase energy efficiency education and labelling programs.

10. MANAGING LAND SUSTAINABLY

Calls on governments to develop policies that take into account the land-resource base, population changes, and the interests of local people; improve and enforce laws and regulations to support the sustainable use of land, and restrict the transfer of productive arable land to other uses; use techniques such as landscape ecological planning that focus on an ecosystem or a watershed, and encourage sustainable livelihoods; include appropriate traditional and indigenous land-use practices, such as pastoralism, traditional land reserves, and terraced agriculture in land management; encourage the active participation in decision-making of those affected groups that have often been excluded, such as women, youth, indigenous people, and other local communities; test ways of putting the value of land and ecosystems into national reports on economic performance; ensure that institutions that deal with land and natural resources integrate environmental, social, and economic issues into planning.

11. COMBATING DEFORESTATION

Calls for concerted international research and conservation efforts to control harvesting of forests and "uncontrolled degradation and conversion to other types of land use," to develop the values of standing forests under sustained cultivation by indigenous technologies and agro forestry, and to expand the shrunken world-forest cover have been made. Governments, along with business, nongovernmental and other groups should: plant more forests to reduce pressure on primary and old-growth forests; breed trees that are more productive and resistant to stress; protect forests and reduce pollutants that affect them, including air pollution that flows across borders; limit and aim to halt destructive shifting cultivation by addressing the underlying social and ecological causes; use environmentally sound, more efficient and less polluting methods of harvesting; minimize wood waste; promote small-scale enterprises; develop urban forestry for the greening of all places where people live; and encourage low-impact forest use and sustainable management of areas adjacent to forests.

12. COMBATING DESERTIFICATION AND DROUGHT
Calls for intensive study of the process in its relation to world climate change to improve forecasting, study of natural vegetation succession to support large-scale re-vegetation and afforestation, checking and reversal of erosion, and like small-and grand-scale measures, have become necessary. For inhabitants whose perilously adapted livelihoods are threatened or erased, resettlement and adaptation to new life ways must be assisted. Governments must: adopt national sustainable land use plans and sustainable management of water resources; accelerate planting programs; and help to reduce the demand for fuel wood through energy efficiency and alternative energy programs.

13. SUSTAINABLE MOUNTAIN DEVELOPMENT
Calls for study, protection, and restoration of these fragile ecosystems and assistance to populations in regions suffering degradation, have seriously been made expedient. Governments should: promote erosion-control measures that are low-cost, simple, and easily used; offer people incentives to conserve resources and use environment-friendly technologies; produce information on alternative livelihoods; create protected areas to save wild genetic material; identify hazardous areas that are most vulnerable to erosion floods, landslides, earthquakes,

snow avalanches, and other natural hazards and develop early-warning systems and disaster-response teams; identify mountain areas threatened by air pollution from neighbouring industrial and urban areas; and create centres of information on mountain ecosystems.

14. SUSTAINABLE AGRICULTURE AND RURAL DEVELOPMENT
Rising population food needs must be met through: increased productivity and co-operation involving rural people, national governments, the private sector, and the international community; wider access to techniques for reducing food spoilage, loss to pests, and for conserving soil and water resources; ecosystem planning; access of private ownership and fair market prices; advice and training in modern and indigenous conservation techniques including conservation tillage, integrated pest management, crop rotation, use of plant nutrients, agroforestry, terracing and mixed cropping; and better use and equitable distribution of information on plant and animal genetic resources.

15. CONSERVATION OF BIOLOGICAL DIVERSITY
Recognizing the need to conserve and maintain genes, species, and ecosystems, urges nations, with the co-operation of the United Nations, nongovernmental organizations, the private sector, and financial institutions, to conduct national assessments on the state of biodiversity; develop national strategies to conserve and sustain biological diversity and make these part of overall national development strategies; conduct long-term research into importance of biodiversity for ecosystems that produce goods and environmental benefits; protect natural habitats; encourage traditional methods of agriculture, agro forestry, forestry, range and wildlife management which use, maintain, or increase biodiversity. Cost of implementation is: $3 billion.

16. MANAGEMENT OF BIOTECHNOLOGY
Calls for the transfer of biotechnology to the developing countries and the creation of the infrastructure of human capacity and institutions to put it to work there are urgent. Highlights need for internationally agreed principles on risk assessment and management of all aspects of biotechnology, to: improve productivity and the nutritional quality

and shelf-life of food and animal feed products; develop vaccines and techniques for preventing the spread of diseases and toxins; increase crop resistance to diseases and pests, so that there will be less need for chemical pesticides; develop safe and effective methods for the biological control of disease-transmitting insects, especially those resistant to pesticides; contribute to soil fertility; treat sewage, organic chemical wastes, and oil spills more cheaply and effectively than conventional methods; and tap mineral resources in ways that cause less environmental damage.

17. PROTECTING AND MANAGING THE OCEANS

Sets out goals and programs under which nations may conserve "their" oceanic resources for their own and the benefit of the nations that share oceans with them, and international programs that may protect the residual commons in the interests even of land-locked nations, such as: anticipate and prevent further degradation of the marine environment and reduce the risk of long-term or irreversible effects on the oceans; ensure prior assessment of activities that may have significant adverse impact on the seas; make marine environmental protection part of general environmental, social, and economic development policies; apply the "polluter pays" principle, and use economic incentives to reduce polluting of the seas; improve the living standards of coast-dwellers; reduce or eliminate discharges of synthetic chemicals that threaten to accumulate to dangerous levels in marine life; control and reduce toxic-waste discharges; stricter international regulations to reduce the risk of accidents and pollution from cargo ships; develop land-use practices that reduce run-off of soil and wastes to rivers, and thus to the seas; stop ocean dumping and the incineration of hazardous wastes at sea.

18. PROTECTING AND MANAGING FRESH WATER

This system sets out measures, from development of long-range weather and climate forecasting to cleanup of the most obvious sources of pollution, to secure the supply of fresh water for the next doubling of the human population. Focus is on developing low-cost but adequate services that can be installed and maintained at the community level to achieve universal water supply by 2025. The interim goals set for 2000 include: to provide all urban residents with at least 40 litres of safe drinking water per person per day; provide 75% of urban dwellers with sanitation; establish standards for the discharge of municipal and industrial wastes; have three-quarters of solid urban waste collected and recycled, or disposed of in an environmentally safe way; ensure that rural people everywhere have access to safe water and sanitation for healthy lives, while maintaining essential local environments; control water-associated diseases.

19. SAFER USE OF TOXIC CHEMICALS

Seeks objectives such as: full evaluation of 500 chemicals before the year 2000; control of chemical hazards through pollution prevention, emission inventories, product labelling; use limitations, procedures for safe handling and exposure regulations; phase-out or banning of high-risk chemicals; consideration of policies based on the principle of producer liability; reduced risk by using less-toxic or non-chemical technologies; review of pesticides whose acceptance was based on criteria now recognized as insufficient or outdated; efforts to replace chemicals with other pest-control methods such as biological control; provision to the public of information on chemical hazards in the languages of those who use the materials; development of a chemical-hazard labelling system using easily understandable symbols; control of the export of banned or restricted chemicals and provision of information on any exports to the importing countries.

20. MANAGING HAZARDOUS WASTES

This seeks international support in restraint of the trade and for containing the hazardous cargoes in safe sinks. Governments should: require and assist in the innovation by industry of cleaner production methods and of preventive and recycling technologies; encourage the phasing out of processes that produce high risks because of hazardous waste management; hold producers responsible for the environmentally unsound disposal of the hazardous wastes they generate; establish public information programs and ensure that training programs provided for industry and government workers on hazardous-waste issues, especially use minimization; build treatment centres for hazardous wastes, either at the national or regional level; ensure that the military conforms to national environmental norms for hazardous-waste treatment and disposal; ban the export of hazardous wastes to countries that are not equipped to deal with those wastes. Industry should: treat, recycle, reuse, and dispose of wastes at or close to the site where they are created.

21. MANAGING SOLID WASTES AND SEWAGE

Governments should urge waste minimization and increased reuse/recycling as strategies toward sound waste treatment and disposal; encourage "life-cycle" management of the flow of material into and out of manufacturing and use; provide incentives to recycling; fund pilot programs such as small-scale and cottage-based recycling industries, compost production, irrigation using treated waste water, and the recovery of energy from wastes; establish guidelines for the safe reuse of waste and encourage markets for recycled and reused products.

22. MANAGING RADIOACTIVE WASTES

Calls for increasingly stringent measures to encourage countries to cooperate with international organizations to: promote ways of minimizing and limiting the creation of radioactive wastes; provide for the sage storage, processing, conditioning, transportation, and disposal of such wastes; provide developing countries with technical assistance to help them deal with wastes, or make it easier for such countries to return used radioactive material to suppliers; promote the proper planning of safe and environmentally sound ways of managing radioactive wastes, possibly including assessment of the environmental impact; strengthen efforts to implement the Code of Practice on the Trans-boundary Movements of Radioactive Wastes; encourage work to finish studies on whether the current voluntary moratorium on disposal of low-level radioactive wastes at sea should be replaced by a ban; not promote or allow storage or disposal of radioactive wastes near seacoasts or open seas, unless it is clear that this does not create an unacceptable risk to people and the marine environment; not export radioactive wastes to countries that prohibit the import of such waste.

SECTION THREE: STRENGTHENING THE ROLE OF MAJOR GROUPS

The issues of how people are to be mobilized and empowered for their various roles in sustainable development are addressed in chapters 23 through 32.

23. PREAMBLE

"Critical to the effective implementation of the objectives, policies, and mechanisms agreed to by Governments in all program areas of Agenda 21 will be the commitment and involvement of all social groups..."

24. WOMEN IN SUSTAINABLE DEVELOPMENT

Urges governments to face the status question; give girls equal access to education; reduce the workloads of girls and women; make health-care systems responsive to female needs; open employment and careers to women; and bring women into full participation in social, cultural, and public life. Governments should: ensure a role for women in national and international ecosystem management and control of environmental degradation; ensure women's access to property rights, as well as agricultural inputs and implements; take all necessary measures to eliminate violence against women, and work to eliminate persistent negative images, stereotypes, and attitudes, and prejudices against women; develop consumer awareness among women to reduce or eliminate unsustainable consumption; and begin to count the value of unpaid work.

25. CHILDREN AND YOUTH IN SUSTAINABLE DEVELOPMENT

Calls on governments, by the year 2000, to ensure that 50% of their youth, gender balanced, have access to secondary education or vocational training; teach students about the environment and sustainable development through their schooling; consult with and let youth participate in decisions that affect the environment; enable youth to be represented at international meetings, and participate in decision-making at the United Nations; combat human rights abuses against youth and see that their children are healthy, adequately fed, educated, and protected from pollution and toxic substances; and develop strategies that deal with the entitlement of young people to natural resources.

26. STRENGTHENING THE ROLE OF INDIGENOUS PEOPLES

Urges governments to enrol indigenous peoples in full global partnership, beginning with measures to protect their rights and conserve their patrimony; recognize that indigenous lands need to be protected from environmentally unsound activities, and from activities the people consider to be socially and culturally inappropriate; develop a national dispute resolution procedure to deal with settlement and land-use concerns; incorporate their rights and responsibilities into national legislation; recognize and apply elsewhere indigenous values, traditional knowledge and resource management practices; and provide indigenous people with suitable technologies to increase the efficiency of their resource management.

27. PARTNERSHIPS WITH NONGOVERNMENTAL GROUPS [CIVIC GROUPS]

Calls on governments and the United Nations system to: invite nongovernmental groups to be involved in making policies and decisions on sustainable development; make NGOs a part of the review process and evaluation of implementing Agenda 21; provide NGOs with timely access to information; encourage partnerships between NGOs and local authorities; review financial and administrative support for NGOs; utilize NGO expertise and information; and create laws enabling NGOs the right to take legal action to protect the public interest. Cost of implementation has no estimate.

28. LOCAL AUTHORITIES

Calls on local authorities, by 1996, to undertake to promote a consensus in their local populations on "a local Agenda 21;" and, at all times, to invite women and youth into full participation in the decision-making, planning, and implementation process; to consult citizens and community, business, and industrial organizations to gather information and build a consensus on sustainable development strategies. This consensus would help them reshape local programs, policies, laws, and regulations to achieve desired objectives. The process of consultation would increase people's awareness of sustainable development issues. Cost of implementation is: $1 million.

29. WORKERS AND TRADE UNIONS

Challenges governments, businesses, and industries to work toward the goal of full employment, which contributes to sustainable livelihoods in safe, clean, and healthy environments, at work and beyond, by fostering the active and informed participation of workers and trade unions in shaping and implementing environment and development strategies at both the national and international levels; increase worker education and training, both in occupational health and safety and in skills for sustainable livelihoods; and promote workers' rights to freedom of association and the right to organize. Unions and employees should design joint environmental policies, and set priorities to improve the working environment and the overall environmental performance of business and develop more collective agreements aimed at achieving sustainability.

30. BUSINESS AND INDUSTRY

Calls on governments to use economic incentives, laws, standards, and more streamlined administration to promote sustainably managed enterprises with cleaner production; encourage the creation of venture-capital funds; and co-operate with business, industry, academia, and international organizations to support training in the environmental aspects of enterprise management. Business and industry should: develop policies that result in operations and products that have lower environmental impacts; ensure responsible and ethical management of products and processes from the point of view of health, safety, and the environment; make environmentally sound technologies available to affiliates in developing countries without prohibitive charges; encourage overseas affiliates to modify procedures in order to reflect local ecological conditions and share information with governments; create partnerships to help people in smaller companies learn business skills; establish national councils for sustainable development, both in the formal business community and in the informal sector, which includes small-scale businesses, such as artisans; increase research and development of environmentally sound technologies and environmental management systems; report annually on their environmental records; and adopt environmental and sustainable development codes of conduct.

31. SCIENTISTS AND TECHNOLOGISTS

Indicates that governments should: decide how national scientific and technological programs could help make development more sustainable; provide for full and open sharing of information among scientists and decision-makers; fashion national reports that are understandable and relevant to local sustainable development needs; form national advisory groups to help scientists and society develop common values on environmental and developmental ethics; and put environment and development ethics into education and research priorities. Scientists and technologies have special responsibilities to: search for knowledge, and to help protect the biosphere; increase and strengthen dialogue with the public; and develop codes of practice and guidelines that reconcile human needs and environmental protection.

32. STRENGTHENING THE ROLE OF FARMERS

To develop sustainable farming strategies, calls on governments to collaborate with national and international research centres and nongovernmental organizations to: develop environmentally sound farming practices and technologies that improve crop yields, maintain land quality, recycle nutrients, conserve water and energy, and control pests and weeds; help farmers share expertise in conserving land, water, and forest resources, making the most efficient use of chemicals and reducing or re-using farm wastes; encourage self-sufficiency in low-input and low-energy technologies, including indigenous practices; support research on equipment that makes optimal use of human labour and animal power; delegate more power and responsibility to those who work the land; give people more incentive to care for the land by seeing that men and women can get land tenure, access to credit, technology, farm supplies, and training. Researchers need to develop environment-friendly farming techniques and colleges need to bring ecology into agricultural training.

SECTION FOUR: MEANS OF IMPLEMENTATION
Chapters 33 through 40 deal with the ways and means of implementing Agenda 21.

33. FINANCING SUSTAINABLE DEVELOPMENT
At UNCED, countries committed to the consensus of a global partnership, holding that the eradication of poverty "is essential to meeting national and global sustainability objectives;" that "the cost of inaction could outweigh the financial costs of implementing Agenda 21;" that "the huge sustainable development programs of Agenda 21 will require the provision to developing countries of substantial new and additional financial resources;" and that "the initial phase will be accelerated by substantial early commitments of concessional funding." Further, the developed countries "reaffirmed their commitments to reach the accepted United Nations target of 0.7% of GNP for concessional funding... as soon as possible."

34. TECHNOLOGY TRANSFER
Economic assistance would move from the developed to the developing counties principally in the form of technology. Developing countries would be assisted in gaining access to technology and know-how in the public domain and to that protected by intellectual property rights as well, "taking into account developments in the process of negotiating an international code of conduct on the transfer of technology" proceeding under the United Nations Agreement on Tariffs and Trade. To enhance access of developing countries to environmentally sound technology, a collaborative network of laboratories is to be established.

35. SCIENCE FOR SUSTAINABLE DEVELOPMENT
Sustainable development requires expansion of the ongoing international collaborative enterprises in the study of the geo-chemical cycles of the biosphere and the establishment of strong national scientific enterprises in the developing countries. The sciences link fundamental understanding

of the Earth system to development of strategies that build upon its continued healthy functioning. "In the face of threats of irreversible environmental damage, lack of full scientific understanding should not be an excuse for postponing actions which are justified in their own right."

Countries need to develop tools for sustainable development, such as: quality-of-life indicators covering health, education, social welfare, and the state of environment, and the economy; economic incentives that will encourage better resource management; and ways of measuring the environmental soundness of new technologies. They should use information on the links between the state of ecosystems and human health when weighing the costs and benefits of different development policies, and conduct scientific studies to help map our national and regional pathways to sustainable development. When sustainable development plans are being make, the public should be involved in setting long-term goals for society.

36. EDUCATION, TRAINING, AND PUBLIC AWARENESS

Because sustainable development must ultimately enlist everyone, access to education must be hastened for all children; adult illiteracy must be reduced to half of its 1990 level, and the curriculum must incorporate environmental and developmental learning. Nations should seek to: introduce environment and development concepts, including those related to population growth, into all educational programs, with analyses of the causes of the major issues. They should emphasize training decision-makers; involve schoolchildren in local and regional studies on environmental health, including safe drinking water, sanitation, food, and the environmental and economic impacts of resource use; set up training programs for school and university graduates to help them achieve sustainable livelihoods; encourage all sectors of society to train people in environmental management; provide locally trained and recruited environmental technicians to give local communities services they require, starting with primary environmental care; work with the media, theatre groups, entertainment, and advertising industries to promote a more active public debate on the environment; and bring indigenous peoples' experience and understanding of sustainable development into education and training.

37. CREATING CAPACITY FOR SUSTAINABLE DEVELOPMENT

Developing countries need more technical co-operation and assistance in setting priorities so that they can deal with new long-term challenges, rather than concentrating only on immediate problems. For example, people in government and business need to learn how to evaluate the environmental impact of all development projects, starting from the time the projects are conceived.

Assistance in the form of skills, knowledge, and technical know-how can come from the United Nations, national governments, municipalities, nongovernmental organizations, universities, research centres, and business and other private organizations. The United Nations Development Program has been given responsibility for mobilizing international funding and co-ordination programs for capacity building.

38. ORGANIZING FOR SUSTAINABLE DEVELOPMENT

To the existing UN system, the General Assembly as the supreme deliberative and policymaking body, the Economic and Social Council as the appropriate overseer of system-wide coordination reporting to the General Assembly, the Secretary General as chief executive, and the technical agencies seeing to their special functions, Agenda 21 proposes to add a Commission on Sustainable Development to monitor implementation of Agenda 21, reporting to the General Assembly through ECOSOC. The Conference also recommended that the UN Secretary-General appoint a high-level board of environment and development experts to advise on other structural change required in the UN system. The United Nations Environment Program will need to develop and promote natural resource accounting and environmental economics, develop international environmental law, and advise governments on how to integrate environmental considerations into their development policies and programs.

39. INTERNATIONAL LAW

The major goals in international law on sustainable development should include: the development of universally negotiated agreements that create effective international standards for environmental protection, taking account of the different situations and abilities of various countries; an international review of the feasibility of establishing general rights and obligations of nations as in the field of sustainable development; and measures to avoid or settle international disputes in the field of sustainable development. These measures can range from notification and talks on issues that might lead to disputes, to the use of the International Court of Justice.

40. INFORMATION FOR DECISION -MAKING

Calls on governments to ensure that local communities and resource users get the information and skills needed to manage their environment and resources sustainably, including application of traditional and indigenous knowledge; more information about the status of urban air, fresh water, land resources, desertification, soil degradation, biodiversity, the high seas, and the upper atmosphere; more information about population, urbanization, poverty, health, and rights of access to resources. Information is also needed about the relationships of groups, including women, indigenous peoples, youth, children and the disabled with environment issues. Current national accounting reckons environmental costs as "externalities." Internalisation of such costs, the amortization of non-renewable resources, and the development of indicators of sustainability all require not only new data but also new thinking.

GLOSSARY OF TERMS

Biblical

Gen	Genesis
Heb	Hebrews
Jn	John
Kgs	Kings
Lk	Luke
Matt	Matthew
Ps	Psalms
Rom	Romans
Wis	Wisdom

Ecclesiastical

AAS	*Acta Apostolicae Sedis*
ARCCWO	African Regional Conference of Catholic Women Organization
CBCN	Catholic Bishops Conference of Nigeria
CCC	Catechism of the Catholic Church.
CCEE	Catholic Episcopal Conferences of Europe
CELAM	Episcopal Conferences of Latin America
COSMAN	Conference of Major Superiors of Africa and Madagascar
FABC	Federation of Asian Bishops conference
JDPC	Justice, Development and Peace Commission.
RECOWA	Regional Episcopal Conference of West Africa
SECAM	Symposium of Episcopal conferences of Africa and Madagascar
SRS	*Sollicitudo Rei Socialis*
WUCWO	World Union of *Catholic Women Organizations*

Institutions and Organizations

EU	European Union
FEPA	Federal Environmental Protection Agency
NASREA	National Environmental Standards and Regulations Enforcement Agency
NERC	National Electricity Regulatory Commission

PHCN	Power Holding Company of Nigeria
PUU	Pontificia Univerisità Urbaniana
UN	United Nations
UNEP	United Nations Environment Programme
WCO	World Customs Organization
US	United States
WHO	World Health Organisation
NTA	Nigerian Television Authority

Others

ab initio	From the onset
COP	Copenhagen climate conference
EIA	Environmental Impact Assessment
et al	*et alii* (and others)
et cetera	And so on
GEO	Global environment outlook
GHG	Green house gasses
IMPEL	Implementation and Enforcement of Environmental Law
N.G.O.	Non Governmental Organization
RILO	Regional Intelligence Liaison OfficesBottom of Form

BIOGRAPHY OF
JUDE THADDEUS IKENNA OSUNKWO

Born in 1961 into the family of Ezinna Sylvester Mputam and Ezinne Christiana Okwuchukwu Osunkwo, Rev. Jude Thaddeus was ordained a Catholic Priest of the Diocese of Orlu, Nigeria, in 1990. He did his primary education at the St. Anthony Primary School Isiekenesi in Ideato LGA of Imo State, Nigeria; and his secondary education at Holy Ghost Juniorate Ihiala, Anambra State, Nigeria. Later, his graduate and post-graduate studies took him to Bigard Memorial Seminary Enugu Nigeria, Pontifical Urban University Rome and Graduate Theological Foundation IN (an affiliate of the Oxford University of London).

Rev. Osunkwo, who has his specialization in Environmental Studies and Pastoral Catechesis, holds the *PhD* honors in Theology (First Class Division). He also holds the M.A. honors in Missiology (First Class Division) and the B.A. honors in Philosophy (Second Class Upper Division).

Rev. Osunkwo has had vast pastoral experiences. He had served in seven Parishes in the Orlu Catholic Diocese of Nigeria: St. Gregory Parish Amaigbo; St. John Parish Urualla; St. Theresa Parish Mbato; St. Paul Parish Amiri; St. Paul Parish Isu; All Saints Parish Ebenator and St. James Parish Arondizuogu.

He had also served his Diocese, Orlu, as Diocesan Director of Religious Education and Diocesan Chaplain of Orlu Diocesan Catechists Association for four years respectively. He was a member of the National Association of Directors of Religious Education (NADRE) Nigeria for four years.

Presently, Rev. Osunkso is a *Fidei Donum* priest to the Archdiocese of Boston, MA, USA. He is currently the Parochial Vicar of the St. Katharine Drexel Parish Boston, and the Chaplain of Nigerian Catholics in the Archdiocese of Boston. Rev. Osunkwo is also a fourth degree member of the Knighthood of Columbus International and Chaplain to *Council* 15292, USA.

Printed in the United States
By Bookmasters